Me......
For the History
Of the War In Texas

By Division General and
The Present President
Of the Supreme Tribunal of War
And the Navy of the Republic

Don Vicente Filisola

Mexico City

Volume I

1848

Translated by
Wallace Woolsey

EAKIN PRESS
Austin, Texas

FIRST EDITION

Copyright © 1985
By Wallace Woolsey

Published in the United States of America
By Eakin Press
An Imprint of Sunbelt Media, Inc.
P.O. Drawer 90159 / Austin, TX 78709-0159

ISBN 1-57168-034-9

Library of Congress Cataloging-in-Publication Data

Filísola, Vicente.
    Memoirs for the history of the war in Texas

    Abridged translation of : Memorias para la historia de la guerra de Tejas.
    Includes index.
    1. Texas — History — Revolution, 1835–1836 — Personal narratives, Mexican.
    2. Texas — History — To 1846. 3. Filísola, Vicente. 4. Generals — Mexico —
    Biography. 5. Mexico. Ejército — Biography. I. Woolsey, Wallace. II. Title.
    F390.F4913   1985   976.4'03   85-16101
    ISBN 1-57168-034-9

For my wife Elizabeth,
my daughter Patricia Haughton,
and my grandchildren,
Ric, Anna Beth and Chuck Haughton

Contents

Foreword to American Edition   xiii

Preface to American Edition   xv

Biographical Sketch to American Edition   xvii

References to the Original Spanish   xxi

Translation begins

Editors' 1848 Prologue to Mexican Edition   xxv

Introduction to 1848 Mexican Edition   xxxi

Chapter 1   1

Discovery and occupation of Texas by the Spanish from the seventeenth century on, whereby it is demonstrated that the United
States of North America had no right whatsoever upon which to
base its claims to the ownership of the territory. — The boundaries
of the territory of Texas with that of Louisiana.

Chapter 2   9

The peace that prevailed in Texas for the long period when the
ownership of Spain was recognized, up to the time of the hostile advances of Philip Nolan; the death of the latter and of all who accompanied him. – Desires of the North Americans to establish themselves in that territory. – The policy of the government of Spain. –
The establishment of presidios. – Missions. – Dispositions concerning land concessions in Texas. – The cession of Louisiana to France.
– The sale of this province to the United States. – New attempts of
the latter to obtain new lands in Texas. – The expedition of Colonel
Aaron Burr. – Mustering of troops in Béxar in 1806. – Don Simón
de Herrera on the frontier. – Alarm on the part of the United States
on account of this, and the agreement celebrated between this
leader and General Wilkinson.

Chapter 3   15

Attention and care of the Madrid cabinet for the preservation of
Texas. – Don Bernardo Gutiérrez de Lara: his expedition to Nac-
ogdoches on behalf of the independence of Mexico; he takes the Bay
of Espíritu Santo; he repels the siege laid by Governors Herrera and
Salcedo of Béxar and Texas; the retreat of these men to Béxar. –
The Battle of Salado. – Surrender of Béxar.

– Establishment of a provisional government. – The imprisonment
of Governors Herrera and Salcedo; the execution of these two and
other individuals. – Consequences of these events. – Expedition and
rout of the governor of Coahuila Elizondo against the insurgents of
Texas.

Chapter 4   24

Effects of the conduct of Gutiérrez de Lara on public opinion in the
United States and on that of the Mexicans favoring the revolution.
–The nomination of Don José María Alvarez de Toledo to replace
Gutiérrez in the Texas command. –The departure of the leader for
the United States. –The mustering of new independence forces in
Texas. –Menchaca, rival of Toledo, and difficulties arising out of
that rivalry. –Don Joaquin de Arredondo named general of the
Eastern Internal Provinces. –His march to Béxar. –He joins Eli-
zondo. –The Battle of Medina River. –The capture of Béxar.
–Arredondo's cruelties. –His return to Monterrey.

Chapter 5   34

Armiñan governor of Texas. –New inroads of the Comanches into
that province. –The adventurer Lafitte in Galveston. –Sketch of
this island. –The adventurer Aury. –General Mina. –Colonel
Perry.

Chapter 6   38

Varela succeeds Armiñan and Martínez succeeds Varela in the government of the province. –Expedition of the French General Lallemand. –He is thrown out of the lands that he had occupied in
Texas, the same as the other colonists who had settled within its
boundaries without the permission of the king of Spain.

Chapter 7   40

Chapter 7 has been omitted in translation because it relates, in detail, boundary lines and treaty agreements covered in many easily
obtained documents and sources.

Chapter 8   41

New attempts by the citizens of the United States to take over
Texas, notwithstanding the demarkation of boundaries which had
just been signed between that government and Spain on February
2, 1819. –General Long: his tragic end in Mexico in the year 1822.
–Moses Austin's plan which laid the foundation for the North
American colony which was established for the first time in Texas
with the permission of the government of the Eastern Internal Provinces. –Conditions of that permission. –Death of Moses Austin. –
He is succeeded in the enterprise by his son Stephen.
–The latter's journey to Mexico City. –From the independent government established in that capital in 1822, he obtains the ratifica-
tion of the permission to establish the colony which his father had
planned. –Provisions with reference to the colony.

Chapter 9   44

Fall of the empire in Mexico. –New government. –The latter confirms the grant of lands for Austin's colony. –His return. –He takes
possession and gives a name to his colony. –Difficulties with which
he struggles again in founding it. –His war and peace with the savage Indians.

Chapter 10   46

New colonization laws. –Critical judgment that is made of them.
–Dire consequences of their abuse by the Texas colonizers, and tol-
erance of the authorities charged with enforcing them better.
–A military command is demanded for Coahuila and Texas.

−Leaders who followed each other in this post. −They become subordinate later to the general command of the Eastern Provinces. −The naming of General Bustamante. −New inroads by the savages. −Vain attempt to make Texas independent under the name of the Republic of *Fredonia*. −Peace signed with the savage tribes.

Chapter 11   52

Order and government in the recently founded colonies. −The State of Coahuila and Texas is formed. −New concessions granted to Austin. −Excessive trust on the part of the Mexican authorities in Texas towards the new colonists. −Extraordinary affluence of the latter. Sad consequences of their admission and the tolerance for them in the country. −Scandalous smuggling that they carried on there. −March of Colonel Piedras to Nacogdoches.

Chapter 12   56

Government officials in Texas in the year 1828. −Montaño's Plan. −General Terán. −Boundary commission. −General Gaona. −The Jalapa Plan. −Visit to the frontier and coasts of Texas. −Election of General Bustamante as vice-president of the Republic. −Ratification of peace with the savage tribes. −General Bustamante's return to Mexico City. −General Garza succeeds him in his general command.

Chapter 13   59

Rumors of the expedition of the Spanish to invade the Republic. −Information from Havana which confirmed them. −General Garza'a preparations. −Landing of the Spanish on Cabo Rojo. −Brilliant action at El Paso de los Corchos. −Meeting of Generals Terán and Santa Anna with General Garza for the defense of the country. −Decisive victory over the Spaniards at Tampico.

Chapter 14   62

Foresight and measures of General Terán for the security of Texas. −Reasons for his fears on this point. −Projects and proposals for the purchase of that territory by the United States. −Condition of the troops of Coahuila and Texas after the war with the Spanish. −General Terán's efforts to fill the ranks and get them ready for service. −Excise taxes that he planned. −Establishment of customs and military posts.

Chapter 15   67

Plans for colonization by Mexicans and preparations by General Terán that proved ineffective. −He continues, however, with the setting up of a military line. −He arranges the customs posts for the country. New difficulties that are caused him by Don Francisco Madero and the latter's outrages.

Chapter 16   72

Lack of respect on the part of the colonists for Mexican institutions. −Their conduct towards the authorities, employees and troops. − General Terán's wisdom and the tact with which he tried to establish order in the Texas colonists. −He sets up the maritime customs at the mouth of the Brazos River. −He locates a detachment there. −A notable event in the transport of these troops.

Chapter 17   76

Declaration of Veracruz in 1832. −Movements to support it in the State of Tamaulipas. −General Terán's measures to restrain them. −Emissaries sent throughout Texas promoting Independence.

–Stephen Austin's profound dissimulation and craftiness.
–General Terán's comprehension, and the policy with which he counteracted these things. –A letter from this general.

Chapter 18   80

The disorders among the colonists and the smuggling in the ports continue. –Stephen Austin's crafty policy to avoid measures against his people. –The arrival of Lieutenant Colonel Ugartechea with troops to reinforce the military positions and the customs houses in the colonies. –New emissaries promoting the spirit of rebellion among the colonists. –An uprising where they hatched up excuses for the rebellion of the colonists. –John Austin, the new leader of the rebels. –Boldness and excesses of these people.
–Invasion of *Anáhuac*.

Chapter 19   88

Movements of the colonists using as a pretext the declaration of Ve-racruz. –Attempt at a revolutionary government in Brazoria.
–Activity and success of Lieutenant Colonel Ugartechea's prepa-rations for subduing the rebels. Attack on Fort Velasco.
–Bravery of the garrison. –Their commander's integrity.
–Surrender and evacuation of Fort Velasco.

Chapter 20   90

Surprise and mistakes of Colonel Piedras in his conduct with the rebels. –His communication with Colonel Davis. –His departure from Anáhuac for Nacogdoches. –Account of the events in Aná-huac by Colonel Davis until the end of April of the following year.

Chapter 21   93

Colonel Mejía's expedition. –Movement in the colonies because of the Declaration of Veracruz. –Letter from Stephen Austin to Gen-eral Terán.

Chapter 22   98

Observations with regards to Stephen Austin's letter that was in-cluded in the previous chapter, and clarification of the matters to which he refers, and of the true purposes that he had in mind when he wrote it.

Chapter 23   103

Continuation of Colonel Mejía's expedition. –Stephen Austin's conduct on this occasion. –The capture of Matamoros. –Colonel Guerra's retreat. –Death of General Terán. –Palo Blanco agree-ments entered into between Colonels Guerra and Mejía.
–Reembarkation of Mejía on his way to Texas. –The consequences.
–General Moctezuma raises new forces, conceives a new plan which is carried out by the Italian Averzana. –The capture of Ciu-dad Victoria and the reinstatement of the government and authori-ties of Tamaulipas who had fled previously.

Chapter 24   110

Continuation of events in Texas up to the period that coincides with the revolution of General Santa Anna and Mejía's expedition.
–Conduct of the latter with Austin and the Texas colonists. –The escape of Villasana and Palacios in order to win over the Texas troops. –New rebel movements directed by John Austin. –Attack on Nacogdoches. –Evacuation of this place by Colonel Piedras.

–Declaration of the latter's troops upon their withdrawal from Matamoros. –Assembling in this place of the different groups with which General Moctezuma brought about the success of the Veracruz Plan in Tamaulipas and the other Eastern States.

Chapter 25   116

The Texas colonists take advantage of the revolution which divides the Mexicans in the year 1832, and call a *convention* in Austin.
–They make their first attempt at government by proclaiming their independence and the formation of a state. –The very remarkable statement which they sent to the legislature of Coahuila and circulated to other States. –The error in the thinking of the Mexicans living in Texas, and the fatal consequences which it brought about. – The unworthy treatment of the latter by the Texans and the open opposition of the Texans to the government and laws of the nation.

Chapter 26   124

General Filisola is named commanding general of the Eastern States. –Troops and resources that were placed at his disposal in January 1833. –Grave difficulties that began to present themselves to the general. –His efforts to overcome them. –Conditions in which he found those states upon his arrival according to notable communiqués that he received en route. –His arrival in Monterrey. –Good reception and favorable opinion which he encountered in that city.

Chapter 27   129

Arrangements of General Filisola to maintain discipline in his troops. –Aid given to him by the governor of Nuevo León.
–Refusal of the governor of Coahuila. –Remarkable communications between the latter and the prefect of Béxar. –Aid provided by some private citizens. –General Filisola's march with his troops from Monterrey to Matamoros. –His arrival in the latter city. – Surprising communications which he received from the government there and some simple reflections concerning these.

Chapter 28   137

Official information from General Filisola denouncing to the government the true aims of the Texas colonists. –Their resources and what the general command had for checking the rebels, at the same time asking for the things that they needed most.
–Description of Texas with regards to population, etc., in 1833.

Chapter 29   141

General Filisola sees through the hidden purposes of the colonists to separate Texas from the Mexican nation. –He calls the attention of the general government to this point, the situation in Texas, the troops and ports of that state. –He prepares to open a campaign against the rebellious colonists and does not receive the necessary supplies for which he had asked. –He explores the coast and military points there and issues several provision for putting a stop to smuggling. –At this time Don Stephen Austin presents himself in Matamoros. –Correspondence between them on this occasion.

Chapter 30   146

Observation on Austin's notes and the allegations of the Texas colonists, with an idea of the facts on which these notes are based, and which conceal the things to which they refer.

Chapter 31   151
Austin's conduct — the exact opposite of what he said to General
Filisola in Matamoros. – He turns his steps towards Mexico City;
hidden designs that he had in mind there. – General Filisola's fore-
sight in this matter. – Loyalty shown by the Béxar council.
– Document to prove it.

Chapter 32   155
The manifesto of Escalada in Morelia and of Generals Arista and
Durán in nearby areas of Mexico. – Defeat of these in Guanajuato.
– Influence of that revolution on the military personnel of the East-
ern States. – Preparations of the commanding general of those states
to prevent or delay a movement that would hinder the impending
Texas campaign. – Manifesto of the Texas division.
– Conduct and plans of the rebels.

Chapter 33   164
Various combinations of General Filisola in order to contain the
progress of the revolutionaries and to bring them back to order.
– Revolt of the garrison sergeants against their leaders and officers.
– Pacification of Monterrey, and General Filisola's return. – His
grave illness. – Preparation for the defense of the city against the
rebels.

Chapter 34   171
Indecision on the part of Cortina. – *Cholera Morbus.*
– Communication from General Filisola to Colonel Cortina to bring
him back into line. – Its satisfactory effects. – Colonel Piedras's
march on Ciudad Victoria. – Encounter in the old pass of Pilón
River with General Fernández's troops. – Colonel Piedras's surrender. – Colonel Praga's detachment, his conduct, and his action
whereby he submits to the supreme government. – He is not given a
great deal of credit. – Outrages by General Moctezuma. His arrival
in Cadereita. – The disarming of General Filisola's troops.

Chapter 35   179
General Filisola becomes ill and temporarily resigns the command
in favor of General Moctezuma. – The tyrannical conduct of the lat-
ter. Communications that prove it. – Persecution which he declares
against those whom he considers as his enemies.
– Treatment that he gave Colonel Praga's section. His march from
Monterrey to Saltillo. – His conduct towards General Filisola.
– Lack of discipline in his division.

Chapter 36   184
Communication from Colonel Ugartechea to General Filisola, in-
closing another from the government concerning various steps that
should be taken for the preservation of order in the Eastern Interior
States. – Difficulties of carrying them out. – Letter from General Filisola to the minister of war with very important observations concerning this material.

Chapter 37   188
General Moctezuma's conduct in places along his route. – General
Filisola resumes general command. – He immediately annuls Moctezuma's decrees. – Character and conduct of the governor of Tamaulipas.

Chapter 38   191
    Idea of the scheming of General V. Fernández and his followers.
    – Story concerning the employee Leal which demonstrates the lack
    of order in those of his class in the treasury department. – Finally,
    Señor Filisola's campaign against Texas is frustrated. – The causes
    are pointed out in three communications that are included from the
    general to the government of Mexico.

Chapter 39   195
    Outline of the situation of the colonies at the end of the year 1833.
    – General Lemus relieves General Filisola of the command of the
    general command of the East. – Instructions that the latter drew up
    for information to his successor concerning the situation in all
    branches of the military administration that he was going to turn
    over to him.

Summary and Observations   197
Index   223

General Santa Anna
Courtesy The University of Texas

Foreword

Following his defeat at the Battle of San Jacinto, General Antonio Lopez de Santa Anna signed two treaties at Velasco on May 14, 1836. Only one was made public and it provided that the Mexican forces would withdraw beyond the Rio Grande. The other remained secret and stipulated that General Santa Anna would personally issue orders for the Mexican evacuation of Texas and would work for another treaty to provide that the Texas boundary would not extend south of the Rio Grande. These provisions gave Texas a claim to all territory north of the Rio Grande and had enormous future ramifications.

Mexico continued to recognize the Nueces River, the southern boundary of its former state of Coahuila and Texas, as the official boundary, while the new independent republic claimed the Rio Grande as its limits. The claim was aggressively asserted when Texas was admitted to the Union. United States troops occupied the disputed territory in 1845 and invaded Mexico during the Mexican War of 1846 to 1848.

Under the treaty of Guadalupe Hidalgo — which ended the Mexican War — the Rio Grande was recognized as the boundary of Texas. But the price of peace had increased substantially between 1836 and 1848. In addition to giving up all claims to the disputed area, Mexico was forced to cede to the United States all of its territory from the western boundary of the Louisiana Purchase to the Pacific Ocean.

Vicente Filisola played his role in this drama and earned his niche in history by obeying Santa Anna's orders to conduct the retreat of the Mexican armies from Texas. He felt that his loyalty and duty of obedience required that he follow his superior's commands, but Santa Anna later said that he never expected Filisola to obey his orders to evacuate Texas.

On May 31, 1836, the Mexican Secretary of War issued an order relieving Filisola of his command and on June 25, ordered him to return to Mexico to stand trial for his actions. By August 1836, public sentiment had turned in his favor and he was later exonerated at his trial.

During the summer of 1836, Filisola wrote his *Representation to the Supreme Government in Defense of his Honor,* which was largely responsible for his vindication. A dozen years later he wrote his much lengthier *Memorias.* Although a translation of his *Representation* was published in Texas in February 1837, his *Memorias,* until now, has not been translated.

Filisola's *Memorias* is one of the most important sources on Texas, from the beginnings of American colonization in the early 1820s through the military campaign of 1836. It is an especially valuable source for the events of the entire 1836 campaign, including the siege of the Alamo, the advance of the Mexican armies across Texas, and the retreat of the armies following the defeat at the Battle of San Jacinto.

The appearance in English of the most comprehensive history of the Texas Revolution by Santa Anna's second-in-command and successor as Commander-in-Chief should lead to a wider understanding of the Mexican side. While the Revolution has been interpreted from the Texas standpoint it has been ignored from the Mexican view.

A comprehensive history of the Texas Revolution is not yet written, and Filisola's *Memorias* is a vital part of the essential Mexican source material, much of which has been discovered or republished only within the last thirty years. Eugene C. Barker called the *Memorias,* "the only comprehensive history of the colonization of Texas and the Texas Revolution from the Mexican point of view." Wallace Woolsey's translation of General Filisola's *Memorias* is a valuable contribution to Texas history and to the Texas Sesquicentennial Celebration of 1986.

DAN KILGORE

Preface

Memorias Para la Historia de la Guerra de Tejas was first published in 1848–1849, one hundred thirty-six years ago, and it was long well known in Mexico. Most recent reprints that I have seen have been in 1952 and 1968; however, I have not been able to find a copy at the present time outside of a very few rare exceptions. In all this time there has never been an English translation of the work aside from the excerpt discussed in the introduction on the life of Filisola.

When this project was first suggested to me by Miss Jean Carefoot, Archivist in the Texas State Library, and I saw the work involved, it gave me pause. A two-volume work of twelve hundred pages was not something to be undertaken lightly. However, with more enthusiasm than good sense perhaps, I decided to get on with the translation. Since the *Memorias* is one of the very few Mexican works on the subject of the Texas Revolution, and certainly a primary source of material, it seemed to be a worth while project. Furthermore, with the sesquicentennial coming up on the horizon this was evidently something that should be done. There was also a considerable amount of encouragement from various quarters. So, for better or for worse, I began the task, and now six years later, it is about to be published.

Because of the length of this work and the rather limited appeal there was a need for some aid, and the Texas Educational Education has seen fit to give a grant toward the publication.

In light of the length and also of the rather verbose and prolix style of the author, the translator has shortened the text somewhat by condensing and summarizing a number of the letters included, especially several of those written by Filisola. There is also quite a bit of repetition. In addition, some material that is easily available from other sources, such as boundaries and limits and the provisions of the Treaty of 1819, have been omitted. Also, Spanish spelling was not always consistent in Filisola's day. His, to say the least, was rather innovative on occasion. Frequently his versions of proper names will be at variance with the more usual forms.

There is to be found at the end of this Preface, a list of all matulal summarized or omitted. For each item there are indicated the page numbers of this translation together with those of the Spanish original.

Any time that one puts forth a work of any kind there will always be a considerable number of people without whose help and encouragement the project would not have been carried out. When I asked my friend Dan Kilgore, past president of The Texas Historical Association, if he would write a Foreword for this translation, he was glad to do so. Although a CPA by profession, he is a student of Texas history with the best of them and is well acquainted with Filisola's *Memoirs* in the original Spanish. I am indeed grateful for his contribution.

I wish to acknowledge my sincere appreciation to Miss Jean Carefoot, Archivist in the Texas State Library and a former student of mine, who suggested the project to me; to Mrs. Elizabeth Snapp, Texas Woman's University Librarian, and her capable staff for their helpful aid and assistance; to Mr. Beverley V. Thompson, Director of the Texas Educational Association, who granted aid for the publication for the work; to Dr. L. Tuffly Ellis, Director of the Texas Historical Association, for his encouragement; to Mr. Ed Eakin, of Eakin Press of Austin, Texas, for his faith in me by publishing the work; to Ms. Shirley Ratisseau, editor of the Eakin Press, for her work with the manuscript and her expertise and many helpful suggestions; to my friends of the Texas Woman's University for their genuine interest in my project; and finally, though really first, to my wife Elizabeth for her patience and continued encouragement at those times when it seemed that the end was not in sight.

GENERAL VICENTE FILISOLA
SECOND IN COMMAND UNDER
GENERAL SANTA ANNA
DURING THE WAR WITH TEXAS

Biographical Sketch
By Translator Wallace Woolsey

From the early age of fifteen, General Vicente Filisola was dedicated to the military, and was thoroughly imbued with its regimen
of duty, obligation and obedience. This lifelong sense of loyalty and
deference to a superior officer shed a great deal of light on the actions of General Filisola immediately following the surprising rever-
sal of fortunes that came to General Santa Anna on April 21, 1836,
at the Battle of San Jacinto.

Filisola was born in Italy, in 1789, and went to Spain, presum-
ably with his family. The fact of his Italian origin was not infre-
quently the object of various snide remarks by officers of the Mexican army in later years — perhaps out of jealousy because of his
success as a military leader.

On March 17, 1804, at the age of fifteen, Vicente Filisola joined
the Spanish army and was in the military for the rest of his life. Because of his dedication and his conduct in a number of battles he
rose through the ranks to become a second lieutenant. The following
year, in about November of 1811, he went to Mexico, or New Spain
as it was then called. When he arrived, a movement was already on
foot for the separation of Mexico from Spain. The year before, Miguel Hidalgo had proclaimed independence in the famous *Grito de Dolores* on September 10, 1810.

As a loyalist the young lieutenant fought with great devotion for
the Spanish cause, and with quick promotions. In June of 1813 he
was made Captain of Artillery. On May of the following year he was
also made Captain of Grenadiers. As a result of his actions, and because of his zeal in his career, Filisola won the confidence and
friendship of Agustín Iturbide. Through this association from 1815

on, he became a leading military figure in Mexico. Even then, these two men had ideas of ultimately seeing a Mexico independent of Spain.

Filisola was completely supportive of Iturbide in his "Plan de Iguala" pronouncement and his declaration as emperor of Mexico. Filisola was in command of some four thousand soldiers of the *Trigarante* or "Three Guarantees" army. These guarantees were for liberty, the Catholic religion and equality of creoles and "peninsulares" — native born Mexicans and those born in Spain. In recognition of these activities, Filisola was promoted to Brigadier General and then ordered to Central America, with a view to bringing this region into Iturbide's empire.

After a long and arduous march to Central America, Filisola was successful in his campaign and won the allegiance of Central America to the Mexican empire. However, this came at the time of Iturbide's overthrow and the fall of the empire, and Filisola released the southern region from its ties to Mexico. Because of this there was some strong criticism of the general in certain quarters.

With the abdication of Iturbide, Filisola was again able to come out on the right side and served in a number of important posts in the Republic of Mexico during the period of the 1820s. This was a time of expansion for the Texas colonies, and also in 1831–1832, there were various revolts and *pronunciamentos* in Mexico. With the final arrival of peace between the various factions in 1832, there was an awareness of the condition of the frontier area and of the political and military situation in the Texas colonies. Consequently, serious thought was given to try to correct any evils brought about by the recently ended revolution. Thus in January 1833, Brigadier General Vicente Filisola was named commander of the Eastern Internal States.

The general had a good understanding of the situation, aware as he was of the concern for the continued loyalty of many for the former government. It was decided that the best thing would be to remove from the capital those who held such feelings and to busy them in places where the national interest would cause them to forget their partisan feelings and the resentments of the moment. This plan was carried out and apparently proved to be effective.

In August 1833, General Filisola became so ill on the march to Monterrey that he temporarily resigned his commission over to General Estevan Moctezuma. Although Filisola was aware of the cruelty and lack of judgment on the part of Moctezuma, he felt that he could not do otherwise. Filisola was desperately ill, and they even gave him the last rites of the church. The nature of his illness was not indicated, but he did recover. As soon as possible he took back the command from General Moctezuma, and immediately General Filisola set about countermanding orders and attempting to remedy the ills brought about Moctezuma's handling of the situation.

Before his illness Filisola had received a grant to settle six hundred families in Texas on lands bordering on the colonies of Arthur G. Wavell, Stephen F. Austin, and Daniel G. Burnet. There was, as in many cases, the provision that the colonists were not to come from the United States. However, there is no evidence that any effort was ever made to do anything to carry out the contract.

A clipping from *The Recorder* of Richmond, Texas, dated May 6, 1854, quotes a letter from Stephen F. Austin to Captain Wiley Martin, dated Matamoros, May 30, 1833. This letter is included in Volume II of *The Austin Papers* of the Annual Report of the American Historical Association, 1922, edited by Eugene C. Barker, and published in Washington, D.C. An excerpt reads as follows:

> The Com. Gen'l Filisola is a blunt, honest candid and prompt soldier. He has been over thirty years in service; has been Com. Gen'l. at various times, with important powers entrusted to him — and what is rather uncommon, he has not made a fortune. His principles are liberal and republican, and he wishes that the practice of all the authorities should conform with the true spirit of the constitution and the laws. Says that there is a great want of moral honesty, and great abuses in the revenue. He is the friend of the farming and agricultural interests — a decided enemy of smugglers and lawyers, for he thinks they demoralize the community by placing temptations before weak or avaricious persons, etc. He will be unpopular with all who wish to make money by evading the law. He thinks well of the idea of making a State of Texas, and has a good opinion of the Colonists in general, but he believes they have more enemies amongst themselves than anywhere else. The reason he thinks so, is that he says a quiet and prudent course is the best for them and a rigid adherence to all laws, so long as they are in force, etc. They are gaining yearly, and the republican principle[s] they have been accustomed to are also gaining all over the nation, so that a little patience will place all right without any difficulty, etc.

When General Santa Anna organized his campaign to subdue the Texas colonists and set out for Texas with his troops, he designated General Filisola as his second in command of that campaign. Thus it was that with the capture of Santa Anna by Sam Houston's men, Filisola was faced with the most far reaching decisions of his career. Dispatches sent from the president general ordered Filisola to withdraw his forces to Béxar while General Urrea was to march his division to Guadalupe Victoria. These dispatches also stated that negotiations were under way for the complete cessation of hostilities.

Although the other generals opposed the idea, Filisola felt that his loyalty and sense of obedience demand that he follow Santa Anna's directions. There was also the fear that was felt for the safety and even the life of the Mexican commander. This fear was felt especially in light of the massacre of Fannin's men at Goliad earlier. In any event Filisola did follow Santa Anna's instructions and carried out the retreat of all Mexican forces, first to Guadalupe Victoria, and then on to Matamoros.

Filisola was accused of being a coward and a traitor in his actions after the Battle of San Jacinto, and the Mexican General José Urrea first leveled charges against him in May of 1836. Filisola's response has long been well known; this was his *Representación Dirigida Al Supremo Gobierno en Defensa de su Honor* (Representation Addressed to the Supreme Government in Defense of His Honor) in the following August.

The *Representación* was translated and published by George Louis Hammeken in 1837, and a part of the material was published by Carlos E. Castañeda in his book *The Mexican Side of the Texas Revolution* in 1928. Most recently the entire translation of the *Representación* was published by James M. Day in 1965, and bears the title of *Evacuation of Texas*. This was accompanied by an introduction giving a brief sketch of Filisola's life.

After the events in Texas, in 1836 General Filisola went back to Mexico City where he was later accused of betraying his country because of his actions in withdrawing his troops from Texas. The accusation was an outgrowth of the charges made by General José Urrea. Filisola was arrested in 1840, but after almost a year he was freed and continued his army career, later commanding one of three divisions in the war between the United States and Mexico.

During an epidemic in Mexico City, Vicente Filisola became ill with cholera and died July 23, 1850, at the age of sixty-one. Here was a military man who was truly remarkable for his organization and tactical abilities in the face of enormous geographical obstacles, lack of finances and supplies, and a complete absence of any comprehension of the problems on the part of the members of the Supreme Government of Mexico.

REFERENCES TO THE ORIGINAL SPANISH
OF OMITTED AND SUMMARIZED MATERIALS

These references are to MEMORIAS PARA LA HISTORIA DE LA GUERRA DE TEJAS, Volume I, by Don Vicente Filisola, México, 1848.

Numbers in the left hand column indicate the pages of each item in this translation.

Chapter and page numbers to the right are from the original Spanish text given above. These page numbers are in italics.

ff. 83   Chapter VII — pp. *90–108*. Treaties on boundaries, etc., omitted.

106   Chapter VIII — pp. *112–123*. Summary of permit to Moses Austin for colonization.

ff.141   Chapter XIII — pp. *151–157*. Ode *Aniversario de Tampico* and also paragraph immediately preceding the ode omitted.

175   Chapter XVII — pp. *185–189*. Summary of letter from Manuel de Mier y Terán to Austin, dated Matamoros, January 27, 1832. The paragraph following is omitted.

194   Chapter XIX — pp. *205–216*. Summary of letter from Colonel Ugartechea to Colonel Davis, July 1832. The paragraph following is omitted.

ff. 206   Chapter XX — pp. *219–224*. Summary of letter from Colonel José de las Piedras to John Davis Bradburn, Anáhuac, July 4, 1832.

Chapter XX — pp. *224–230*. Summary of letter from Colonel John Davis Bradburn to General Filisola, Matamoros, April 28, 1833. Next paragraph omitted.

223   Chapter XXI — pp. *237–242*. Summary of letter from Stephen F. Austin to General Manuel de Mier y Terán, Matamoros, June 27, 1832.

241   Chapter XXIII — pp. *256–259*. Summary of agreement between Colonels José Mariano Guerra and José Antonio Mejía, Rancho Palo Blanco, July 6, 1832.

247   Chapter XXIII — pp. *255–256*. Note omitted.

261   Chapter XXV — pp. *279–301*. Summary of Circular Letter from the city councils of the Department of Béxar, December 21, 1832. The petition is dated December 19, 1832.

288   Chapter XXVI — pp. *308–312*. Summary of letter from Second Adjutant Cortina to the governor of Coahuila to be sent on to Filisola, written in February (?) 1833.

297   Chapter XXVII — pp. *317–319*. Summary of note from Saltillo from the lieutenant governor of Coahuila and Texas to Filisola.

299 Chapter XXVII — pp. *319-322*. Summary of communication from prefecture of Béxar to Governor Ramón Músquiz of Coahuila and Texas. Béxar, March 11, 1833.

313 Chapter XXVIII — pp. *334-347*. Summary of communication from General Filisola to the Secretary of War and Navy, Matamoros, May 9, 1833.

331 Chapter XXIX — pp. *354-360*. Summary of note from Stephen Austin to General Filisola, Matamoros, May 24, 1833.

337 Chapter XXIX — pp. *361-366*. Summary of letter from General Filisola to Austin, Matamoros, May 27, 1833, and of that from Austin to Filisola.

342 Chapter XXIX — pp. *352-353*. Note omitted.

356 Chapter XXXI — pp. *378-380*. Summary of note from Filisola to the governor of Coahuila and Texas, to be sent to the Vice-President of Mexico, Monclova, May 20, 1833. Two preceding sentences omitted.

400 Chapter XXXV — pp. *425-429*. Summary of two letters from Estevan Moctezuma to Colonel José Domingo Ugartechea, Cadereita, First letter, August 14, 1833; second letter, August 15, 1833.

409 Chapter XXXVI — pp. *435-436*. Summary of portion of letter from Colonel Domingo de Ugartechea to General Filisola, Monterrey, September 2, 1833.

412 Chapter XXXVI — pp. *439-445*. Summary of letter to José Joaquín de Herrera from General Filisola, Monterrey, September 19, 1833.

ff. 421 Chapter XXXVII — pp. *449-456*. Summaries of letters to General Filisola from: Vital Fernández, Matamoros, August 3, 1833; Colonel Luciano Muñoz, Matamoros, August 12, 1833; Colonel Stáboli, Matamoros, August 18, 1833.

ff. 432 Chapter XXXVIII — pp. *460-477*. Summary of three communications from Filisola to the Ministry of War and Navy, Monterrey, September 12, September 25, October 9, 1833.

450 Chapter XXXIX — pp. *479-495*. Summary of letter to Brigadier General Pedro Lemus, named as successor to Filisola, from the latter as an instructive memorial, Monterrey, December 30, 1833.

ff. 508 Apéndice del Tomo I e Índice del Tomo Primero — pp. *541-601*. Omitted.

Translation of the
First American Edition

Editors' Prologue

What! You feel not the trembling lance
Bloodthirsty in your murderous hands!

Espronceda
Song of the Cossack

From the time in 1842, when we had been informed that a *history* with the title *Concerning the Republic of Texas* just written by Mr. Doran Maillard had been printed and published in London, we had had the desire to confront it with another history from the pen of a Mexican or with data and notes that he might obtain instead, to which there could be ascribed no note of excessive zeal or lack of exactitude. This we had wished to do so that with the truth of the matter set straight and made manifest these items should be available to our compatriots and that they would at all times avail themselves of the important revelations.

With this in mind we had planned to reproduce at the present time the commendable articles published by "El Espannol" which was edited in tht same year and in this same capital by the renowned Don Luis Manuel del Rivero, with the intelligence and courage which characterize all his productions. But we had been granted through the generosity of the Most Excellent Señor General Don Vicente Filisola the favor of reading and having available the MEMOIRS which we are now publishing and which we have been working on for some time. Since in this narration and in these justifying documents our people in government and our fellow citizens of all classes will find the most important and impartial information on the events and the consequences that have been linked to them to produce the conflict in which we have finally seen our independence and our national existence compromised, we have definitely decided to choose these MEMOIRS for the greater service of our subscribers and to facilitate the execution of our first thought already indicated.

The noble and glorious role that fell to the lot of General Filisola from the time when this nation was fighting for its independence from the mother country, which he carried out as a general and as second in command of the forces that on several occasions operated in the rebellious colony, which he has likewise upheld in his long military career and in the high magistracy to which he still belongs, the integrity of his character and the loyalty and good faith with which he has guided his pen have created in us a duty to give him the preference indicated. These relieve us in our opinion of any other apology or recommendation which we might wish to add to our works and give us reason to expect that our fellow countrymen will receive them with the same kindly thoughts and the same interest which their objective inspires in us, and that these must increase in proportion as our difficulties have increased. We find ourselves in the necessity of overcoming these difficulties if we are to continue to be counted in the catalogue of nations, whatever have been our misfortunes otherwise in the sad period through which we have just passed, and with which our publishers must occupy themselves for a long time to come.

One of these publishers under the title of NOTES FOR THE HISTORY OF THE WAR BETWEEN TEXAS AND THE UNITED STATES has just begun to present in August of the present year one of the productions of that type, whose first chapter we might well designate as the compendium or synopsis of the material that we propose to develop in these MEMOIRS. Consequently they may serve as a reenforcement or the extensive prologue to the terrible scenes which are to be described in the notes referred to.

The MEMOIRS that we shall be dealing with will come out in the form presently seen, serving only as material for the publication EL UNIVERSAL, and without being involved in or affecting in the least the principles or the political coloring that people may wish to attribute to that newspaper. Our goal is the truth, and our only objective in this regard also is nothing more than to embellish and to recommend the paper to which it is attached, repeating the concepts which EL ESPAÑOL printed in 1842, and which we have seen to our greater sorrow in 1848, to have been so accurately stated. We desire with all our hearts to help prevent in this manner the complete realization of the mad prediction which is included therein without there even having been made the efforts demanded by patriotism so that Mexicans may at least have the rights which with the greatest injustice have been denied to them or put in doubt in these trying days. Such is the respect and the sympathy for which unhappy circumstances cry out.

"The New World," said Señor Rivero, and we remember with affection all our compatriots, "is wide indeed and gives space for the human family to extend itself without its individuals rubbing elbows in uncomfortable proximity, the origin of disturbances and wars. However, we have here the fact that the members of this family having departed some points extremely distant one from the other *approach and seek out each other, not to embrace* BUT TO DESTROY EACH OTHER, for man is the same here that he was there without the novelty and the grandeur of his situation contributing in any way in this magnificent dwelling place to erasing from his heart *the thirst for blood that besets him, nor from his thoughts* THAT FIXED IDEA OF DESTRUCTION AND OF DEATH WHICH DOMINATES HIM.

"*The man of the South and the man of the North meet here again face to face just as they are in the ancient world and have been for all time across the whole span of history.* IT SEEMS IMPOSSIBLE FOR THERE TO BE ANY FUSION BETWEEN THEM, EACH REPELLING THE OTHER AS THEY DO ON ALL POINTS, AND IMPOSSIBLE AS IT IS FOR PEACE TO BLESS THEIR RELATIONSHIPS SO LONG AS A GREAT DISTANCE DOES NOT SEPARATE THEM. *Their physical and moral being, their affections and their ideas concerning man, concerning society, concerning life and concerning death,* EVERYTHING IS DIFFERENT BETWEEN THEM, EVERYTHING CONDEMNS THEM TO SEPARATION.

"The immensity of the unoccupied lands seems to guarantee even here for many years their peaceful relations, but this barrier is beginning to fall before the intrepid march of the people of the North, who though stopped for a moment in that majestic valley of the Mississippi, so full of the future, have sent out advance parties in all directions to take possession of the land that they believe has been promised to them.

"These mysterious movements of peoples have never been subject to any regulations of morality or of politics; they are regulated by other laws of a separate order and obey only the instincts which God has put into the races of mankind. *They are not to be stopped except by physical obstacles capable of resisting them* or of turning them from their way, like the flood that nothing can prevent from covering the plain, so that at times it is impossible to direct its course. *To think that morality or politics can contain the march of a great people* toward the fulfillment of their destinies, *is to ascribe to the net spread out to check the flight of a little bird the power to check the charge of a bull in the full vigor of youth.*

"It is not our intention as we give this aspect of a great question to intimidate one of the interested parties, *but to draw back the veil that conceals the danger in order to infuse into this question the spirit which always inspires such knowledge and insight in warm hearts.* THAT THE PEOPLE OF THE UNITED STATES LOOK UPON MEXICO AS THE EAGLE DOES ITS PREY FROM THE LOFTY SKIES IS A TRUTH IN FACT *which breathes through all the acts, sayings and writings of that people who certainly do not worry much about hiding their designs.* THAT IN SPITE OF ALL THE IMAGINABLE PRETEXTS ON THE PART OF ITS GOVERNMENT THAT SAME PEOPLE WILL CARRY OUT THEIR PROJECT THE DAY THAT ITS EXECUTION IS MATURE IS ANOTHER TRUTH, *although not precisely historic since it belongs to the future which can be declared* AS IF IT ALREADY BELONGED IN THE DOMAIN OF FACTS. This is because according to the laws of history and human nature that which must be fulfilled we can with all assurance consider as being already fulfilled.

"And what can be done? *Trust perhaps in words and sleep* IN THE SHADOW OF TREATIES *and in the hope of aid from foreign sources? It is well to strive for all these supports* BUT IT IS BETTER YET TO RELY UPON ONE'S OWN STRENGTH AND FIND SALVATION IN ONE'S OWN SACRIFICE. *Prudence dictates this — the instinct for self-preservation which never deceives either the individual or peoples,* especially in times of great trouble. *We have here then the great need of the moment — to build this dike which will cause the border to be restricted, forcing the torrent that descends from the North not to retreat but to continue its peaceful course towards the West,* which is the one that Providence has marked out for it. It is the method and materials that are to be employed that can give rise to excellent combinations or else to great and far reaching errors.

"Immediately one begins to see that *frontiers are not defended without population*; to attempt this first element of defense should be, therefore, the first matter of attention of those who govern. But inasmuch as the Mexican population does not possess the necessary expansive quality, and much less in that direction, for one is to be able to expect that this great objective will be taken care of through a spontaneous movement, *it is requisite that the government remedy this defect* by employing in this respect all its energy after maturely combining all means.

"But defense, and especially one so determined as that which is being made, demands furthermore a great center of action, a wise and strong government capable of uniting all forces and of utilizing all resources. And this is the great question of the definitive organization of the country that the nation has just commended to its representatives and of the solution of which must depend the future fate of the same.

"Mexico is today making before the universe its final and decisive proof of the capacity that serves it for governing itself. If after twenty years of misfortune and blunders and in the presence of a formidable enemy her sons have not been able to learn from experience and lack sufficient will to make upon the altars of the fatherland the sacrifices of their own purposes and their private ambitions, one must despair of the health of this unfortunate nation."

Firm in these convictions and noble purposes, we offer then to our compatriots the lessons of experience in the MEMOIRS which follow.

The Editors

Mexico City, November 16, 1848

Introduction

It is very difficult for contemporaries to possess the impartiality and other talents that go to make up the good historian, and perhaps it would be better for them to limit themselves to setting forth in their writings, faithfully and in detail, the actions to which they have been witnesses, *together with the documents that substantiate them*, and leave to care of the writers of the future the extracting of the most valuable materials from this great depository, the wise and harmonious arrangement of them, and the formation with them of a lasting monument. When there are many Suetoniuses or faithful compilers, although they may be as dry as the chroniclers of the Middle Ages, there will always be later a Tacitus, a Hume or a Montesquieu who will compose a philosophical situation and morality with the torch of observation and experience.

— Fernández de Angulo

"The dominant thought of the United States of America from the period of its political infancy has been the occupation of a large part of the territory that formerly belonged to the Spanish . . . And since the distinctive character of the American government is *desire, hope* and *work*, no other civilized world equals it in unbounded pursuits. Once the object that can satisfy its cupidity has been conceived, it is on the alert for just the right occasion, pretending a lack of interest and concern that it is far from feeling. When the set of circumstances that seems useful to it arrives on the scene, it does not hesitate in the selection of means to achieve the desired end. This is an historical fact, a truth available to every one, a truth as clear as the noonday sun."

In these terms Señor General Don José María Tornel expressed himself in the material which he published in 1837, under the title of *Texas and the United States of America and their relations with the Republic of Mexico.* In relation to this we can also state that since our independence on, other event of such interest or so productive of consequences of all kinds has presented itself as the uprising of the Texas colony, as ungrateful as it was deceitful, nor has there been anything which should have received as much attention from our governments as the necessity of reconquering it and the means that should have been sought out to achieve this and to preserve the colony in the obedience from which it had removed itself in so criminal a manner.

With these objectives continual and considerable quantities of men and money have been dedicated to this for more than a dozen years, and the nation has not ceased to make the greatest sacrifices, less to maintain the indisputable rights which have not been recognized than to vindicate its honor so unworthily insulted by a group of rebellious and treasonous newcomers, who in recompense for the undeserved hospitality which they found in its midst, rose up with the immense expanse of territory that had been granted to them with the greatest of generosity, and have aspired later to usurp by force all that which belonged to the Mexicans.

To the misfortune of the latter and the good fortune of the former, thanks to our underdeveloped ways and education, the greater part of our men, and even of the best informed that have been in the forefront of our destinies, have scarcely recognized, and that very recently, the great importance of those lands, and how with their natural endowments and special products they should have, together with the capital and the rest of the Republic, influenced the increase in the commerce, the wealth and the power of the whole nation.

There are still people who are unaware of the geographic situation of those countries and are likewise without knowledge of the wise laws and exceptional regulations with which they were governed by the mother country, in whose underlying policy were not concealed the advantage and benefits of keeping them separate as well as the other internal provinces of the government of the viceroyalty. These persons came to be persuaded that such laws and regulations were neither useful nor necessary for the provinces from which the Mexican Republic was later formed.

But nevertheless, since there are insults for the righting of which it is still the duty of the individual man to be unmindful of his own existence, that which the Texan adventurers have inflicted upon our Republic is undoubtedly one of those for which all civilized nations who know the value of their rights and their dignity have abandoned all that they possess and all that they are, putting their honor ahead of everything else, in order to obtain the satisfaction that fits the insult.

Such was the situation in which we came to find ourselves, on the surface, with respect to the rebellious colony, and positively with respect to the power that had inspired and aided it in its criminal defection. Thus it is that in order to punish this colony, no Mexican could stop to consider anything else, nor calculate the physical importance of that reconquest, nor the greater or lesser convenience that might result from it. As the author cited above has said, aptly and in agreement with our own ideas: "An Alexander or a Napoleon ambitious for conquests to extend his dominion or his glory is not the one who inspires in the proud Anglo–Saxon the desire to destroy us, that fury of usurping and dominating what belongs to some one else. It is the entire nation which, possessed of the restless nature of the barbarians of the north of Europe and of another period in time, tramples underfoot all those who oppose its course of aggrandizement."

With this in mind, growth of the Mexican Republic would be impossible if it did not attempt with all the means at its disposal to check and put an end to such boundless and illegal projects. Desirous of contributing for our part to such a noble and inescapable obligation, we have undertaken the painful and even superior task that we shall strive to carry out in the following pages.

The existence and ownership of the province of Texas, although better known and valued by the Spanish government than by that of Mexico, were not, however, sufficiently appreciated until Napoleon sold Louisiana to the United States, and as a consequence passed on to the Republic the rights of France, and with them her former claims as to the extent and boundaries of that province. Such circumstances made it necessary for the Spanish to place the province in a state of defense and to begin to colonize its vast territories. The undertaking of Don Bernardo Gutiérrez de Lara in the early years of this century working on behalf of Mexican independence made even clearer to the Spanish crown the need and the advantage of preserving those lands. Also, from that time on the government in Washington began to make much more evident its determination to acquire them at any cost.

Although when the great task of our emancipation was accomplished in 1821, a veil of subterfuge was pulled across that undertaking, and one might even be led to believe that it had been forgotten or rejected by the very ones who never dreamed of abandoning it, experience has opened our eyes to the exact opposite and to the fact that everything done by us from that time on with respect to a border fraught with so much interest and danger was more propitious to preparing the way for the loss of Texas than to avoiding it.

The nature and circumstances of the turbulent times in which we live have made it natural and inevitable that the Mexican Republic has not been able from the earliest days of its existence to fix

its constant and systematic attention on that objective. This is another circumstance which our greedy guests have been able to make
use of for the takeover that they had planned so far in advance. This
was true because more urgent and pressing demands necessarily occupied our nation from the time that she gained her independence
and entered upon the difficult and dangerous problem of establishing herself, charting her course and assuring her future. The first
tasks that were laid out for her were to combine the old with the
new, customs with origins, public interests with those of the party,
those of the party with those of influential persons, and those of
these persons with those of the people as a whole, private aspirations
with honor and the true national interest, the consolidation of her
political system with respect to the outside world.

All these stumbling blocks must not only have slowed the forward movement of so new a society, but must also have set it aflame
with continual internal strife and exposed it to and even made necessary the unending change of leaders, and consequently of direction. Here then is the reason why one could not demand of her what
might be expected of an older and well organized nation whose public opinion, interests and purposes were identified and rooted
equally in all classes and in all individuals.

On the contrary, the care and attention of the new Republic
had to be extended to the far reaches of an immense territory with
divergent interests, manners and customs, and only in the simple
early days of its occupation by the Spanish race could it be feasibly
brought into unity and harmony with the rest of the viceroyalty. But
they could not fail to be in opposition and strike a note of discord
under the new order of things which opened the territory and all
Mexican ports to the men and projects of all the nations of the
world. Under such circumstances relations with the interior, which
were so scant even before, were later bound to be extremely difficult
to centralize and to maintain from the ancient capital of the viceroys; to the hindrance and the obstacle of inhospitable and extensive
desert lands there had to be added the lack of roads and of centers of
population. The latter were far apart and scattered in a dispropor-
tionate manner and as though by chance, which prevented obtaining from them any other materials than those that they could provide for their own defense and which could not suffice for the defense
of the frontiers, when the colonies that had just been established
there were made up not only of foreigners but of the dissembling
enemies sent there by the neighboring nation, the only one on our
continent that could be a threat to us. But trusting in their good faith

and friendship we were lulled to sleep and even came to believe one day that we would find aid in the event of a conflict with the crown of Spain or against any other European power that might try to invade us.

And how could anything else be asked of the government of a country in constant turmoil because of party violence which from the beginning of its political existence has been keeping it stirred up? Was not its first duty to look after its own existence, assuming that it was indispensable for the existence of the Republic itself, since no country in the world can maintain itself without a government? Let us not be surprised then that as long as the projects and the influences of our neighbors were not recognized, the attention of the Mexicans could not have been fixed on Texas except incidentally and from time to time. And still less should one wonder that with the latter divided in opinions and constantly upset by political passions (the third element of interference which owes its existence to the cabinet in Washington, and of which this cabinet has been able to take advantage with a cunning equal to that manifested by the minister that caused it beginning in 1827, and to which was added the war in Texas in 1836) this ill fated territory should become the apple of the gods. These same political passions have given rise among us to an inexhaustible fountain of mutual recriminations, causing ferment in the parties, creating thousands of hard feelings and causing the flare-up of a thousand hatreds. These hatreds were sometimes between individuals and those who were leaders in politics, sometimes between the latter and those who had directed the military operations, and finally among the general population of the nation, causing dissatisfaction and lack of trust among themselves as well as hatred against every one.

Therefore, since the nation has been unable to decide in which direction reason lies because it has been unable to obtain accurate knowledge of the facts, little use can be made of what has been written on this subject. Most often the writing has been done with no other motive than to discredit the facts and to charge faults and errors that have not existed. On other occasions the only objective has been to forestall or to reject the latter which were suggested with evil intent, and of necessity the only result has been always to defame or to slander. Such accusations, when they do not confuse completely, put merit in doubt and cause hesitation concerning the best of reputations of men or of things against which the darts are directed, and they likewise make most difficult the clarification of the most certain things as well as the exercise of good criticism against the censure of the deeds. Then the whole situation degenerates, and everything is believed to be slander or flattery, and the output of the printing press does nothing more than weary the readers, prejudice them more and more, and confuse the most vital and most important truths. There is no nation in the world that can forget or ignore them with impunity.

Herein then lie the need and the usefulness of the essay which we are undertaking concerning this period of our contemporary history as well as the need and usefulness of focusing public opinion upon the causes and upon the events, upon the faults and the errors of which they should be aware and upon which the present and future generations must make their judgment. Otherwise, our painful task would be purposeless and to no avail.

Indeed, without the examination, without the knowledge of the truth of the events, or in an attempt to prove that what was done was the best, we would not dare to take up our pen; rather would we be afraid to have a part in the immense responsibility of the mistakes and faults that we might try to cover up or that might continue to be committed through lack of enlightenment.

Impartial and correct judgments of opinion and revelations of the truth which history is due may be delayed, but never avoided completely. Truth or falsehood, error or malice, ignorance or exaggeration will be disclosed in the end because in the great crises of nations there is never a lack of men who write, although what is written may not be allowed to be published in every period. These are men who unceasingly discover and gather material, and generally these men do not do it without a purpose; they are reflective and farseeing. If they can be deceived by what they do not find sufficiently explained, the deeds themselves, without the need of interpreters or of interpretations, put them within reach of the very thing which through lack of more explicit indications the mind is able to discover when sharpened by the desire to penetrate the most secret places, and this is generally their torment and their greatest stimulus.

But for our part this examination will rely upon data that we have been able to gather with constant effort in the calm of a conscientious and a dispassionate consideration. With such purpose in mind, we shall attempt to present the available facts, beginning with that time when Texas was unknown not only in Mexico but in Spain itself. We shall go back to its discovery, and we shall observe the progress of its colonization, slow in its beginnings, but always gradual and constant. We shall make mention of the rights which France alleged in order to extend her boundaries that far, and we shall analyze her treaties of cession to the United States to come at last to the events of our days and for which our nation is responsible as an independent nation and sovereign over Texas.

In this manner our readers will be able to judge without great difficulty whether or not everything that was done to save that department and to reincorporate it into Mexico after its rebellion was the most correct and the most fitting for the objectives which for one consideration or the other the Republic should have proposed; also whether or not the means employed were the most adequate and all that were at the disposal of our government. They can judge on the contrary whether or not there was a lack of knowledge in the cabinet, or whether the most opportune and best directed use was made of those resources which they had at hand and upon which indeed they relied to carry out so important an enterprise. Likewise, it will be deduced whether or not the adverse results of the Texas campaign flowed from unforeseen antecedents, from inevitable causes, or whether they depended upon the knowledge and the ability of those charged with directing the operations, and what the responsibility was that each one had to carry for the success of those operations.

With such end in mind we shall make use of all trustworthy information and documents that it has been possible for us to gather, and we shall present them in their entirety so that the truth of what we write can never be doubted. We shall leave to better managed pens than ours the purification of what may be believed to be superfluous in these *Memoirs*, as well as the use of the most substantial and important material that may be found in them to write a complete history of Texas and of the war which its rebellion occasioned that may be useful to our descendants since it could not be so for our contemporaries. This is the only ambition which impels us to take upon ourselves so arduous a task. If it should bring some benefit or enlightenment to our country, we shall consider ourselves abundantly repaid and shall even look upon it as a happy circumstance that can satisfy the greatest ambition of a good patriot.

General Vicente Filisola
(2nd in command of Mexican Troops in Texas)

Courtesy Prudhomme, C.L.; *Album Mejicano.*
Mexico, C.L. Prudhomme, 1843

[1]

To serve as a beginning and basis for these *Memoirs* nothing has seemed more valuable, more apropos and more authentic than what was set forth by Don Luis de Onís,* minister plenipotentiary from the king of Spain to the government of the United States of the North, and commissioner extraordinary for the treaty fixing the boundaries between Mexico and that Republic, which treaty was signed in Washington on February 22, 1819.

"It is not to be disputed (he said) and is to be found in most trustworthy documents that the Spanish nation long before any other European nation, discovered Florida during the first expedition made by Juan Ponce in the year 1512; in the second by Lucas Vásquez de Ayllon in 1525; in the third by Pánfilo Narvaez in 1527; and in the fourth, by Hernando de Soto in 1538, who was followed by Luis Moscoso in 1542 and Pedro Meléndez three years later. The latter then remained as governor of Florida. These Spanish explorers and conquistadors landed in the Bay of Santa Rosa, in that of El Espíritu Santo or San Bernardo, and at various other points. They went as far as the lands of Hirrihigua, Mōscoso, Umbarracuxi, Amera, Orali, Apalachi, Alsapalia, Cofia, Mobile, Chasquin, Guigate, Uhanque and Cuachoya, where Hernando de Soto died after having crossed the Mississippi and gone as far as the Black River in the year 1542.

"In all those countries at that time the Spanish established missions, small settlements and forts. In 1562, the Frenchman Ribaut came to Florida with a small force and built there a fort called Char-

[* Memorial concerning the negotiations between Spain and the United States of America which produced the treaty of 1819. Printed in Madrid in 1820 and reprinted in Mexico in 1826. — TRANS.]

1

lesfort, but the Spanish governor Meléndez attacked him, captured the fort and took Ribaut and all his people prisoners. Under the name of Florida at that time was included all the country from the Río de las Palmas, which is the boundary of Pánuco as far as the 48th parallel, in an extension of land of more than 600 leagues, crossing the Mississippi.

"At the same time the Spanish were extending their explorations in the provinces of Mexico, that is the new kingdoms of León and Santander, around the year 1595, in the province of Coahuila around the year 1600, and around the year 1690 they advanced into the province of Texas. There they established several towns, small settlements, missions and forts which were called presidios or garrisons such as that of San Antonio and of El Espíritu Santo in the interior of that province, and that of Nacogdoches and of Los Adaes on the frontier, where the dividing line has always been considered to be the right bank of the Carient or Carcacine (Calsieu) River, which flows into the Mexican Gulf at 284 (93.5) degrees longitude and 30 degrees latitude. There is the beginning of the territory of the French with the name of Louisiana.

"The Spanish continued progressively extending and perfecting their settlements, but neither they nor the French were ever unaware of that boundary line, nor did they ever cross it; it has always existed as the definite limit which separated the territory of one nation and the other. To demonstrate that the statements of the American minister with respect to the settlements that he claims were made on the banks of the Mississippi and the Bay of San Bernardo, to the west of the Colorado River, under the authority of France in the year 1685, and to destroy the other data or gratuitous assumptions upon which the government of the United States bases its rights in order to extend their Louisiana boundaries to the Río Bravo del Norte (Río Grande), it is sufficient to point out that all their claims and assumptions rest upon the following data and bases:

"1. The patent of Louis XIV to Mr. Crozat and the French company in which it is implied that the lands possessed by France on that continent extend as far as New Mexico. Furthermore, they declare in favor of said concession the territory, lakes and rivers which flow directly in the direction of the Saint Louis or Mississippi River. But can this vague concession, made without knowledge of the territories which it embraces, and in prejudice to the possession which Spain exercised over many of them, a concession always refuted and never agreed to by Spain, perhaps give the least right or any other value than a preposterous claim carelessly expressed without knowledge of the geography of the country?

"2. The supposed discovery of the Bay of San Bernardo by M. de La Salle in 1685, and the establishment of the fort of St. Louis, and the declaration of possession of that bay in the name of France by La Salle, who has already been mentioned.

"3. The maps of the French geographer Dalille and others, who without any other reason than their own fancy, or guided by the tenor of the patent of Louis XIV, placed the boundaries of Louisiana at the Río Bravo (Río Grande). However, there were also French geographers, such as Danville, Janvier and Bonna, who fixed them with more accuracy. They also took advantage of the errors committed on the maps of the geographer Don Tomás López and Don Antonio de Arcedo, who made them while Louisiana belonged to Spain, and consequently they did not bother to mark out the true limits of the western part.

"4. The lies and falsehoods that are contained in the history of Louisiana by Mr. Duprast concerning the journeys of the Frenchman St. Denis from Mobile to Mexico, and concerning the agreements which he claimed to have made with the Viceroy the Duke of Linares.

"To demonstrate and prove the absolute lack of force and of reason behind these presumed bases, there is such a volume of indisputable documents and facts on Spain's part in her archives that the difficulty lies rather in having to pick and choose the most outstanding than in finding incontrovertible and convincing foundations upon which to base the rights of Spain and to refute the chimerical claims of the United States. I shall limit myself here to giving a very brief resumé of the essential points.

"Centuries before France had thought of establishing herself on the Mississippi and even long before she had established herself in Canada, Spain was in possession of the whole circumference of the Mexican Gulf, which extends from the peninsula of Yucatán to the southernmost cape of Florida. If the western part of that gulf as far as Pánuco, all of it then known by the generic name of Florida, was not physically populated with Spaniards, there is no doubt that it had been explored by them from the time of Juan Ponce de León in 1511, nor that the same coast of present day Florida as far as Pánuco in 1518 was explored by Francisco Garay and also by Hernando [de] Soto, and without interruption by other Spanish leaders up to the year 1561 in which it was traversed and explored by Angel de Villafañe and Jorge Serón, whose description (which exists in the original in the archives of Mexico) was ordered to be made by virtue of a royal decree issued concerning it. With the circumference of the

3

Mexican Gulf in the possession of Spain, who allowed no foreigners to approach it, there was no point whatsoever on said gulf that was not thought to belong to the crown of Spain, even though settlements had not been physically extended to all points. This was in accord with the principle generally recognized that the possession of a lake or narrow sea, surrounded by one's own lands, in which no other foreign power has any part, is acquired by the occupation and possession of the principal points.

"With this assumption, the establishment of the French, even in Mobile and on the Mississippi, where they first came down from Canada, could only be considered as a usurpation which was tolerated until there was an opportunity to expel them. In this light are conceived the various opinions of the Council of the Indies, the reports of the viceroys of Mexico and the royal decrees of the king Charles II. In the year 1684 the Frenchman La Salle, who had already descended the Mississippi from Canada, made his way to France where he was granted an expedition of four ships under the command of Captain Beanjin to continue his explorations, departing from La Rochelle August 1 of that same year.

"This expedition entered the Mexican Gulf the 12th of the following December. La Salle, deceived by the calculations of the currents of that area as he sought the mouth of the Mississippi, found himself in the Bay of San Bernardo February 20, 1685. However, he continued in his error of believing that he was at the mouth of the Mississippi.

"During his crossing Spanish cruisers had taken one of his boats; in the bay he lost another; and with the rest Beanjin returned to France, while La Salle with some men and ten artillery pieces remained behind. They established a small fort which they constructed, and their situation varied for three months.

"The nearby Tonkawa Indians molested the French to such a degree that La Salle found himself obliged to leave the fort and travel inland in search of the fabled mines of Santa Barbara. On this journey he was assassinated by one of his companions, and shortly after his death, with the resultant confusion in the fort of St. Louis, the Indians attacked and captured it, massacring almost the entire garrison. This is what it came down to, and this is the famous expedition and the declaration of ownership by the French of the Bay of San Bernardo, or El Espíritu Santo, upon which the Americans base their rights as far as the Río Grande of the North or the Río Bravo.

"As soon as they knew about the attempt of the French and of La Salle in Mexico, it was feared that there might be a repetition. To

4

carry out the royal decrees of King Charles II who was continually calling for the elimination of all foreigners from the Mexican Gulf, the war council held July 23, 1688, ordered that Captain Alonso de León, with the necessary forces, should set forth in search of the French who might still be there. To accomplish this he set out from Coahuila with 100 men, and on April 22, 1689, he arrived at the place where La Salle had founded the fort of St. Louis; on the 24th at the mouth of the bay he found the remains of the lost boat. From there, with the knowledge that some of the French from among the companions of La Salle were lost and had sought refuge from the Indians, he went on to the nation of the Hasinais, where he was received with friendship. He called them *Tejas*, which in their language means friends, and that has come to be the name of that province.

"Alonso de León wrote to the viceroy on May 16, 1689, that there remained no trace of the French colony; he gave information concerning the good disposition of the Tejas Indians, and he asked for prisoners and the construction of presidios to maintain the conquest of the country. In Mexico it was agreed that in accordance with the royal decrees of His Majesty all signs of the French nation that might be feared should be destroyed and laid waste, and on May 22, 1690, the mission of San Francisco de Los Tejas was founded, thus subjecting that territory to His Catholic Majesty Charles II. The latter, when he was made aware of all this, ordered that they continue the settlement and conversion of the Tejas Indians. For this purpose they sent out another expedition under the command of Don Domingo de Terán. When a new royal decree on the same subject dated November 12, 1692, arrived, a new expedition with the same purpose and under the command of Don Gregorio Salinas set out on May 3, 1693. From that time on the province of Tejas remained peacefully under the crown of Spain, and the French were completely eliminated from all those parts, remaining only in Mobile and the vicinity.

"Twenty-two years later, in 1715 when the Duke of Linares was viceroy in Mexico, with passport and under pretext of buying cattle from the Spanish missions of Texas, the Frenchman St. Denis and three others came from Mobile as far as the Spanish presidio of San Juan Bautista. In reality they came for the purpose of smuggling and to explore the country. These Frenchmen were taken to Mexico City, and later a new expedition to Texas was decided upon to be under the command of the leader Don Domingo Ramón, who was the commander of San Juan Bautista, and whose niece the Frenchman St. Denis had married. On this new Texas expedition the afore-said Frenchman St. Denis was employed by the Spanish government in the capacity of quartermaster with a salary of 500 pesos. This in-dividual, as much in order to be employed on this expedition as for success in a lawsuit that some time later landed upon him in Mexico where he was in jail, always claimed to be a Spaniard since he was married to a Spanish woman. However, the Council of the Indies upon the proposal of its attorney sharply disapproved of the conduct of the viceroy, the agreement and the Judge Olivan for his easy han-dling of the Frenchman St. Denis, whom the Council labeled an ex-plorer for the French from Mobile. Later he was confined with his wife in Guatemala.

"This historical monument is very curious and interesting as a means of giving the lie to the falsehoods of Duprast in his HIS-TORY OF LOUISIANA. During the new expedition to Texas under Captain Don Domingo Ramón there were founded the four missions of San Francisco, La Purísima Concepción, San José and Our Lady of Guadalupe a short distance from Nachitoches, at a time when the French had not even built New Orleans, the capital of Louisiana. When war broke out with France during the regency of the Duke of Orleans, the Frenchman St. Denis, suffering no doubt because of what had been brought against him, seems to have fled and appeared in the French port of Nachitoches, attacking the Span-ish missions of the Tejas Indians, whose people because of those hos-tilities found it necessary to flee to the presidio of San Antonio de Béjar.

"But the Marquis de Valero, named general and governor of Texas, or the New Philippines, with 500 dragoons which he re-cruited at his own expense and two companies of cavalry, set out for Texas in 1719. Meeting no opposition he arrived at Los Adaes, and the French withdrew to Nachitoches. When the king Philip V re-ceived word of this, he ordered that an attempt be made to fortify the province of Texas and that the war should be continued against the French.

"The Marquis de Aguayo reestablished the old missions and founded some new ones, among them the presidios of Our Lady of Pilar de los Adaes, that of Loreto on Espíritu Santo or San Bernardo Bay, and that of Dolores which is known by the name of Orquizaco. He improved the situation of San Antonio de Béjar with no incident along those borders other than two expeditions against the Indians of the north — one in 1730 from the presidio of Béjar, and the other in 1758 under the command of Colonel Don Diego Ortiz de Parrilla.

6

"Some time later an attempt was made to organize a general and uniform establishment of presidios to defend all the interior provinces of New Spain, and finally a commission was given to the Marquis de Rubí to go out and visit them and examine the state of affairs there. As a consequence of this commission there was set up September 10, 1772, general regulations for those presidios by which a line of them was established from the coast of Sonora to the Mexican Gulf, setting up in the province of Texas, those of San Antonio de Béjar and San Bernardo Bay; those of Los Adaes and Orquizaco had been terminated since Spain was then owner of Louisiana, and that was no longer a frontier and would be of no subsequent use.

"Furthermore, there is contained in the parochial records of Los Adaes, Nacogdoches, etc., not only the year when the establishments referred to were founded, but also the records of baptisms and burials of the parishioners from the time of the foundation until the year 1805 when the bishop of the new kingdom of León, Don Primo Feliciano Marín, made a visit to that diocese. No more positive and authentic proof of Spain's continued possession of those territories can be given. It is proven by other documents that even the possession of the port of Nachitoches, the only point that the French occupied in 1719, west of the Mississippi, was held precariously and through the tolerance of Spain.

"In the expedition of Captain Don Domingo Ramón to Texas, which has already been mentioned, where he had entered as a friend the French port of Nachitoches, he did so with his mace and royal insignia as a sign of the jurisdiction of Spain. It is likewise stated that when Don Manuel de Sandoval was governor of Los Adaes for Spain, the French governor of Nachitoches *asked* him for *permission* to move the French fort a short distance towards the Spanish area on the banks of the Red River at Nachitoches because the old fort had been destroyed by flooding from the river. This permission was *granted* by the Spanish governor since he considered it a matter of little importance. When the viceroy learned of this, he ordered Don Francisco Benito de Luby to go from Mexico City to Los Adaes and publicly seize Governor Sandoval and bring charges against him, which was done. This was in spite of the fact that according to the declarations in the trial it appears to have been about a gunshot's distance from the land *granted* by Sandoval to the French.

"To this collection of documents, against the possession by Spain for centuries of the Mexican Gulf and the permanent settlement of Spaniards in Texas for a century and a half, always respected by the French, the American government can oppose noth-

7

ing more than the temporary settlement by the Frenchman La Salle on the Bay of San Bernardo in 1685, which expedition in its origin, progress and end appeared to be more refuge sought by a ship-wrecked person or an adventurer or an unknown shore than a dec-laration of possession as a representative of a government. But even though that temporary occupation should be supposed to have given some right to France, no one can doubt that this was lost from the moment that they abandoned the country in 1688. This is even more true later when in that and following years the Spanish Captains León, Terán, Salinas, Ramón and Aguayo were sent one after an-other by the government and by virtue of orders from the king with armed forces to uphold the rights of Spain and to repel the usurpa-tion by the French even to their total extermination in that province. This they carried out in the manner that has been related.

"To these facts there may be added what is on record in the DESCRIPTION OF LOUISIANA, which Mr. Kerlerk, who had been governor there for the last eleven years that it was in the pos-session of France, set forth by virtue of an order from the Most Christian King who communicated it to the minister of state, the Duke de Choiseul, so that the aforesaid *description* of Mr. Kerlerk should be made official as an appendix to the act of cession to the king of Spain, the new proprietor of Louisiana, and should serve as a rule for the administration of the colony.

"In fact, any one who wishes to know what Louisiana was *when France had possession of it* — that is the phrase employed in the Treaty of San Ildefonso for the *retrocession* — can find nothing more authen-tic than the *description* of Mr. Kerlerk, who had been its governor for eleven years. He wrote officially under orders from his government, and in the act of delivery to Spain he had no interest in increasing or diminishing the territory. This authentic and official document that can be considered as a part of the treaty of cession lays down as un-deniable that Louisiana ends at the Red River, drawing a perpendic-ular line from this river and the point of Nachitoches between this city, Los Adaes and Arroyo Hondo, to where it empties into the sea, and from the point at Nachitoches to the Missouri.

"In view of this brilliant demonstration all the data that they have tried to establish in favor of the United States are destroyed."

8

[2]

From the time of the events that are outlined by Señor Onys nowhere is there to be found any indication or assumption that other disputes had arisen between France and Spain concerning the rights of the latter nor concerning the boundaries of Louisiana with Texas, and even less when by the cession that France made to Spain of Louisiana in 1763, and the peaceful possession of West Florida in which the latter found herself, as has been stated, there was no longer the least reason for similar questions in the future. Thus it is that that vast territory, from the year referred to on enjoyed a long period of peace which was interrupted only by a few hostile advances of savage Indians, for the pursuit of which the Spanish government adopted a system of presidios which was ordered to be observed as a special law for the interior and border Mexican provinces on September 10, 1772.

The wisdom, experience and good sense that providence willed should be contained in this small set of laws, which we might also call *military colonization,* and the benefits which they brought to those extensive and valuable lands have been of the same magnitude and evidence as has been the increase in population and wealth of the provinces mentioned. Thus in the period of independence they were already remarkable and continued in progress until the year 1832 when the savage tribes rose up after having been held in line for forty years by Mexican arms.

But because of the abandonment of the discipline of the presidio and the drain on the treasury as a result of the war of insurrection they could not maintain the force nor the means upon which those establishments counted to fulfill their purpose. Likewise no attention was paid to the chieftains and the families of the Indians who supported themselves or whose friendship was bought by gifts and

9

favors which the crown of Spain had so wisely dispensed in order to save Christian blood and to make secure the property of people living on the frontier. All this was in addition to the immediate idea of reducing to order and civilization and placing in towns the tribes mentioned, who at the same time opposed all this and were able to calculate their strength and their advantages in order to oppose it. They took up arms and grew proud with the triumphs which they won quickly and easily.

From that time forward they began to rob, destroy and lay waste all the towns, ranches and settlements that had been established and were flourishing in all eight provinces; four of these were called the Eastern Interior Provinces and the other four the Western Interior Provinces, and they were not included in those that were considered as the viceroyalty of New Spain. It is worthy of note to state that even with the aid later of the North American adventurers and in the long course of more than fifteen years they have not been able to bring to an end completely the great elements of prosperity and wealth that they still envy us in those areas of privileged climate. Such were the benefits that the aforementioned arrangement brought with it.

This was scarcely beginning to be observed in the presidios of the western borders when there occurred the mad undertaking by a certain Philip Nolan, a native of Ireland, who apparently had settled in one of the western states of the republic of North America. He and a band of some fifty adventurers and outlaws, stimulated by news of the existence in the mountains of the province of many rich gold and silver mines, thrust themselves into those desert regions in 1789 with the pretext of capturing mustang horses between the Río Grande and the Colorado River. But this came to the notice of the commander general of those eight provinces, Brigadier Don Nemesio Salcedo, whose home was the town of Chihuahua in the province of New Vizcaya, he mustered the forces of the presidios and sent some 400 or 500 cavalrymen to punish Nolan's boldness and to avoid a repetition of such attempts in the future.

The expedition was successful because when they had met the adventurers and ordered them to surrender, with their subsequent refusal, these were attacked and routed completely. Nolan and the greater part of his men died in the fray, and the rest were taken to Chihuahua and given a military trial in that capital.

This example taught them a lesson and for a time held back new attempts by American adventurers. However, the exaggerated news of the fertility and beauty of the land and the rich mines that were thought to be there again stimulated the greed of our neighbors, who up until that time had been almost unaware that there existed such a province of Texas nearby — with the exception of a few of the more knowledgeable and bolder travelers who have always come from among those enterprising people, but whose contacts were not quickly generalized.

Meanwhile, the establishment of the companies and the line of presidios in accordance with the laws of 1772 already mentioned offered the most satisfactory results, and in their shadow caused the growth of towns and the elements with which God had endowed those interior provinces. Thus it is that in the Sonoras, New Mexico, and New Vizcaya were flourishing mining, cattle raising and commerce, which sent torrents of silver and gold to the capital and brought back in return the noble results of commerce with Europe and even with Asia which came into Acapulco. At the same time these activities also flourished in the Western Interior Provinces, the towns of the north, situated on the right bank of the Río Grande in the Department of New Santander, today Tamaulipas, and also in those of Coahuila and Monclova, such as San Fernando, Santa Rosa, etc.

The missions had a large part in this prosperity since they not only conquered the Indians for the vineyard of the Lord with their gentleness and a truly evangelical solitude, but with these virtues they contributed a considerable increase to the population, workers for agriculture and familiar crafts, and in short made these people as useful to humanity as they had been prejudicial formerly in their savage state. As opportunity afforded, they provided aid of all types for the commanders of those companies, and the latter furthermore found in the Indians who had accepted the religion very useful and wise explorers in the frequent forays that the security of the people required to be made by them constantly. But the lack of payment of the benefices to the missionaries and the poverty of the funds destined to religious activities caused these to decline in such a manner that all the influence and benefits that had been produced in times immediately after the establishment of the missions came to be absolutely naught.

Texas was not the province that participated the least in this benefice with the aid of the companies of Béxar, the Bay of Espíritu Santo and the detachment of Cíbolo Creek which was the first. The missions of San José, La Espada, La Purísima Concepción and San Juan in the vicinity of Béxar, and those of El Rosario, Espíritu Santo and El Refugio near La Bahía, were other establishments and houses of instruction invaluable for agriculture, textiles and other

11

useful and necessary crafts in which the neophyte Indians learned to worship God and at the same time to make themselves useful both to themselves and to society. Thus it is that the only three towns in Texas — that is Béxar, Bahía del Espíritu Santo, and Nacogdoches — had immense herds of cattle, horses, mules, sheep and hogs.

The harvest of corn, beans and other cereals and vegetables were abundant, and the inhabitants led a comfortable and happy life while at the same time they were increasing, crossing the Spanish and Indian races, from which resulted one of handsome, agile, wise, brave, loyal, industrious and hospitable men.

Some writers of other nations have criticized this system of religious missions associated to a certain degree with the armed forces to subdue the savage Indians and to populate the country. But how else could both objectives be accomplished with more charity and economy and at the same time guard the security of the settlements against the savage and horrible inroads of the Indians? Has the system adopted by other nations perhaps been more humane, using only arms, steel, liquor that brings drunkenness, deceit and mistrust — pretending to buy from them the lands that they inhabited for some trifle or other in exchange for items that perhaps harmed them instead of being beneficial to them, in order to remove them thus from the tombs of their fathers? Is it better to leave them forever in ignorance and barbarism in order to have in the future new excuses and occasions for once more removing them from the new lands which they possess, or destroying them as a proscribed race unworthy of civilization, whose existence is incompatible with that of the Europeans, with nothing else than extermination in favor of it? And do those who write thus consider themselves as enlightened, philanthropical lovers of the human race?

Furthermore, the government did not deny lands to any family or person of whatever nation provided that he professed the Catholic religion and gave guarantees to the army of some profession, craft or trade useful to society and that he made his request through proper legal channels. Would that the government had never been so trusting and generous!

In the year 1800, Charles IV ceded to France in exchange for the grand duchy of Tuscany and the kingdom of Etruria that same Louisiana that the latter had given him in 1763, but with the condition that if France ever disposed of it again, Spain should have preference for regaining it. However, since the overbearing man who at that time directed the destinies of France did not consider himself obliged to be consistent with anybody, he sold it to the United States

12

of the North in 1803. Although the Spanish government protested the sale immediately, she found herself forced to consent to it and withdrew the protest in 1804, more out of consideration for the government of the United States that had bought it than for Napoleon himself.

The government of the United States ever anxious for territory no sooner found herself in possession of Louisiana than she approached Spain with the claim that Louisiana extended to the Río Grande. This absurd claim opened a broad field to the ambitious spirit of the North Americans who were so fond of moving on to new lands. Very soon this was the occasion for several families to come clandestinely to settle in the lands of Texas, and for Colonel Aaron Burr to conceive the bold project of marching with a considerable force onto Mexican soil to promote a revolution in 1805. This he did not carry out since he had been denounced and even ordered to be prosecuted by the president of the federation. Such attempts and machinations alarmed the government of Mexico to the point of taking adequate measures to avoid them and to assure the peace of their towns.

At the beginning of 1806, about 1,000 to 1,500 reserve troops of the militia were mustered from Nuevo Santander and Nuevo León in the city of Béxar under the orders of Colonel Don Simón de Herrera and of the political and military governor of the province of Texas, Don Manuel Salcedo, a man who was worthy and learned but not very well versed in the military. From the city mentioned they furnished detachments of cavalry for the town of Nacogdoches and Atascosito and the Trinity, Colorado, San Marcos and Guadalupe Rivers where men and horses were suffering a great deal because of the lack of sustenance for both. Because of this, with the exception of the first point, the others were in places lacking in absolutely everything; the pastures were of the worst quality, and it was very costly to transport necessities from where there were any to those distant and isolated places. It was also ordered by the viceroy that the old fort of Los Adaes, abandoned in 1763, should be rebuilt. It was eight leagues distant from Nachitoches to the west of this point, and located on the line that before the acquisition of Louisiana by Spain had been considered as the one that marked the boundaries of the Spanish possessions and those of the French.

For this operation Don Simón Herrera himself marched on Los Adaes; his purpose also was to observe whether the ferment occasioned by the rebellious activities of Colonel Burr had been completely pacified or if there remained some symptoms of uneasiness.

13

This movement spread alarm in the United States to such an extent as to bring about the march of a body of troops and militia to New Orleans, and General Wilkinson, together with Governor Claiborne, advanced as far as the Sabine to protect the frontier of the federation. An outbreak between the two forces seemed imminent. However, when Wilkinson had protested to Herrera that his only intention was to guard the border and in no way to insult Texas, the two of them made an agreement without prejudice as to what their respective governments might decide in the future. According to this the troops on both sides would withdraw to their quarters, leaving only those who would cover the points of Nacogdoches and Los Adaes for Spain and of Nachitoches for the United States. The first were not to cross the Sabine River, nor the second the Arroyo Hondo, with Herrera returning to Béxar and Wilkinson to New Orleans.

[3]

With the same zeal and activity with which the viceroyalty of New Spain and the command of the internal provinces — which are independent of the first — looked after the preservation of Texas and ordered the steps which circumstances demanded, concerning which we have just given an idea, the cabinet in Madrid likewise maintained its constant goals with reference to so important an objective. Mindful of this, since the year 1804, they had ordered the raising of troops that they believed sufficient to maintain the integrity of the territory of Mexico. When by their number and discipline they should be readiness, they were to be put under the orders of Brigadier Don Pedro Grimaret, carrying out thus the triple objective of defending the Texas frontier against the claim of the United States, and at the same time against the rapacious invasions of the savage Indians, and beginning to populate the vast territory with men trained in the use of arms and skilled in trades and crafts of greatest necessity and usefulness so that they might at the same time contribute to improving the situation of those noteworthy colonies just being born.

Thus it is that they chose leaders and officials of honor and outstanding knowledge, not only in the profession of arms, but in all those that could contribute to the indicated objective. They were likewise careful that the sergeants, corporals and soldiers, in addition to being married, should be farmers, carpenters, blacksmiths, etc., and that nothing should be lacking for them to get settled with all comforts and advantages in those unpopulated parts. With the same purpose in mind they enlisted a number of poor but honorable families and a large number of foundlings who made up in all about five thousand persons to begin to build the population of Texas.

15

Such was the wonderful project and the costly and far reaching preparations that were made useless by the break between Spain and England, which happened in the same year of 1804 with the treacherous and surprise capture of four frigates laden with gold and silver sailing from Great Britain. This event made impracticable the movement of all classes of people and especially of troops from the Peninsula to Mexico. Since this difficulty lasted until about the year 1810, in which the cry of independence by the hero of Dolores was heard, it was completely impossible to carry out the colonization planned by the Spanish, and that of the Mexican families could not be put into effect either.

Quite the contrary: scarcely had hostilities begun between the forces led by Señor Hidalgo and those commanded by the viceroyal government when with this war there began the disasters, sufferings and misfortunes that were the consequences of it, and of which the distant and much coveted territory of Texas began to feel the bad effects. Numerous hordes of Comanches and other savage tribes began to spread out and overrun it in all directions with impunity. Thus it was that nothing stood in the way of their laying waste the ranches and settlements that were beginning to be established there. They robbed and killed bands of horses, mules and all types of stock that were flourishing in the fertile and abundant fields. The result was that the inhabitants, filled with sadness and fear because of the large number of deaths and captives that were a consequence without regard to sex or age of the victims, found themselves at last forced to flee and to move to other lands to save their lives and the few possessions which might escape the repacity of the enemy.

Here then in a word is the situation of the people of the Texas frontier in March of 1811, when the retreat from Saltillo to Béxar was attempted by the first leaders of independence. During this time a man about forty years old presented himself to Señor Hidalgo at the Santa María Ranch. His stature was average, but of athletic proportions; he had a quick wit and a warm nature; he followed the trade of blacksmith in the town of Revilla, today the city of Guerrero, a place in that vicinity and where, in addition to his trade he was the owner of broad lands, stock, a business and other not insignificant property that made him a man of great substance in his class. After he had presented himself he declared his great belief in the cause of independence and that he had good connections in New Orleans to provide men, arms and ammunition to continue the war. He indicated that he was disposed to leave for that city, and he strongly urged that he might busy himself in whatever would be useful to that cause.

16

This man was Don Bernardo Gutiérrez de Lara. His offer was well received; he was decorated with rank of lieutenant colonel and provided immediately with the credentials and instructions that he deemed proper so that he might fulfill his mission and that he might be able, if it should be necessary, to present himself to the government of the United States to solicit its aid and cooperation. On the twenty-first of the same month, only a few days after this, the Wells of Baján on the road from Saltillo to Monclova witnessed the deplorable occasion of the capture of Señores Hidalgo, Allende, Abasolo and the rest of the collaborators and leaders of the revolution for independence.

Under these circumstances, Gutiérrez de Lara's commission should have been ineffective; however, carried along by his patriotism and natural spirit he gathered together some of his friends, men who were equally bold and determined in behalf of so great and just a cause, and with them he set out by land on the road to Washington. He arrived there at the end of four months after uncounted sufferings of all kinds and after having faced the risks and dangers of crossing through the midst of savage nations and along routes and roads that were as unknown as they were impassable.

He presented the above mentioned credentials, but since the government of the United States did not consider them sufficient, and the observant Gutiérrez understood immediately that the mind of those people leaned more particularly to the increase of their territory at Mexico's cost than to protecting her independence from the government in Madrid, he limited his plans and his confidence to his own resources. With these and his connections in New Orleans he got together about five hundred men, natives for the most part of the states of Kentucky, Tennessee, Mississippi and Louisiana, with some French and Spanish. Among the first acting as officers were a certain Magie [Magee], Kemper, Lockett, Perry and Ross, bold men with some military training.

With this body of adventurers Gutiérrez headed for Nacogdoches where he was joined by a detachment that was protecting that town, the one from Los Adaes and a considerable number of Coushatta Indians. He immediately issued a proclamation in which he appealed to the patriotism of those inhabitants and succeeded in increasing the ranks of his troops to the number of seven hundred men who were determined and skilled in the handling of arms, and particularly of firearms since most of them were hunters.

After Gutiérrez had stopped for some time in Nacogdoches in order to organize his forces, name officers, distribute arms, muni-

17

tions, etc., he set out on the road to Béxar. As soon as he came to the Colorado River, he made his way as quickly as possible toward the Bay of Espíritu Santo, now the town of Goliad. One reason was because at that place were located the quarters of a company of soldiers of a garrison of that name which was fortified and gave him support for his later operations. Another reason was that since he was only eight leagues from the Cópano squadron he could receive aid of all types by sea from New Orleans.

His unexpected arrival at Bahía del Espíritu Santo at the beginning of November in 1812 gave an immediate result which was that of the soldiers of the garrison that covered it part of them fled, and the others regrouped with Gutiérrez remaining in control from that point on without the least resistance. Since he was aware that there were royalist forces gathered in Béxar, he proceeded immediately to improve the fortifications of the presidio by erecting parapets in the street intersections of the town and gathering together provisions and cattle for the subsistence of his troops in case it became necessary to undergo a blockade.

Indeed it was not long before royalist troops appeared before that post commanded in person by Señores Don Manuel Salcedo and Don Simón de Herrera. The first was governor of Béxar and a relative of the commander general of the eight interior provinces, and he resided in the town of Chihuahua; the second was governor of Nuevo León. When they learned of the penetration of Gutiérrez through Nacogdoches on the road to Béxar, they had gone out to meet him with almost all their forces which came to some two thousand men. Aware also that Gutiérrez had later taken the road to Goliad, they countermarched at once on that point where they arrived on November 7.

The first days were spent in reconnaissance and minor skirmishes with very small losses on either side, but on the fifteenth firing was rather heavy both from cannons and rifles, and the royalist troops launched a serious attack which was vigorously repulsed by the defenders with considerable losses of dead and wounded on the part of the attackers. As a consequence, and since as has been pointed out, Lieutenant Colonel Salcedo was not much of a military man, appearing rather to be very human, he proposed that those under siege be brought to surrender by a regular blockade. This method promised to give complete results in view of the fact that the besieged were short of all types of vital supplies, and trusting to this, he put his plan into action.

Gutiérrez's troops indeed found it necessary in order to obtain

18

corn and cattle to make frequent sallies by day as well as by night, living as the saying goes from hand to mouth, with this state of affairs continuing until February 9, 1813. Those under siege had lost in the continual sallies, scarcity and illness many of their best and bravest soldiers and officers, including the one that they called Colonel Magie [sic]. But the besiegers had not been without losses on their part either, both in men and horses; since in the most cruel season of the year they were forced to be out in the open both night and day, in addition to the men that they had lost in frequent actions with both dead and wounded, a considerable number had become ill or deserted. The horses, lacking in pasture and of necessity tethered in the open and in the mud that they themselves had made beneath their feet, were sick, many of them with infected hooves, and all of them so emaciated that they had become useless.

This and the continued murmurings and complaints of the officers obliged the royalist leader to undertake a decisive assault, and indeed he carried it out on the ninth of February already indicated with all the means at his disposal under those circumstances. The attack was made with all the energy and decision imaginable, and some of the royalist soldiers were already putting their ladders up to the parapets when those within, sorely pressed, raised a white flag, thus indicating that they wished a truce.

Salcedo, who earnestly desired the ending of the siege, granted the truce and had his troops withdraw out of rifle range of the enemy. However, this acquiescence was unfortunate for him because he demanded in the surrender that the five ranking officers of the garrison should be handed over in order for them to be taken to the viceroy. The besieged refused this absolutely, protesting that if all the individuals that made up their ranks, foreigners as well as Mexicans, were not permitted to withdraw to where best suited them with all that belonged to them, they would defend themselves to the limit. Thus it was that when Salcedo refused this, those under siege were highly indignant and broke off negotiations. Immediately the bells of the tiny church of the fort rang out, and they readied themselves again for combat. Although Salcedo launched the attack anew, he was repulsed completely on all sides with very large losses.

This event so glorious for that garrison and due in greater part to their noble and unstinting determination, on the contrary occasioned in Salcedo's division discouragement and extreme dissatisfaction, to such an extent that because of this as well as continued desertions, the poor state of the horses and the lack of provision which was beginning to be felt in the camp, they found themselves forced to undertake their retreat to Béxar after thirteen or fourteen days of siege, this they did by night. A detachment from the garrison went after them as soon as they noticed their withdrawal and took from them several pieces of equipment, mules and horses which were placed inside the fort without their adversaries having tried to regain them. In the retreat Salcedo lost almost a third of the forces which he had, some of them going over to the enemy and the rest deserting to their homes.

Since Gutiérrez had increased his forces and was encouraged with the good success that he had had, he set out after the enemy on the road to Béxar. The latter tried to set up an ambush on March 29 near Salado Creek, but when they were sighted by Gutiérrez they were forced to do battle in the open. The forces that they had left numbered around nine hundred men with all types of arms, with six cannons which they placed in the center of the battle. Those with Gutiérrez were about the same number, although they were more accustomed to gunfire. As we have said before, Salcedo's troops were made up almost entirely of militiamen and auxiliaries from the frontier, while those of Gutiérrez were either soldiers or adventurers from other countries, or North American huntsmen from the states of Kentucky, Tennessee, Mississippi and Louisiana. Gutiérrez dispatched a certain Lockett with a number of selected sharpshooters to fire with their rifles exclusively on the artillerymen who were handling Salcedo's pieces while a certain Kemper and another named Ross, each with a detachment, were to try to turn the flanks and take the enemy from the rear.

These tactics had complete success, for the people of Béxar were anxious to join the independents, and as soon as Gutiérrez was seen with his forces, they got into communication with him and indicated their decision and the moral state of the few troops that were there. Gutiérrez asked that Salcedo and Herrera surrender unconditionally, and the latter, since they had lost the confidence of their troops who were in no mood to defend themselves, accepted without delay, delivering themselves into the hands of Gutiérrez with twelve other officers, natives of Spain. Of the patriot troops and their officers, some joined Gutiérrez's ranks and others were let at liberty to withdraw to their homes.

Salcedo, Herrera and the twelve Spanish officers were placed in a narrow prison cell in the Alamo, not as prisoners of war, but as malefactors. Gutiérrez made his victorious entry on April 1. On the fifth he established a provisional government composed of thirteen leading individuals, nine Mexicans and two Americans, a certain

Masicot and another named Hale. Don Bernardo Gutiérrez y Lara had been named with the pompous title of commander in chief and governor, whom the thirteen named above were to serve as a Council of State. The first question that the provisional government had to settle was the fate of Governors Salcedo and Herrera and the other twelve Spaniards who were arrested with them. Consequently the decree was that they should be charged and judged in a council of war.

According to the attorney who was given the task of bringing the charges and those who were named to make up the council of war it was a foregone conclusion that they would all be sentenced to death because the attorney and the majority of the judges were personal enemies of the two governors. Indeed, that was what happened — the trial was concluded, and the sentence was death. However, they did not decide to carry it out because the North Americans and other foreigners who were serving with Gutiérrez's troops had made clear on numerous occasions their horror and resistance to such barbaric and cruel proceedings. In view of this Gutiérrez had the fourteen unfortunate men taken by an escort of seventy men on the ostensible pretext of taking them to the Ensenada of Matagorda to send them from there on a boat to Spain. However, a short distance from that city in a creek bed they sent them upstream and cut the throats of all of them except Salcedo. He begged them to commute that type of death to shooting, and that was done.

This did not remain hidden for very long and caused almost general indignation against the one believed to be the principal author of it. It was atrocious and repugnant in the eyes of humanity and for the majority of the Americans. It caused in them such extraordinary dissatisfaction that almost all of them, including Kemper who was acting as their colonel, with several other officers, abandoned the ranks of Gutiérrez. They said that they did not wish to be a part of a class of men that showed so little consideration for the rights of war and of nature. Gutiérrez excused his conduct, pointing out in favor of it the treatment that several of his friends, relatives and companions in arms had suffered at the hands of the Spaniards — as if the evil done by another person could serve as an excuse for one who commits the same thing himself.

Because of the withdrawal of Kemper and those with him the forces commanded by Gutiérrez were reduced to a number insufficient to be able to undertake anything worthwhile against the royalist troops that were occupying the district of Monclova. Therefore, they remained where they were in Béxar. It is known that any troops kept in idleness for very long decline in spirit and in discipline, especially where they are made up as these were of different nationalities. Consequently there grew up between the foreigners commanded by Ross and the Mexicans a mutual lack of trust. The former evidenced an insulting scorn for the latter, who did not hesitate to make it clear that neither did they hold the others in the greatest esteem. On the other hand, scarcities of every kind were beginning to be felt, and dissatisfaction and distrust on the part of all were beginning to mount when unexpectedly news was received that the royalist Lieutenant Colonel Don Ignacio Elizondo was just a short distance from the city with more than a thousand men. Consequently they were not long in receiving from this leader an announcement that the city and those who were occupying it should surrender unconditionally.

The Americans and other foreigners at the word from their leaders immediately took up arms and gathered with them at the place indicated. But the Mexicans showed an inconceivable lack of interest and reluctance. At the same time Ross, the leader of the foreigners, received a message in the visit from a young woman with whom he had relations that the people of the city and the Mexican troops stationed there had made an agreement with Elizondo that together they should set upon the foreigners and kill them all. Ross, trusting only in the words and tears of his girl friend, called his officers together for a meeting in which he emphasized the danger that they seemed to be in and declared his opinion which was that they should beat a hasty retreat. But the officers did not share his apprehension and rejected his advice with scorn. Ross was by no means a coward, but whether through the influence of his girl friend or out of shame for what had happened in the meeting, he disappeared from the city the next night; as a consequence the following morning a successor for him in command was named. The selection fell to Colonel Perry.

In a short time this leader received a communiqué from Elizondo according to which he should be permitted to withdraw freely from Texas with all the North Americans and the other foreigners that were under his orders provided that he handed over Gutiérrez de Lara and the other Mexicans who had had a part in the sentencing of Salcedo, Herrera and the rest of the Spaniards who had been put to death. But Perry gave a negative answer with dignity and furthermore made public the demand of the royalist leader. By means of this the Mexicans and the foreigners came to understand that all the disagreements and distrust created between the one group and the other had been kept going by the hidden workings of the royalists. Once rid of all rivalry and mistrust, with one accord they took up arms, and impatient of any delay in giving battle, they got ready on the night of the 17th and 18th to go out to meet the enemy. The morning of the next day, about two leagues distance from Béxar, the independence group found the royalists on the Alazán at the time that the holy sacrifice of the mass was being celebrated.

The action began at once, and the officiating priest fell at the first bursts of gunfire. The royalists, in spite of the surprise, since they were armed, resisted bravely but were never able to recover from the advantage gained by the Béxar troops in the first moments of the attack. Thus, after an obstinate defense disorder began to be evident in their ranks, which were soon disorganized going on in a short time to complete rout with considerable loss of men, horses, mules, equipment, munitions and all the artillery, Elizondo with difficulty saved himself in order to rejoin the remains of his division in Río Grande, today at the town of Guerrero, and to be plagued with remorse over the fact that his overconfidence had been the cause of that disaster. Far from thinking that he might be attacked that morning, he was only waiting for mass to be over to set out on the march to Béxar. Meanwhile, he had had the inexcusable carelessness not to have kept at reasonable distances the corresponding advance guards for the security of the camp while that holy service was being concluded. This omission cost dearly and is one that never fails to bring such fatal consequences to all who fall into it and into others similar.

[4]

The execution of the royalist leaders Salcedo and Herrera and the other Spanish officers of whom we have spoken created in the United States a very unfavorable opinion of the patriot troops in Béxar, and especially of their chief Don Bernardo Gutiérrez de Lara. Many men of those provinces who were well intentioned and desired the independence of the Mexican nation were anxious that there should be at the head of the independence group a man knowledgeable in military affairs, who at the same time possessed the other qualities that were necessary for them to accept his commands and to aid so noble a cause. Because of this lack they had not yet made up their minds to participate openly in the insurrection until they thought that they had found all that they could wish for in the person of Don José María Alvarez de Toledo. He was a native of Havana, from an illustrious family, of just the right age, had a pleasing appearance, good and courteous manner, had been captain of a frigate in the Spanish navy, a deputy who had just been in the Spanish Cortes in which he had made clear his liberal ideas. Because of these ideas, with the return of King Ferdinand VII to the throne, he had been persecuted as many other deputies of his same opinion; seeking safety in Washington, he was at the moment in that capital. It was believed also that since Toledo had offered his services from Washington to the Mexican congress, at that time located in Aptsingan, they had named him as agent to the government of the United States and had sent him some quantities of money to defray his expenses.

To this man then those patriots turned to persuade him to come and replace Gutiérrez de Lara. When he had accepted, he recruited some volunteers, procured arms and munitions, and made his way overland to Nacogdoches; during his journey he was joined by Colonel Kemper with the other Americans who had withdrawn with him from Béxar because of the displeasure that they felt as a result of the execution of the leaders and Spanish officers as we have noted earlier. Together with all of these, in spite of the antipathy that Gutiérrez had made clear to him, he presented himself in Béxar. The good breeding and manners of Toledo soon gained him the good will of the foreign volunteers and most of the Mexican troops. All were unanimous in deposing Gutiérrez de Lara from command and proclaimed Toledo as their general, a proceeding that was not at all unusual with the lack of organization and the instability of the revolutionaries, especially when they found themselves in that country so distant and isolated from the other events that were occurring in the heart of the nation at that time.

Gutiérrez left for the United States, and Toledo busied himself training and organizing his subordinates with a care and enthusiasm that justified his having been chosen. However, there were still some who were dissatisfied with him. The Americans and the other foreigners according to the most reliable data came to about eight hundred infantrymen under Kemper's orders; the Mexican troops, almost all cavalry, numbered about one thousand, commanded by Menchaca who was a brave and impetuous man with a good knowledge of the country. He had been captain of a presidio company of the Alamo, and he suffered without very good grace the authority of a *gachupín* as he called Toledo, one of those against whom they were fighting at the time. This disaffection of Menchaca caused frequent embarrassment for Toledo who could see that this would bring greater difficulties when it should become necessary to have better union and better unity of action, which was not long in occurring.

The defeats suffered by the royalist troops in Texas lent a very great importance to the brave men who had been responsible for them and made the viceroy in Mexico aware that if he did not do something to stop the progress of the independence group in Texas who had troops better trained for war and better led than those that had opposed them up until that time, he should soon fear not only the loss of Texas, but also of Coahuila and other provinces that might follow. Consequently on April 28, 1813, he named Brigadier Don Joaquín de Arredondo, who was with part of the Veracruz infantry regiment in Tamaulipas, as commander in chief of the four Eastern Interior Provinces. With these he was to make his way to Béxar, to subdue that province again and pursue the patriot troops that had made it independent.

At the same time he warned the civil authorities of the four

Eastern Provinces to put forth an effort to aid Arredondo's preparations by providing him with information, foodstuffs, transportation,
horses and anything else that he could. Likewise, he urged the
bishop of Nuevo León, the mayors of San Luis Potosí and Zacatecas
and the commander of Veracruz that nothing should be lacking in
all that they could contribute to the achievement of a complete
triumph over the Texas insurgents. Furthermore, he ordered Arredondo that should he receive reliable news of the death of the governor of Nuevo León, Don Simón de Herrera, he was to assume both
political and military command of the four provinces; this is what he
did.

Arredondo had in part anticipated these orders, for as soon as
the disasters that had occurred in Texas came to his attention, he
hastened to muster in Aguayo all the forces that he could and set out
through Linares, El Pilón and Cerralvo for the town of Revilla on his
way to Laredo. Thus it was that he received the above mentioned instructions in Revilla; he answered them from there on May 27 and
set out for Laredo in the first part of June.

Here he established his general headquarters, gathered together Elizondo's scattered remnants and a portion of the fugitives
that presented themselves to him for the Béxar troops, among them
several officers. He organized his troops, trained, armed, and
mounted and dressed as best he could. He secured means of transportation, foodstuffs, and everything else that he thought necessary
to undertake the march on Béxar, which he did at the end of June.
Before his departure he had dispatched orders to Elizondo who was
on his way to Monclova that he should join him on the road to
Béxar. This was carried out at Cañada de los Caballos (Horse
Creek), otherwise called Cañada Verde (Green Creek).

There he incorporated the infantry that Elizondo brought with
the men under arms that he had with him for greater order and
unity of military operations that might take place; thus he raised the
division under his orders to seven hundred thirty-five foot soldiers,
eleven hundred ninety-five cavalrymen, and eighty artillerymen.
This made a total of two thousand ten men, not counting leaders, officers, those employed in the quartermaster's corps, the care of
arms, munitions, foodstuffs, hospital, medical supplies, etc., and
eleven pieces of artillery of various calibers.

From that point Arredondo continued his march to make more
uniform the training of the troops. He made them exercise every day
as soon as they arrived at the place where they were to stop for the
night since most of them were composed of new militiamen, mus-

tered hurriedly and without training, especially those that Elizondo had brought with him.

Thus things went on until August 13, 1813, a league and a half distance from the stopping place known as *Las Rancherías*, which is about three leagues from the Medina River. His first care was to dispatch a corporal and four garrison soldiers who were familiar with the country to go out in search of news concerning Toledo's troops, with orders to proceed as far as Béxar if necessary. When this party had returned with the information that Toledo had left the city with his troops to encounter Arredondo on the Medina River to give battle there, Arredondo made preparations and set out for the river so that he would cross it at a spot other than the usual one. He had an idea that the patriots would wait in ambush on the left bank which is higher than the right one and heavily covered with big trees and brush, just right for defending the crossing, which is very narrow also.

Before leaving at dawn on the appointed day which was the eighteenth, Arredondo sent Lieutenant Colonel Elizondo forward with one hundred eighty cavalrymen, giving him orders to proceed with the greatest caution and vigilance. As he was reconnoitering the woods along the right and left banks, under no circumstances was he to engage in any action to his disadvantage should he encounter Texas forces. He was only to try to learn the number, types and quality, rushing back any information that he might obtain that would give the general the necessary knowledge to carry out whatever action seemed best. If he should be charged by those forces, he should do nothing more than withdraw as orderly and as cautiously as possible, maintaining his fire as best he could. He was likewise to send messages continually with details of the movements that he was carrying out, all the time making his way to the spot where the general was going to cross the river. With this in mind, he ordered that Elizondo be accompanied by his most trusted and alert aides-de-camp.

From the moment that he first received news of Arredondo's march, Toledo redoubled his care and attention to the best discipline and training of his troops, the good condition of his artillery and munitions, and everything that might contribute to the success of the operations that were coming up. Since he observed the good spirits and determination that was evident in his men, he made up his mind to go out to meet the enemy, both for this reason and to spare Béxar the sad consequences that were to be feared in an unfortunate event. Thus he set out on the morning of the seventeenth and made camp before he got to the Medina River; he took his position on the left bank at dawn on the following day. He realized his good

27

position for waiting for the enemy there because in addition to the advantage of its height and location above the right bank for the artillery and of the woods and brush that were in abundance there for the infantry, without much difficulty they could ford the stream from the right and the left with the cavalry at a proper distance to charge the enemy on the flanks and the rearguard at the most opportune moment of the battle.

His decision was to await the enemy at that spot, but the other leaders — Kemper who commanded the American infantry and the Coushatta Indians, and Menchaca who was at the head of the Mexican cavalry and the Indian tribes of the Lipan Apaches, Tehuacanas, Tonkawas and Tawehashes — refused to follow that laudable and useful decision. They declared that it was necessary to take advantage of the valor of the troops, whose eagerness and enthusiasm would cause them to feel insulted if they were obliged to await the enemy behind natural or manmade fortifications and defenses when they were not inferior in numbers. Thus they compelled Toledo to order the troops to cross the river and to continue their march.

Those who were in the advance guard soon made contact with Elizondo's scouts, who for their part, aware of the approach of the former, had drawn their troops up in battle line, doing no more than to observe their instructions strictly. However, Toledo's men charged them so fiercely that with their superior forces they almost surrounded those of Elizondo, and he began to retreat as he had been commanded by his general. As he was losing ground while he kept up a constant fire, the enemy was gaining as they followed him in an orderly and cautious fashion. Toledo, who feared an ambush, halted his troop and tried to reestablish order in it at the same time making his suspicions known to the leaders Menchaca and Kemper. These, filled with daring and rivalry, said that his fears were groundless and that they were determined to take advantage of the gains already made.

Without waiting longer they charged Elizondo's line again; the latter in the short pause that he had enjoyed had halted his troops to give them some rest and to reorganize them, while at the same time he had sent one of Arredondo's two aides that he had brought with him to take him news of what was happening. Arredondo hastened to his aid with one hundred fifty more horses and two small artillery pieces of small bore under the command of the subordinate Don Manuel Zambrano, telling him to relay to Elizondo his order that under no circumstances was he to expose himself. Rather the contrary, and that by means of an orderly retreat he should draw the enemy on until he made contact with Arredondo who was following Zambrano closely in the direction of the firing that could be heard. He executed this order and commanded his whole division to form a column and march toward the firing line.

When Zambrano had rejoined Elizondo, and Toledo's men had noted this reinforcement, they were convinced that this was the whole force of the royalists. Urged on by such a fatal mistake and casting aside all prudent precautions they charged the enemy with the greatest daring. Elizondo let loose on them the fire from his two small artillery pieces followed by rifle fire. However, since he could not stop such a bold thrust he began an orderly retreat in accordance with the orders that he had received, but this soon turned into a complete rout as they abandoned their two cannons and also their wounded. At this time Arredondo was very near at hand, and when he saw the disorder in which Elizondo's men were about to join his, he immediately ordered his column into battle formation to protect his men who were being pursued and to receive the pursuers with fire at close range.

The land was covered with a rather thick live oak grove, and the soil was a fine sandy dirt such that the horses in their movements kicked up everywhere great clouds of dust. These clouds, together with the thickness of the trees, hid almost completely the royalist battle line. Toledo's troops had gone all-out in the pursuit of Elizondo's men, thinking that the victory was decided in their favor. Thus they were taken completely by surprise when they found themselves facing that battle line and under the destructive rifle fire from it and that of the artillery on their flanks. As a consequence they hesitated and then stopped.

Toledo had foreseen that possibility, and he took advantage of the moment of decision on the part of his men to reorganize them with the aid of the dense woods there; when he had done this, he began the battle anew with indescribable determination, placing his artillery at forty paces and even less from that of the royalists, who for their part were presenting an admirable resistance. The firing lasted for more than two hours, with the most sustained fury on both sides, without any advantage being noted for either of them. When Toledo observed the tenacious and brave resistance and the enormous losses that his troops had suffered, he determined to strike a decisive blow by extending his ranks over both flanks and even the rearguard of the royalists. When Arredondo took note of this maneuver, he wheeled his two flanks backwards, forming almost two right angles with his battle line. He reenforced the escort for his baggage train and munitions with another group under the command of Second Lieutenant Arreola.

The Béxar patriots charged the three fronts with extraordinary valor, even going against the enemy's baggage train, but they were received with the same daring and were unable to gain any advantage over any of the fronts attacked. Finally their own determination proved to be their undoing; since they had extended themselves too much to encompass the sort of quadrangle that the royalist formed, they were weak throughout their whole line, and even in places this line was cut by the passage of the royalists. These were more concentrated and could be overseen and urged on by their leaders and officers who could see them and were in a position to attack with unity and order.

Indeed, when Arredondo saw that Toledo's artillery was supported by very few troops, he launched a sudden movement against it and overpowered most of it at precisely the moment when Colonels Kemper, and Menchaca and several others of the bravest and most influential of the Mexicans and foreigners of Toledo's division had just been killed or badly wounded. This caused some confusion in the troops that was noticed by Arredondo, and he ordered the drums and the band to play the triumphal song. This demonstration of joy, although it might be insignificant in itself under other circumstances, produced an extraordinary change in the combatants on both sides. The royalists, considering it a sign of certain victory, redoubled their efforts, and the patriots weakened by fatigue, the dust, a raging thirst and a blazing sun that beat down upon them, without artillery, ammunition gone, and they themselves scattered in a long line around the enemy, without being able to see each other because of the dense woods and the heavy clouds formed by the dust and gunsmoke, almost without leaders and officers to rally and encourage them for the battle, surprised by that demonstration by the enemy, believed themselves to be routed and began to give ground everywhere, without being able to regroup to make an orderly retreat.

Meanwhile the royalists, encouraged by those signs of an approaching victory, redoubled their efforts, and their cavalry charged simultaneously on all sides. At the same time the enemy was moment by moment becoming more disorganized and losing ground, finally leaving only the infantry in the fight; these at last gave up completely, overcome by weariness and the superiority of the enemy.

The defeat had been one of the most complete, bloody and disastrous because the fray had been engaged to the point that whichever of the parties might lose, there would be nothing less than their total extermination without any hope of refuge or help to sustain them. The pursuit was violent and barbarous with the victorious cavalry continuing on to the Medina River without giving quarter to any one of the many who fell under their onslaught. Of the foreign infantry and of the Indian tribes the Coushattas, the Tonkawas, the Tawehashes and the Lipan Apaches that were in the battle, there were very few that escaped from that terrible fight, and the wounded and the prisoners taken by the infantry were ordered shot the same day.

When the first news of that awful disaster reached Béxar, most of the families abandoned the place, leaving just as they were. Leading ladies on foot, without any means of subsistence, with only the clothes on their backs and their small children in their arms, fled hastily across the deserted countryside, among the wild beasts, to go to beg food on the other side of the Sabine, casting themselves on the generosity of the North Americans, or in the forests on that [the generosity] of the savage Indians. A cruel state of affairs for people who were accustomed to lacking nothing that might be necessary for a comfortable and happy life!

Toledo, wounded, fled to the United States with the few leaders, officers and soldiers — who with the greatest difficulty had been able to save themselves after having made on their part every effort possible to gain for their side the victory that abandoned their ranks. At the same time they carried out the duty of a good general and of a courageous soldier, according to reports of several eyewitnesses and the account which Arredondo himself gave of the encounter.

The following day while the latter was gathering up the spoils from the battlefield, he sent Elizondo with two hundred horses to Béxar with the purpose of taking possession of that city and of the artillery, ammunition and anything that he might find belonging to those who were defeated. He carried also the order to arrest all the wounded and those left behind and all those who seemed suspicious to him. This character did not fail to take advantage of this occasion to avenge himself for the defeat that he had suffered a few months earlier, and he immediately conducted himself in such a manner that he deserved to be classified as not only cruel but also savage and ruthless.

Arredondo made his entry into that unfortunate city with all his forces three days after Elizondo, his satisfaction made complete with the dispatch that he received at almost the same time to the effect

31

that the presidio of Bahía del Espíritu Santo when they received the first news of the defeat of the patriots from some of those who had been able to escape had hastened to declare themselves royalists. They had put to death twelve of the unfortunate men who had thought that they would find safety there.

Immediately he dispatched to that interesting place a force of eighty cavalrymen under the orders of the captain of Nuevo Santander Don Luciano García, with instructions to gather together the remnants of the presidio company that had formerly occupied it, reorganize them and complete the number of men and horses that they should have according to the existing regulations.

In Beśar, Arredondo besmirched his victory and his triumph with acts of a truly barbarous character by ordering a great number of military executions of officers and individuals of the troops who were caught after the battle on the road, in the city or its vicinity, and even those of some private and outstanding persons of the city who had taken no part in the armed action, such as Señor and Señora Arochas and others. To put the final stamp on his cruelty he confiscated a great deal of property and rounded up in a house on the bank of the San Antonio River to the south a large group of women, among them respectable ladies and young girls. These were made to grind materials for the preparation of gunpowder under the insolent rule of a brutal, immoral and cruel sergeant. With a small group of soldiers under his orders, instead of guarding them he insulted and humiliated them in the grossest and most indecent manner. Likewise he brought hatred upon himself with other despicable arbitrary actions that will not be forgotten in that unfortunate city as long as a single inhabitant is left. These characterize him as a scourge of humanity and the prototype of the most savage tyranny which can bring shame to the human race.

Later, he proceeded to send Elizondo, his principal and trustworthy agent, at the head of five hundred men to the town of Nacogdoches, for the purpose of taking possession of it and to see if he could catch up with Toledo and the others with whom he had undertaken his flight to the United States. Elizondo, on the march as well as in the capture of that town, which he carried out without any resistance, repeated his usual cruelties and exercised the most abusive tyranny. He reestablished there as well as in the former fort of Los Adaes at the crossing of the Atascosa River, as well as on the St. Bernard, the former detachments of cavalry and took whatever steps he thought expedient to carry out Arredondo's instructions and even his most secret ideas.

The latter for his part saw to the reestablishment of the political, judicial and economic authorities which for some time had not existed as they had been before the occupation by Don Bernardo Gutiérrez de Lara. He set about reorganizing the presidio company of the capital, and commanded the destruction in Texas of all the establishments that owed their origins to the North Americans and other foreigners who had been living there while the country had been withdrawn from its obedience to the Spanish government. The individuals who did not have the good fortune to take the opportunity to escape were placed in prison and treated in the most cruel manner.

Such was the government of Arredondo in Béxar until the arrival in that city of the Extremadura battalion in January of 1814, whose Colonel Don Benito Armiñán held both the political and military command of the province by the order of the viceroy. When that chief left his command, he likewise left a reputation for his public conduct and private morality — the one as sad as the other was in no way befitting the dignity of his rank and the high functions that he had to fulfill in the Eastern Internal Provinces. Then he returned to the city of Monterrey, capital of the new kingdom of León, with all the troops that he had with him with the exception of fifty cavalrymen that he left in Béxar. These were composed of several groups from presidio companies and auxiliary militia from Coahuila, Nuevo León and Nuevo Santander.

And thus it was that because of the unfortunate battle of August 18, 1813, the glories of the independence patriots in Texas came to an end with the disappearance of that numerous and handpicked group of brave men who were able to count as many victories as there were actions and battles in which they had so bravely taken part. Thus it was also that the province of Texas returned to the obedience and submission to the Spanish government, from which it had freed itself by that same series of triumphs that have been described and by the sacrifices of all kinds of which it was also able to resign itself and to make itself superior along with those who took on the burden of so glorious an enterprise.

That was the fatal and inevitable consequence of the lack of a good system, unity, discipline and subordination to the leaders constituted by themselves in command, and because in those moments when they should only have been attending to the common danger they were not able to guard against any spirit or motive of discord and disunity.

[5]

Colonel Armiñán continued with the greatest zeal the expulsion of all the colonists established in the territory of Texas without the express permission of the Spanish government. He had their houses and crops destroyed and confiscated their stock and all types of property for the public treasury. At the same time the viceroyalty* ordered Colonel Don Manuel Arango to reconnoiter to the best of his ability the province of Texas, and this he carried out carefully and intelligently, later giving an extensive and detailed account of his operations, the valuable document of which was sent to the court in Madrid, with a copy left for the viceroy; this copy later disappeared.

Also it was during the time of Armiñán's government that the Comanches undertook a number of invasions into that country, reaching on several occasions the edge of Béxar, in spite of the constant pursuit of them that was kept up.

In the same year of 1814, there appeared on Galveston Island a certain Lafitte, a famous pirate who under the false colors of the Mexican flag carried out large scale attacks, not only against the boats of the Spanish nation, but against all those of any other when he could do so with impunity. He tried to justify his piracy under the guise of judicial sentences pronounced by other men with no more

_____

[* It has already been said at the beginning of Chapter 3 that the Interior Provinces were independent of the viceroyalty. They depended directly upon the *government* of Madrid, with which they had communication through the *captain* or *general* in command from Chihuahua. But in the area of war they received and obeyed the orders of the viceroy, according to the instructions of the County of Galves, given by authority of the monarch, who made the laws and rules in these matters. (Author's note.) — TRANS.]

mission or titles than he and just as perverse as he. To this group he gave the name of the Admiralty Tribunal; their crimes became such that even the United States saw itself obliged to take measures to force them to abandon that point which was later occupied by Aury. This fellow was another adventurer of French origin, a man capable and daring, who had been named governor and military commander of Texas by Dr. Don Joé Manuel Herrera, agent and correspondent of the revolutionary government of Mexico in the Port of New Orleans.

Galveston was at that time an island totally deserted and uncivilized, on whose sterile sandy soil no type of vegetation was to be seen, and where the adventurers who occupied it and of whom we are speaking could scarcely construct four or five cabins with the remains of boats that had been shipwrecked on that dangerous coast.To these they added a small earthwork to the westward. On this wretched island the aforesaid Lafitte with his small boats caused such serious and repeated damage to commerce and navigation in general, that the English government found it necessary to let Lafitte and his men know that it would treat them as pirates whenever they were apprehended by ships of war of that nation if they did not abandon the island.

At the end of October or the beginning of November of that same year 1816, Don Francisco Javier Mina* showed up there with about three hundred adventurers of various European nations and some North Americans with the intention of preparing a disembarkation at one of the points on the coast of Mexico where he might easily make his way into the interior of the country and effectively contribute to its independence from the Spanish government. He could very well have increased that force with another three or four hundred men, but unfortunately, or rather of necessity, they disagreed, and the only ones who joined General Mina were Colonel Perry and something like one hundred men who had become displeased with Aury.

Mina sailed from Galveston for Soto la Marina toward the end of March in 1817, and Aury immediately abandoned Galveston to

---

[*■ Who is the Mexican for whom the name of Mina does not hold a story and a thousand tender and glorious memories! He is by a law of the constitutional Mexican congress of 1823, associated with the names of the first heroes of independence, and we refrain from repeating here the stories that are generally known concerning the origin, character, etc., of this person in order not to burden our pages with commonplaces and not to stray from our main purpose, and because we could add nothing that would increase the glorious fame of General Mina. (Author's note.) — TRANS.]

go to Matagorda, first setting fire to everything that he had built on that Island. Since his purpose and that of the other pirates with him was not to give any positive service in favor of Mexico's independence but only to enrich themselves by piracy that they carried on in Mexico's name and under the protection of her flag, they did not delay long in abandoning Matagorda also. They disbanded completely, and each one made his way where it suited him or where he could.

Such then were the character, projects and fate of the first men who occupied Galveston Island during the last days of Spanish domination in the Mexican nation.

Mina landed with good luck on the bar of Soto la Marina at the beginning of the month of April. In this town, that is located on the left bank of the Río Nuevo Santander de San Fernando, which forms a bar ten leagues upstream, upon some small elevated places, Mina had a fortification built to enclose his war equipment securely and to defend it from Colonel Arredondo's troops. The latter, as was natural to suppose, as soon as he received news of the arrival of those people made his way there with very superior forces to do battle with them. But since it was not in Mina's calculations to undertake any action on the coast but to provide himself with a theater more extensive and more adequate to the daring and high purposes of that arduous enterprise, he left a small garrison in the fortifications of Soto la Marina and made his way with the greater part of his forces into the interior, in order not to be surprised in a disadvantageous place that was not of his own choosing. Later we shall see just what indeed were the results of his system, and the proofs of his knowledge and valor with which he developed it, as well as the end that fate had in store for this illustrious leader up to that moment. But let us stop a bit to inform ourselves also of the fate that was Colonel Perry's.

Since he thought that the project that General Mina had planned was too risky and rash, he separated from him along with Major Gordon, a few other officers and fifty troops, making his way along the coast and the Bay of Espíritu Santo toward Matagorda. It would not have been difficult for him to arrive with good fortune because the whole country through which he had to pass was then uninhabited, and there was no other town than the one indicated at the Bay of Espíritu Santo. At that time the troops that occupied it were reduced to a small part of the presidio itself; when they saw Perry and his men coming, they shut themselves up in the place and were not sufficient to oppose any sort of resistance to his passage.

However, whether it was because the colonel wished to obtain some supplies or because his troops tried to sack the town thinking that they could do so with impunity, the fact is that they very foolishly insisted on attacking the presidio. When they were in the thick of the action, they were surprised from behind by two hundred men that had been detached and sent with the greatest urgency by the governor of Béxar to that point to strengthen it as soon as he had learned of the landing of Perry. The action was stubborn, and Perry and all his men fell on the field without a single one of them escaping death. This event occurred in the middle of the month of May of the same year of 1817.

[6]

Because during the same month of April when General Mina disembarked, Colonel Arminán had been called to the interior of Mexico, Lieutenant Colonel Don Mariano Varela was left in command in Texas. It was then during the time that this leader was in power that the Perry disaster occurred — with the notable circumstance that at the same place as in the year 1812, Kemper and Gutiérrez de Lara had gained over Governors Herrera and Salcedo a signal victory with forces much inferior to those under their command as has been related in Chapter 4. However, Varela did not last long in the command, for almost immediately after the Perry affair Brigadier Don Antonio María Martínez was named governor and military commander of Texas.

During the remainder of this same year 1817, a considerable number of leaders and officers and even a few individuals of the troops that had belonged to the last army of Napoleon, had escaped the disastrous end which their companions in arms had met in Europe, and which put an end likewise to the deeds and the power of that unusual man. Since these men did not wish to give allegiance to the new regime under which France now was, as a consequence of the triumph of the allies, they had enlisted in the United States under the leadership of General Lallemand with the purpose of founding a colony in the United States.

The government in Washington gave them a grant of lands proportionate to their numbers to the west of the state of Alabama. However, the bleakness and sterility of the country quickly made the French dissatisfied with those parts, and they moved into the territory of Texas. They settled between the Sabine and Trinity Rivers in the vicinity of Galveston Bay, as various North American families had done in several other places in the same province without the notice or knowledge of its governor — although they were motivated only by their natural mobility, restless spirit and their ambition to own land.

As soon as Brigadier Martínez learned of what had happened, he sent a detachment to the area occupied by Lallemand, and ordered him either to vacate the land or to recognize the sovereignty of the king of Spain. When the French general refused to do so and found himself without sufficient forces to resist, he abandoned the settlement. Those who were following him had to disperse in order to seek subsistence somewhere else.

However, since the instructions of the commander of the detachment were not limited to this, he carried out a similar ousting of the other families who were in the same situation scattered among other points along the borders of Texas. Their homes were destroyed, and they were dispossessed of the stock of all kinds which they kept there as had been the practice formerly of other colonizers that had preceded these in the same sort of illegal occupation of the land.

To these penalties is due in our opinion the fact that during the rest of the year and throughout the whole of the following year 1818, no other similar impresarios appeared, nor did there occur in the territory of Texas other notable events beyond what might be called ordinary, such as the attacks by the savages. These, because the people were so accustomed to seeing them and because of the military forces that occupied the presidios of that province, were much less dangerous and much more easily repelled.

[7]

[Chapter Seven has been omitted since it relates in detail boundary lines and treaty agreements covered in many easily obtained documents and sources.]

[8]

It was only fair to expect that because of due respect to this treaty the endeavors of the North Americans to settle clandestinely in Mexican territory would cease, but it was soon noted that such was not the case. No sooner had the treaty been published when in the same year several families again settled in Texas. In Natchez, on the Mississippi, there was a gathering of more than eighty adventurers under the orders of General Long, and these gradually increased to the number of three hundred men who then set out with plans to invade the town of Nacogdoches. But the governor and military commander of Texas found out about that plan and caused them to be attacked between the Brazos and Trinity Rivers. Routed completely, they scattered in all directions.

Long, a fugitive, made his way to the place called Bolivar from where, after having joined those that were scattered, he went on to New Orleans in search of more men and aid. When he had again gotten together a little more than two hundred men and provisions sufficient for this force, he decided to march a second time and first of all to attack the presidio of La Bahía del Espíritu Santo which had a very small garrison. Thus it was that he overpowered this presidio without the slightest resistance, although for a very few days. The matter was known in Béxar within forty-eight hours after it occurred, and immediately all the troops that the governor could dispose of were made ready and went to the defense.

The invaders, after a vigorous resistance, had to surrender in the number of one hundred eighty men that had remained; these and their leader were sent to Mexico City at the beginning of the year 1820, in which capital they were held as prisoners until the year 1821, when they were set free by the independent government. General Long was properly recognized. However, one day when he tried to enter a guard post where a man condemned to death was being held, the sentinel prevented him from doing so, and Long, indignant, slapped him. The soldier answered this with a shot which left him dead on the spot.

This happened in 1822, as a sign perhaps that Providence destined for all the entrepreneurs in Texas a disastrous end, and that the occupation of Texas was to be the cause of the horrible and damaging bloody scenes that have occurred following the treaty of 1819.

Moses Austin, a native of Durham, on the continent, more than fifty years old, a man of uncommon capability and learning, enterprising and persevering in his projects, in spite of the poor success that he had had in all the business deals in which he had been involved in the United States, as a result of the signing of the treaty between Spain and the United States, in which it was provided that those individuals in Louisiana who wished to move to territory of the king of Spain would be admitted there as individuals of that nation, Moses Austin, we repeat, conceived the plan to be also a colonizer in Texas to see if in this manner he might recover his previous losses.

Consequently, he made his way from New Orleans to San Antonio de Béxar, arriving there in December of 1820. Although at first he was received with some mistrust, later, through the mediation of Baron de Bastrop, his petition was heard and even recommended by the governor Don Antonio María Martínez and the city council of Béxar to the governor of the four Eastern Internal Provinces, Brigadier Don Joaquín de Arredondo, who was the one to grant or deny it. The grant had to do only with permission to enable Austin to settle three hundred families in Texas. But while that business was being transacted, Austin found himself out of money and decided to return to the United States to get the necessary funds. Leaving the previously mentioned Baron de Bastrop in Béxar as his proxy, he took his departure in January of 1821.

The country that they had to cross was absolutely deserted because the Spaniards had taken care to destroy, as we have said, all the dwellings that had been established there in order to avoid in the future mutual claims and counterclaims between the government of Spain and that of the United States. Thus it was that the trials and tribulations suffered by Austin were beyond belief, and they were increased in the extreme by the disloyal rapacity with which he was robbed and abandoned in the wilderness by those who were with him. This fateful event weakened him to the degree that after becoming ill as a result, he died June 10, 1821, before arriving in the

42

United States, and before concluding the preparations for the transport of the families of the colony. The permit for this was sent to him at the time of his departure from Béxar, with the date of January 17 of the said year 1821, and this he left as an inheritance for his son Stephen Austin, charging him to carry out the undertaking.

SUMMARY OF PERMIT:

The conditions were: Three hundred families to be brought by Moses Austin to Louisiana, Roman Catholics or becoming such prior to entry, with documentary proof of good character. They were to swear allegiance to the king of Spain and Constitution of 1812. In the beginning political government was to be subject to Moses Austin. Documents delivered to Moses Austin and by him to Stephen Austin, who subsequently selected land on the Brazos River.

Meantime, Mexican Independence was achieved, and Stephen Austin's authority was easily transferred to the new government. Approval was given to Austin and distribution of land is designated, but amount of land was not increased. Austin, together with governor of Texas and some approved commissioners, was to divide and allot land. Any additional families from the U.S. must settle in the interior of the province. Request for personal land by Austin was granted. Authorization was given for the establishment of a "center of population" of families brought in, and these must give evidence of being good Catholics. They were to receive doctrinal instruction.

Austin asked for certificate of citizenship and for authority to organize a national militia body to preserve peace and tranquility. Points indicated were generally approved by the government of the Empire. Austin was to apply for citizenship to the national organizational council.

[9]

After the occurrence within a short time of the abolition of the monarchy, which was followed by a different order of things and the prevailing of ideas of republicanism, which were immediately generalized throughout the nation, producing later the adoption of the federal system, there was an increase in the obstacles that the aforesaid colonizer from Texas had to face in order to carry forward his enterprise. Since the acts of Señor Iturbide as emperor and those of the organizational council as a legislative body had been nullified and submitted to the revision and approval of the new congress that was to organize the nation, it was necessary that the concessions granted to Austin also be considered defective. But when they had been upheld and confirmed by the supreme executive power which was newly installed to take the place of the emperor by the decree of April 14, 1823, Austin was able to return with this new advantage to his colony, and so he did after a year's stay in Mexico City.

During this same period of time, Brigadier Don Gaspar López was named commander general of the Eastern Internal Provinces, and Colonel Don José Félix Tres-Palacios governor of Texas — the former to replace Arredondo and the latter to replace Martínez. However, because of the fall of the imperial government, both were relieved of their posts, one by Brigadier Don Felipe de la Garza, and the other by Lieutenant Colonel Don Luciano García; the latter was the one who with all the formalities that are observed in such cases solemnly put Austin in possession of the lands that had been granted to him for his colony. To its capital he gave the name of San Felipe de Austin as it is known even now. Likewise, while the laws which were to govern the above mentioned colony were being drawn up, Austin was granted almost all-embracing powers to dictate what-

44

ever he thought proper for the order, security and progress of the new settlements, and was also given the rank of lieutenant colonel in the Mexican army.

But it is worthy of note concerning this individual that the labors that the carrying out of this enterprise were to cost him did not end here, but there still remained many material and painful trials that followed him later. These included the clearing of lands, building houses, etc., etc., which operations were all the more difficult because of the great and deplorable lack that he experienced with regard to all kinds of implements, tools and even those things necessary for the subsistence and comfort of those families. The boat that was to have brought them in through Matagorda Bay never put in an appearance, either because it lost its way or for some other cause that we do not know.

On the other hand, it was almost necessary for those people always to have their arms at hand in order to defend themselves from the attacks of the savage Indians by whom they found themselves surrounded, sometimes native tribes from Texas itself, sometimes those that the United States had thrown out into Mexican territory for the takeover of the lands which they possessed, with the appearance at least of buying them for insignificant sums. But those that gave the most trouble to the colony were the Karankawas who lived along the lagoons of Matagorda, Lavaca Creek, and the mouth of the Guadalupe. Their cruelties and depredations reached such a point that they made it necessary for Mr. Austin to take the offensive in order to be free of them.

He placed himself then at the head of sixty of his armed colonists and managed to defeat the Indians, leaving some of them dead, and obliging them to sign a treaty by which they bound themselves never to pass the left bank of the Colorado River. When this was happening in 1824, the federal constitution had been adopted in Mexico by which Texas became an integral part of the State of Coahuila and Texas, and Mr. Austin had brought in all of his three hundred families and raised the local militia of the colony of which he had been named commander.

[10]

Following the chain of events that from those first days of the Texas colony paved the way for the troubles and sorrows that have later come to the Mexicans because of them, it seems fitting to observe at this point that contributing no little to the fateful results were the excessive permissiveness and bounteousness with which the laws concerning colonization were granted in January of 1823, and August of 1824. They could not protect against the enormous frauds that were committed in their name, nor the fact that a host of families from the United States would come to take over either clandestinely or with false documents the lands of Texas.

In New Orleans, and also in New York, there were hordes of individuals who, pretending to be proprietors or commissioners of the general government of the Republic or of that of Coahuila and Texas, sold to others as evil as they, or at least [as] unwary, considerable portions of those territories. In this manner so many and such repulsive irregularities were committed that it is impossible for us to understand how they could have been tolerated by the authorities of Coahuila and Texas or to attribute it to anything other than a beneficent and poorly understood generosity. But that was not the way it was on the part of the colonists who thought of nothing less than they did of reciprocating in due manner for such outstanding favors. In addition to profiting from the major exemptions of the liberal system that the nation had just adopted, they came to act so absolutely on their own volition that they wound up by denouncing all the other laws that were not to their liking.

Exempt from all sorts of imposts and burdens in favor of the country that was taking them in, nothing could motivate the hatred that they have later manifested against Mexico; neither could they lack anything for the progress of their colonies except the virtues, the love of work and the loyalty to which they were obligated toward a nation that had so generously admitted them into its midst. Thus it was that although under the conditions of colonization it had been established that the families that were to take part were to give faith previously that they professed the Apostolic Roman Catholic religion and that they were of good character, that the impresarios should not permit among them the presence of criminal individuals, vagabonds of bad conduct or reputation, that they should also establish Spanish language schools, churches for worship, provide them with ornaments, and sacred vessels, and seek out priests for the administration of the sacraments and for the discharge of other religious functions, nothing of this was carried out — either by the impresarios or by the colonists, nor were the constant endeavors of the authorities of the State sufficient to accomplish it. What could be expected from all this? Just what has been seen since that time.

About the middle of the year 1825, General Don Felipe de la Garza was relieved of the command of the Eastern Internal Provinces, which have since been elevated to the rank of a free and independent State by the constitution of 1824; Colonel Don Bernardo Gutiérrez was named in his place. The government of Texas and Coahuila was also united as we have said; this command was given the title of principal command and placed under the direction of Captain Don José Domingo Castañeda, who took the place of Lieutenant Colonel Don Luciano García so that the latter might return to Tamaulipas to the garrison where he served.

At the end of the same year, under the orders of His Excellency the President of the Republic, General Don Guadalupe Victoria, a new force was organized to garrison the department of Texas, and it was composed of two hundred infantrymen of the twelfth battalion and one hundred dragoons of the ninth cavalry; the command of this was intrusted to Lieutenant Colonel Don Mateo Abumada, who was also in charge of the principal command of said department.

A few months later, in accordance with a law put into effect by the general congress on March 21, 1826, Division General Don Anastasio Bustamante was named commander general and inspector of the Eastern Interior States. General Bustamante set out at once; he arrived in Saltillo at the end of the following August, and immediately he began to exercise his duties with the greatest acceptance on the part of those people. His first tasks were the reorganization of the presidio companies and the carrying out of all the other objectives according to the law cited above. Since frequent information had been received about the repeated invasions by the savage Indians, who were taking advantage of the approach of winter which was beginning to make itself felt, the general decided to leave hastily to go to the aid of the city of Monterrey. He did so because this season was the most favorable for the Indian raids, and they not only made inroads across the frontier, but came into the vicinity of Monterrey more than at any other time.

Scarcely had he taken his position in that city when he received news form the principal commander of Texas, in which he was informed concerning an American named Hayden Edwards, a resident of Nacogdoches, who was extremely resentful because his contract which was contrary to the colonization laws had been canceled. He wanted to get revenge and had made an agreement with Dr. John Dums Hunter, also a North American who had the same intentions because he also had been denied lands that he wanted on the frontier where he had just arrived in the company of two Cherokee agents. These were Richard Fields and Bowles, who were in search of possessions with which to compensate his constituents for those of which they had been divested in the United States of America. The plan of the men was that while Fields and Bowles were stirring up the country with their Indians and followers, Edwards would work in the United States to get reinforcements in men, arms and provisions sufficient to sustain the war and to make Texas independent under the name of the *Republic of Fredonia*.

With such purposes in mind they had planned also to begin by taking over the only stone house in the town of Nacogdoches and proclaiming the *Republic of Fredonia*. For this ceremony they raised a peculiar flag spotted with white and red, colors that were supposed to indicate the union of Indians and whites. Then they spread abroad a large number of proclamations to the colonists settled on the Brazos River, and to the inhabitants of the banks of the Red River, inviting them to participate in the infamous plan. But one of those proclamations was intercepted by Stephen Austin in his settlement at San Felipe before it reached its destination. Immediately he had the leader arrested, and notified the commander Don Mateo Abumada of those developments, and that leader on his part passed the information on to General Bustamante. Without the loss of a moment Ahumada set out, accompanied by the political leader Don José Antonio Saucedo, for Nacogdoches with a force of one hundred thirty men to nip that treasonous attempt in the bud.

General Bustamante also made his way with all haste in the direction of Lampazos in order to organize there a respectable unit with the dual objective of aiding Commander Ahumada, and in case it should be necessary, of using this force to undertake a formal campaign against the savages who were continuing to harass the frontier.

As Ahumada with his troops passed through San Felipe, Austin joined him with several other armed colonists to cooperate in pacifying the country. On their march from San Felipe to Nacogdoches they had found out that the rebels had disbanded. Bowles as well as others of his group had gone into that project with the purpose of obtaining lands on which to settle, and some of his people had persuaded him that they could do so without having to expose themselves to so many risks and difficulties by embracing the cause of the Mexican government and delivering to it the leaders of that desperate criminal undertaking. Bowles, convinced of how well timed and preferable this means must be, had separated from the rebels with his Indians, had had Hunter killed and pursued Fields, who had managed to escape. The latter was caught at the crossing of the Sabine River and was killed as Hunter had been. The rest of the adventurers who had made up that crowd fled to the United States, and those who did not were pardoned. Thus ended a revolution that if it had succeeded in taking form would have ended forthwith from then on the rising Texas colonies.

Commander Ahumada, however, continued on to Nacogdoches to reestablish order in that place. Later he designated lands for Bowles's Cherokees in the area of the road that leads to Béxar, and leaving a detachment of infantry and a small band of cavalry in the town, he returned to his residence by way of the road from San Felipe and Bahía del Espíritu Santo, now Goliad. Upon his arrival at this presidio he found General Bustamante, who with a corps of four hundred cavalrymen had advanced to that point in order to reinforce it in case there was need, as we have indicated previously. But since this was not necessary, the general was glad to see that he could devote himself to carrying out his preplanned expedition against the Comanches, Yamparicas, Wacos and Tehuacanas — Indian tribes of the four provinces under his command.

With this in mind he began to set up the necessary provisions for opening the campaign as soon as possible. He joined forces with Chihuahua, New Mexico, Nacogdoches and the volunteers from Austin's colony, who offered to accompany the general in the number of two hundred mounted and armed men, supported on their own account and headed by Stephen himself.

About this time news came to General Bustamante that the Karankawas, Cocos and Kohanis who were to remain as rearguard had renewed their hostilities against the colonists of Victoria, Gonzales and Austin, and were proceeding with the greatest bloodthirstiness. In order to give support to this new emergency, he called together at the rising colony of Martín de León on the Guadalupe River the leading chieftains of the rebellious Indians and the impresarios and influential people of those colonies. With all of them present in Guadalupe Victoria, he harangued them, urging them to peace and harmony, and threatened harsh punishment for any one who in any manner should attempt to make a disturbance between the two parties. He said that in an atmosphere of peace they could prosper, but on the contrary it would be impossible to exist and to organize societies of free and virtuous men.

This reasoning produced the most felicitous results that its author could have desired. All were in agreement and united cordially; as an indication of this he had them embrace in his presence and invited them to eat at his table, to which came also all the chieftains and officers who were with them. Finally he made them sign a reciprocal peace treaty in which were set forth the boundaries which they were to respect, and the conditions under which they were to enter each others' possessions. He was likewise careful, of course, to mark out lands that had belonged to the natives from time immemorial and which should be respected and remain forever exempt from colonizing undertakings.

At the same time that this was happening General Bustamante also received the commissioners that had been sent to him by the Cherokees, Kickapoos, Coushattas and other tribes that had settled secretly in the neighborhood of Nacogdoches, seeking permission to remain there in peace and security. The general granted them this so long as the government of the union did not decide otherwise. He offered to recommend their request and later did so in order that the matter might be dispatched as quickly and as satisfactorily as possible, but with the definite condition that they be always faithful to him and maintain peace among themselves and with the other inhabitants.

He returned to La Bahía, and when he was getting ready to begin the campaign of which we have spoken previously, the above mentioned general received from Béxar a message in which he was advised that another commission sent by the principal chieftains of the Comanches and of the Tehuacanas had presented themselves there asking peace for their people, and also in the name of other tribes. This unexpected event caused General Bustamante to suspend the orders given and all the arrangements that he had been making for the campaign. Making his way to Béxar with all his forces reunited, he busied himself at once in formalizing with the chieftains concerned the preliminaries of the general peace, which was later ratified by the government of the Mexican Federation.

[11]

Meanwhile many additional grants of land in Texas were still being made, and among these the ones to Stephen Austin himself on April 27, 1825, in order that he might bring in and settle three hundred more foreign families. The former groups had increased notably, and consequently Austin directed that for their better government and administration of justice they should be divided into two districts, to which he gave the civil and criminal regulations to which they should be subject. These were approved and ordered to be observed as of a temporary character by the political head of the Department or district to which the colonies belonged in the State of Coahuila and Texas.

On March 7, 1827, still a third grant of lands was made to Austin which permitted him to settle another five hundred families and which designated for him in it, an immense expanse of the most valuable and fertile part and closest to the sea in the state. Thus, if the labors and risks that Austin had faced up to that time had been great, the reward and profit that he was getting from them was turning out to be much greater. Now indeed, after a few years, with conduct that was prudent, wise and loyal, he would have been the most powerful citizen, not only in Texas, but in all the Mexican republic. But his adherence to his theories of independence and exaggerated liberty for himself and his people, if not less noble and less excusable purposes, the mystery of which it is possible will not be known, caused him at last to lose the fruits of his anxieties and sufferings. These were in truth snatched from him later by the new wave of adventurers and criminals who came in, whereby the population was increased, and these people took over his lands. Neither were these in their turn able to enjoy them, as perhaps those who call themselves the owners of them now will probably not be able to do so in peace.

On March 11, 1827, the political constitution of the State of Coahuila and Texas was published in Saltillo, and although there was promise that this charter would bring an end to all the abuses and lack of order and economy that were being experienced relative to the land grants and rule in the colonies, unfortunately such was not the case. The reason was that the power to distribute the grants was given to the legislature and government of the state, no doubt so that they might proceed with more interest in and knowledge of the matter, but just the opposite was seen. The fact is that if up until that time the lands had been given without sufficient care, afterward they were squandered in the most heedless manner. Instead of the order and good system that was so needed in this area, it may be said that Texas was handed over to frightful depredation and to the most lamentable state of anarchy into which all the other branches of its interior administration later fell.

Those authorities, either because of lack of experience in these matters, or perhaps for other reasons that we do not perceive nor wish to insist upon, gave lands without moderation and with no precautions whatsoever to all North Americans who came forward to ask for them. With things as they were, prudence would have counseled that they should have preferred to see these lands stand empty to the extreme of populating them with such dangerous guests.

The evils, however, did not stop only with such grants that were no doubt unwise because of the way in which they were made and the persons who obtained them. Other ills no less grave were to follow also, and these prepared the way for and even precipitated the time of the terrible conflicts in which the whole nation saw itself involved, with all the imaginable obstacles to coming out of them victorious. A multitude of families and peoples of all classes, religions and customs flooded the territory of Texas and settled wherever it suited them to do so. Hordes of adventurers, curiosity seekers, vagabonds and people capable of every sort of undertaking roamed the country in all directions, with no other property or trade than their rifles on their shoulders and their ammunition bags.

The criminals from all parts of the United States selected Texas as their place of refuge and asylum as did the first founders of Rome. They found shelter and a warm welcome among their compatriots, and were even invited by the latter to augment the population, fortify themselves and make themselves secure on the lands that they were usurping with a treachery as evident as it was premeditated.

53

Since the colonization laws already mentioned granted them absolute exemption for seven years from all duties on importation into the Texas territory for the effects, provisions and tools and implements that they might need, and even for all that the colonists could consume and export, the result was of necessity that under the shelter of this privilege smuggling was carried on in an outrageous and barefaced manner, without excepting a single point along the coast from Corpus Christi to Galveston, for the states of the interior. It is impossible to calculate how much this damaged the interests of the nation and decreased and demoralized commerce, especially in the matter of tobacco, although the contraband trade carried overland with the United States of the North in the exportation of horses and mules was no less harmful; these were scarce there and were held in high esteem.

Thus passed the first days of the existence of the colonists in Texas, favored also by an uninterrupted peace that was provided for them and assured them by General Bustamante, as has been related. In this likewise they were supported by the endeavors of the natives and the inhabitants of the state, without the latter's having been given any indication or suspicion whatever to the contrary unless it might have been the prudent amazement that must have been produced naturally by the studied mission that they noted in the exact following of the conditions of colonization, and the displeasure and reproval with which the treacherous attempts of Edwards, Fields and Hunter were viewed. These began to make apparent the ambitious plans that were wrapped up in the seemingly peaceful and friendly undertakings that the colonizers from the United States and other foreigners who likewise coveted the territory of Texas were entering into.

This justifiable distrust alarmed somewhat the general government and made the officials aware of the necessity that existed of thinking seriously about occupying with sufficient forces the frontiers and ports of that territory, especially when the United States of America had just evidenced the greatest eagerness that this should be sold to them (a proposition that was made to the government of Mexico through the ministers of the former republic), and if they could not acquire it in this manner, then by any means that might be possible.

Thus as soon as news was received from General Bustamante notifying the general government of the happenings in Nacogdoches, he had Colonel Don José de las Piedras make his way to that point with three hundred men of the twelfth infantry regiment that was

54

stationed in San Luis Potosí, and the detachment of the same branch which Ahumada had left in Nacogdoches, together with an artillery company and two light pieces.

Colonel Piedras made his march by way of Tamaulipas, Matamoros (where he left the two pieces), La Bahía del Espíritu Santo and San Felipe de Austin, arriving in Nacogdoches at the end of June in 1827. Immediately he personally assumed the military command of that frontier as far as Galveston Bay, a measure certainly most proper under the circumstances, if Piedras had taken with him at least three thousand instead of three hundred men. However, with this reduced number it could do no more than cause alarm to the colonists and make the neighboring republic cautious and put it on the lookout.

[12]

Well aware, watchful and prudent with respect to all that was happening, General Bustamante remained in Béxar until the end of December of 1827, when he left that city. Nothing else happened that is worth mentioning here, unless it be those who followed him in the command. The post of military commander of Coahuila and Texas he turned over to the assistant inspector of the presidio companies of that state, Colonel Don Antonio Elozúa. Likewise he intrusted that of Nuevo León and Tamaulipas to Colonel Ahumada who within a few days set out for the state to fulfill his duties.

General Bustamante had stopped in Laredo during the first days of the month of February in 1828, where he received a communiqué sent to him from Saltillo by General Don Manuel de Mier y Terán, advising him of his arrival in that city and that he was continuing on to Béxar. His purpose was to carry out the commission that the supreme government had given him to explore and define the boundaries of the Republic and the United States of America in conformity with the agreement on this point by both cabinets and as a consequence of the treaties signed with Spain in 1819.

General Bustamante had just received information through the government in Mexico City of the movements that were being observed in the capital, its vicinity and other points in the Republic, as a result of Montaño's Plan. At the head of this Division General Don Nicolás Bravo, the vice-president, had placed himself, and since it was suspected that General Terán was also in agreement with Señor Bravo, Bustamante undertook to keep watch over his conduct. This general wrote to Terán with great tact and discretion, inviting him to make his journey to Béxar by way of Laredo since it seemed to him safer and more comfortable, and because it would give him the pleasure of greeting him and conferring with him concerning matters of importance that he wished to communicate to him.

Terán understood what was at the bottom of that amiability, and in order to dispel all suspicion concerning him, he did go to Laredo, where he stopped for a very few days with Bustamante, who remained, however, heartily disposed in his favor. Terán continued on toward Béxar, taking an escort that was offered to him and which he needed in that vast deserted area in order to defend himself against the savages who roamed it and who might attack him any day.

Because of the political movements indicated that had taken place in Mexico City and in other parts of the Republic, about the end of December of 1827, or the first of January of 1828, Lieutenant Colonel Don Antonio Gaona of the eleventh infantry battalion was made prisoner by his own soldiers in Horcasitas. He had been an adherent of the principles that were being put forth, and consequently the garrison of Tampico had been stirred up, and the discipline of all the troops occupying the state of Tamaulipas had been relaxed.

General Bustamante, in order to prevent other disorders to which the circumstances might give rise, and now having nothing to fear because of Texas, Coahuila or Nuevo León, decided to march from Laredo to the port of Matamoros which had just been opened to foreign trade; he arrived there without anything unusual happening about the middle of April of 1828. He learned to his satisfaction that order had been reestablished everywhere and that the conditions of the general government had changed from dangerous to favorable. In light of this he decided to remain in Matamoros until November of that year, taking part in the arrangement of the affairs of the new port that we have mentioned and improving the organization of the presidio companies active in that general command. This was very urgent considering the state of disorder and lack of discipline that were to be found there.

The following December he planned to pay a visit by way of Tamaulipas as far as Tampico in order to explore the coast and to see for himself whether his orders had been carried out. However, when he was in San Fernando de Presas in January of 1829, he received news of the events of the capital of the Republic in the previous December.

These had been brought about by the opposition to the election of the president by Don Manuel Gómez Pedraza and to that of the vice-president by General Don Vincente Guerrero. The declaration was made in favor of the latter by the general congress, and was also extended to Señor Bustamante himself for vice-president with his subsequent call to Mexico City to fulfill his new duties. Because of this he went on to Ciudad Victoria, and there with the approval of the general government he ratified the peace treaties that he had approved in Béxar the year before with the Comanches. He turned over the armed command of those states to General Felipe de la Garza and returned to the capital of the Republic at the end of April of 1829.

[13]

Later great and glorious were the events of the year that we have just cited, vast the field that was opened up for the prowess and deeds of bravery and patriotism of the Mexicans, as we are going to see. Scarcely had General Bustamante departed from the state of Coahuila and Texas, with his successor still detained in Soto la Marina, when rumors began to be general there of an early arrival of Spanish troops that had set sail from Havana for the coasts of the Republic with the purpose of invading it. Indeed, these rumors were not without foundation, for General Garza had received previous dispatches concerning the day when the troops were to embark, and the ships that were bringing them.

Consequently, he began to dictate the measures that were in his power to gather the forces of the State and so dispose them that they could be brought to the point where the enemy might attempt to land. However, it was not possible for him to obtain sufficient troops immediately to prevent it. Nevertheless, as soon as he knew, positively that they were landing at Cabo Rojo on July 28, 1829, he took care to give this information to General Terán who was in Matamoros. He invited him to take command of those states and of the military forces occupying them and to march at once for the port of Tampico. He had given orders immediately also that all the permanent, active and civilian troops that could be mustered should proceed to that place, where he himself was going.

He left at once, but when he arrived at that city on August 5, the invaders were already occupying the right bank of the Pánuco River, and they had taken possession of the artillery pieces that were in place and without a sufficient garrison for the defense at various points along that same bank.

In the meantime the action called that of *Los Corchos* took place, in which Colonel Don Andrés Ruiz de Esparza and the aide R. Juan Cortina with a small number of soldiers of the battalion from Pueblo Viejo of Tampico, the company of cavalry from there also, and several other civilian militia groups from the nearby towns held back for more than four hours a body of three thousand Spaniards, at the same time causing them a large number of losses. The valor and determination of those brave defenders of the independence and nationality of the Mexican Republic could only give way to the hundredfold numbers and the superior training of their adversaries, but they never conceded victory to them.

After General Garza made every effort in his power to prevent the invaders from crossing the river and occupying Tampico, Tamaulipas, and since it was impossible for him to face the great superiority in numbers of troops and resources of the enemy, he abandoned Tampico and retired to Altamira. In command he left Colonel Don José Mariano Guerra Manzanares, his second in command, with orders that he should lead to the former city all the troops that he had been able to muster up to that time, and even the country people who had come there from the points that had been occupied or that they feared would be occupied by the Spaniards.

General Terán, as we have said earlier, had gone to Béxar in January of 1828, taking with him Colonel Don José Batres, Lieutenant Colonel Don Constantino Tarnaba, Lieutenant Don José María Sánchez and Engineers Don Rafael Chowel and Don Luis Berlandier to carry out the mission of defining the boundary between Texas and the United States of the North. He had explored completely that boundary and all the coast from the mouth of the Sabine to the Nueces River and had returned to the port of Matamoros at the beginning of that year 1829, with all those who had gone with him.

The sufferings and difficulties of that expedition were endless, as can be envisioned by anyone who is acquainted with those extensive and frightful deserted lands — the lack of auxiliary support of all kinds that were experienced there and the aversion that the colonists had always demonstrated towards the Mexicans. But overriding everything was the intense desire on the part of the above mentioned general and his associates to carry out their mission, and they did so insofar as it was in their power. However, with the necessity of inspecting and improving their scientific labors, they stopped in Matamoros, awaiting at the same time the latest orders from the government for the subsequent operations of that commission. This was a good spot to observe because if they did not get all the results, it was because the commissioners for the government of the United States of the North were not at the boundary line at the prearranged time.

When General Terán received the invitation from General Garza, he set out at breakneck speed with Colonel Don José Batres and Lieutenant Colonel Tarnaba, arriving at Altamira a week after the above mentioned Garza had gotten there. This general again insisted that Terán take charge as commanding general of the brigade; since Garza was only in an acting capacity in his rank and at the same time a man of science, he recognized Terán as of higher rank, which indeed he was. But Terán continued to refuse, although this did not stop him from indicating the measures that without a moment's loss it was proper for him to dictate in order to harass the enemy in every way available and that circumstances permitted.

During those same days Brigadier General Don Antonio López de Santa Anna arrived in Pueblo Viejo by way of the Tuxpán road with the troops that he had managed to muster in Vera Cruz. Since he had seniority over the two mentioned, he took supreme command of all the forces that were arriving and were being quartered in Tampico. He immediately named General Terán as his second in command and dispatched General Garza to Mexico City with the commission to communicate in person some observations to the government of the Union that were believed to be conducive to the greater success of the country.

Because of this, through the ministry of the law the military command of the Eastern Interior States fell upon General Terán. He had not wanted to accept this previously with the resignation of General Garza; the general government confirmed the appointment also as soon as there was a happy conclusion to the war operations against the Spaniards in the memorable month of September of the above mentioned year. Concerning these we will not permit ourselves to speak further since they are not concerned with our general purpose, and because there is no Mexican who is not well versed in what they were. Any one who is not will be able to find them out by referring to the many well written accounts that have been done from that time to the present.

* [Final paragraph and *Ode* of original Spanish, has been omitted in the translation as of little or no value in the story of Texas. — TRANS.]

[14]

One of the principal worries that particularly occupied the thoughts of General Terán after the war, invasion and consequent victory in Tampico against the Spanish was the establishment of order in the colonies that had just been settled in the Texas territory, and the security and defense of this area, which he considered to be in danger because of the indications that the government of the United States had given of how much it was interested in adding it to that republic, as we shall relate. Because of this, as soon as circumstances permitted, the first thing to which he turned his attention was the building up and bringing order to the troops of the general command under his charge. As a consequence of the actions and the difficulties of the campaign through which they had just passed as well as the plague that overtook them later, they had suffered a considerable reduction in numbers. There were many who were sick and convalescent, all of them were without horses, saddles or uniforms, and the arms that they had were almost useless.

It is worthy of note that the government of the United States, ever covetous of new acquisitions of territory, instead of being satisfied with Louisiana, longed to take over the fertile and extensive lands of Texas as far as the Río Grande, or the Nueces, or the Colorado, or even the Brazos, if it were not possible to obtain more. Because of this it gave instructions and the necessary powers to Mr. J. R. Poinsett on March 26, 1825, which were repeated and amplified in 1827, authorizing him thereby to make the corresponding proposals to the Mexican government since there was the idea that the latter held those possessions in very low esteem when it was granted them in large and excessive parcels to all who came forward to ask for them.

The first of these proposals was that the department of Texas should be sold to the United States, and in addition those lands belonging to Tamaulipas and Coahuila on the left bank of the Río Grande. The second was that for all the lands of Texas and of the Colorado River of the North, they would pay one and a half million dollars — for the first one million, and for the second a half million.

When these proposals had been rejected, they were made again, in spite of everything in the year 1829, in the following terms:

First. That there be sold to the United States all the territory that is to the north, halfway into the plains between the Río Grande and the Nueces from the coast to the mountains.

Second. In the same manner from the Lavaca on.

Third. From the Colorado.

Fourth. From the Brazos.

For the sale of the land which was contracted in the first proposal Poinsett was authorized to offer up to five million dollars, and for the rest increasing according to what might be granted. However, since this official was recalled by his government before he could present the terms, this was done by the one who relieved him, Mr. Butler, without any results whatever, as had happened in the action of 1827.

Such insistence on the part of the United States to acquire the Department of Texas, the extreme liberality of the laws, the character and nature of their regulations and the provisions that had been set forth relative to the colonization of Texas, the great affluence of the North Americans, and the lack of foresight with which the authorities of Coahuila gave so abundantly of their lands at last brought the general congress to an awareness of the necessity of attending more effectively to the security of that valuable part of the Republic and of dictating opportune provisions for avoiding immediately the difficulties that might arise in time. To this end there was issued on April 6, 1830, the law which contained the suspension of the admission of colonists who were natives of the United States and other measures conducive to the security and good order of that country.

A few months earlier had occurred the change brought about by the declaration made in Jalapa on December 4, 1829, by General Bustamante, who as vice-president placed himself at the head of the new administration of the Republic. In January of 1830, General Terán had had to move out of Tampico and go to Ciudad Victoria to quell the disturbances that had broken out in that city because of the understanding that must be given to Article 4 of the plan which was proclaimed in the Declaration of Jalapa, which was made general and accepted throughout the whole Republic. Although General Terán was successful in achieving his noble objective peaceably, it was not without great risk even to his very life. By virtue of this he ordered some of the troops that had rebelled to march to Matamoros and other points, and decided to go on to that port after short stops in the towns along the way.

Terán arrived in Matamoros in April of 1829, and scarcely had he done so when with the determination and attention that were characteristic of him he devoted himself to organizing a military expedition with which he planned to go personally to Texas (from which he had never for a moment taken his eyes), because of the importance he saw in attending immediately to the regulation of the colonies and the necessity for placing a garrison there and securing the territory. In this connection he was in the habit of saying, very correctly and with knowledge of what he was talking about, that the Texas territory would some day be the apple of discord between Mexico and the United States. In confirmation of this he added that during the year that he had remained on the boundary commission he had had occasion to deal with the leading and most influential colonists and had read their minds and guessed their ulterior motives.

To carry out this idea it was necessary first for him to bring to full strength the permanent battalions that were under his command. These were the eleventh, twelfth and ninth cavalry regiments and a small force of artillery, the presidio companies and civilian militia from the three eastern states. Next he had to set up the maritime and land customs of the port of Tampico on whose products he had to depend for providing himself with the most essential supplies. As we observed before, not only had the troops been reduced by war and the plague, but the ones that were left had their ranks depleted and were barefoot, naked and poorly armed.

The general lacked the cash to remedy all these faults immediately, and to take care of the lack of men he had to allow time for the arrival of the replacements that they were supposed to send him from the states of the interior. Consequently it was indispensable that the customs be well organized and faithfully serviced, for without what it produced nothing could be undertaken, and at that time this was the only resource that the general could count on. It was urgent that the indicated plan should be carried out promptly, and the government had charged the general especially that he should see to it that in Texas due compliance was given to the law of April 6, 1830.

He was to take a hand in the colonization, taking care that this should not be in the twenty leagues of border territory nor in the ten along the coast that were to remain closed. He was to be sure that the enterprises that had been set up had complied with their contracts and to declare illegal and void those that had not been put into effect.

There was even more: The end of that same year 1830, was supposed to see the last of the exemptions and privileges granted to the districts of Texas, Monclova and Río Grande for the importation free of duties of all that they might need for the use of those inhabitants and for the extraction of products from the soil —favors of which the colonists almost without exception had taken advantage of and had abused. It was then indispensable to establish customs on sea and land at all points in the state that were considered as proper for this purpose. Since this could not be accomplished without the use of force, as long as this was insufficient, the measure however advantageous it might have been, had to be delayed, as was true also of the aid that the general had promised himself therefrom for the accomplishment of his principal objective.

For their part, the colonists had continued in absolute freedom, governing themselves as they saw fit, or according to the laws that best suited their particular interests and whims. Their population had increased considerably, and their business dealings and enterprises were going along with astounding promptness and rapidity. At the same time the conditions of the state, which was daily more prodigal and unwise in the grants of lands and in the persons to whom they were made, found itself in the greatest decline because of the smuggling which the colonists were carrying on with the knowledge and patience of officials and citizens of Texas with the United States and the interior of the Republic, using as a pretext the exemptions which they enjoyed. As a consequence they could not even bear the idea that some day an end would be brought to irregularities which were as pernicious as they were liable to punishment.

Intent upon correcting these irregularities, General Terán — whose learning, prudence and tact in his dealings were as well known as were his honesty and patriotism — included in his plan the establishment of military posts properly fortified and garrisoned with the necessary troops in sufficient numbers at the following points: On *Lavaca Creek* where it empties into St. Bernard Bay or *Matagorda*, at the south of the *Brazos River*, on *Galveston Bay*, at the town of *Nacogdoches*, in the far western part of the *Austin* colony on the Brazos River also, and on the road that leads from Béxar to the town of Nacogdoches. He did this in order that the old presidio of La Bahía del Espíritu Santo, to which the legislature of Coahuila and Texas gave the name of *Goliad*, anagram of *Hidalgo*, and the city of Béxar, residence of the principal commander and the political head and which had been recognized in earlier times as the capital of Coahuila, might serve as aids to all these points. It was done also so that the general headquarters might be located in Matamoros where the general was residing at the time.

Also he busied himself in occupying the line from Goliad to Matamoros (eighty leagues of deserted lands) by establishing on the right bank of the Nueces River a military post on the road itself, which post he called *Lipantitlán*. This was in order to stimulate the Lipán Indians politically, as he wished, to begin to take on the ways of civilization and to abandon peacefully and gradually the life of wanderers and the savage customs that they followed.

He also wanted them to settle in *Lipantitlán* as a point of their land, under the shadow, protection and watchful eye of the second active company of Tamaulipas. This under the command of Captain Don Enrique Villareal was ordered to station itself there as was done with the unassigned and presidio troops on the border, according to the regulations of 1772. Finally, he ordered that a war frigate with full crew should serve to convoy with the necessary security all that was to be sent by those towns to *Matagorda, Brazos* and *Galveston*.

[15]

With the military posts located at the points indicated in order to defend the inhabitants from the inroads of the savage Indians, General Terán, always one with foresight and caution since he was aware of the still concealed tendencies of the colonists, was successful and obtained from the general government the power to dispose of half a million pesos to carry out the duties imposed upon him by the above mentioned law of April 6 of that year. At the same time, in order to put into effect his first idea, also pointed out in Chapter 13, he sent a circular letter to the governors of the states of the federation in which he asked and insisted that each one of them should send him twenty poor families to colonize the frontier. Thinking that it would facilitate and speed up the execution of this plan, he had placed in each capital commissioners who would supply those people with the necessary means for their transfer to Monterrey or Saltillo and would assure that their trip should be made with all possible comfort and safety.

In all seriousness he added that they would not be limited to those benefits, but that they would continue to enjoy them until they arrived at the place designated for them. There also they would enjoy not only the use of the lands but would have all the privileges provided by the colonization laws, and indeed they would be given oxen, cows, farming implements, etc., ten pesos per month during the first year, plus one hundred twenty that would be given immediately to each family for them to build their houses in the places set aside for them.

Three months passed without any one of the governors of the states giving an answer to the general's circular. Because of this he sent them out again, but still did not receive a single answer. Never-

67

theless, persisting in his project, he sent them out for a third time, including also this time a very thoughtful and courteous letter in which he clearly developed his well thought out plan for the security of the Texas colonies. The general said that he was doing this because:

> with four hundred fifty Mexican families gathered from the states and a thousand or more soldiers that were located at the military posts, some with their families and others who might acquire them, they would make up a total of eight hundred Mexican families, and this number should produce about four or five thousand inhabitants which would no doubt be sufficient to defend themselves against the inroads of the savages with the aid and protection of the military posts. At the same time they would serve as a counterbalance to the foreign population, could observe their movements and quickly put down any attempts of rebellion or disorder.

Although all of this was quite correct, unfortunately the officials who could do the most to aid in the realization of ideas that were so useful and patriotic did not look at it in this manner.

The amazement and discomfiture of General Terán as he received the personal answers of the governors were such as may be imagined when we learned that unanimously, as if they had made an agreement, they were saying that

> they had not sent nor would they send the families that he had officially requested because they did not wish with the blood of their states to enlarge another that might become more powerful.

Thus did the governors of the states understand the principles of the federation, and thus also unfortunately did they give aid to the treacherous purposes of Texas colonists, although without believing or perhaps having the least suspicion that they were doing so.

Otherwise, from then on the ambition plans for illegal seizure of lands that the colonists had would have failed, and in any move that they might have attempted to make after that they would have quickly encountered more than eight thousand armed Mexican inhabitants who were determined in their defense of the country. These would have been placed strategically in the coastal as well as the border areas, and also in the central part between Béxar and Nacogdoches, which served as a boundary marker for the savages. Furthermore, they could have counted on the effective cooperation of the Cherokee, Kickapoo and Coushatta tribes and another that lived between the Trinity and the Sabine Rivers. Since Mexico had legalized the clandestine possession that they had taken of those lands, they were very grateful and supportive.

Such was the vast and profound plan that was dashed to earth by the immediate negative of the state governors, with whose cooperation with a very few years the happiness of a considerable number of families would have been achieved. Today these people are probably groaning in poverty, and perhaps many of those individuals will increase the number of criminals in the territory of the Republic. With the proposed plan they would have been transformed from proletarians into property owners, from unfortunate people into those who were well to do, and from colonists into citizens of Texas. But let us go back to the account of what was going on in that territory during the period to which we have arrived.

Gaining time and carrying out his plans, General Terán ordered fifty militiamen from Pueblo Viejo and the twelfth regular infantry under the command of Colonel Don Juan Davis Bradburn to embark in Brazo de Santiago on a schooner for Galveston. He commanded that thirty men of the presidio company of Espíritu Santo should join them by land and locate themselves without a moment's delay in their fortified post on Galveston Bay. On Lavaca Creek he ordered the stationing of another small detachment of infantry and cavalry, and on the Brazos River, on the Nacogdoches road, in a place that he called Tenoxtitlán, he stationed the presidio company from Alamo de Parras which had sixty men, and as many more from the presidio company of Béxar, so that all these detachments might give each other mutual aid and reinforcement when necessary.

With the purpose of putting the town of Nacogdoches in communication with the post built at Galveston, which is called *Anáhuac*, he ordered the placement of two detachments, one on the Neches River and the other on the Brazos River, the first to be known by the name of Fort Terán, and the second as Fort Velasco; both were to be in communication with the military post at *Anáhuac*.

Immediately he named the employees for establishing a maritime customs at Galveston and a collection office in *Velasco*, as well as the maritime customs for the port of Matagorda, which was set up, although the latter ones were of an interim character.

This was the state of affairs when he thought it opportune to declare that the only contracts to be considered legal and correctly drawn would be those of the Austin colonies located between the San Jacinto and Colorado Rivers and between the coast and the Nacogdoches road; that of Green DeWitt between the Colorado and Guadalupe Rivers, and that of Martín de León between the left bank of the Guadalupe and Lavaca Creek to the coast. All the other grants made by the authorities of Coahuila and Texas would be considered as held in abeyance until it was made clear whether they had complied with the terms and conditions prescribed by law and stipulated in the contracts.

The customs and collection offices began gathering taxes with the greatest caution; the colonists with some difficulties received the property titles of their respective grants; the claims and even the insults of the impresarios were answered satisfactorily. These were to the effect that they had made colonization contracts with the State of Coahuila and Texas. In short, everything was moving along in the colonies in an orderly and prosperous manner. However, unfortunately, to disturb the fine order of things at that time Don Francisco Madero appeared on the scene. In the role of commissioner for the state he made his way to a point within the limits of Anáhuac, where there were a few American homes. Using the powers that he said he had been given to issue land titles and set up town councils at points that he considered appropriate, he began by founding a town which he called *Liberty*, and he set up a council there.

Madero was accompanied by a secretary whose name was J. M. J. Carbajal, a native of Béxar, but who was raised and educated in the United States, and to this circumstance may very well be attributed the error and untimeliness of such deeds. Colonel Davis immediately informed General Terán of the facts, and at the same time protested to Madero for his actions and the disturbance that the latter was causing to his authority in those places that were under his jurisdiction.

But Madero answered him haughtily, telling Davis that on the contrary he was attacking the sovereignty of the State of Coahuila and Texas. In this fashion he added other reproaches that gave greater encouragement to the colonists, whom he had taken under his protection, and who with this support paid very little heed to the military authority and showed the greatest hatred and scorn for the treasury employees of Galveston. That was all that was needed.

In fact, from the moment that the council was set up, the alcaldes and councilmen began to oppose Colonel Davis and the customs administrator Fisher; their boldness went so far as to threaten the latter with pistols in his own office which he had established on San Luis Island. The commander of Anáhuac, in accordance with General Terán's orders and instructions, and in view of the excesses stated, decided to hold Madero and Carbajal until by the new decisions made by General Terán, who wished to avoid anything upsetting and alarming, they were set absolutely free. However, the ungrateful and persistent Madero, insisting upon his mad projects, instead of withdrawing from them, did nothing less than sow discord between the people of *Liberty* and the authorities of *Anáhuac*, and between the colonists and the *military and the clerks*. How sad the results have been!

[16]

Also contributing to the beginnings of the expression of the intentions of the Texas colonies was the new occurrence which we shall relate. Two Negro slaves from the United States fled from that country and entered ours, placing themselves under the protection of the constitutional laws of Mexico in order to gain their freedom. Their masters made claim for them; the colonists wished them to be handed over. However, Colonel Davis consulted with General Terán, who answered that this affair should be worked out diplomatically between the two nations and not by subordinate authorities. Consequently the slaves were not returned, and because of this the thankless colonists made very evident their insubordination and animosity against the Mexicans and their government.

Therefore, in November of the same year, General Terán, to still if possible such discord, and to calm their emotions, embarked at Brazo de Santiago on the national war schooner *Constante* bound for Galveston. At *Anáhuac* he reviewed everything that had been done by Colonel Davis, and since he found it worthy of approval, he turned his attention to bringing about harmony between the colonists and the Mexican troops. After twelve or fifteen days there he embarked with the same objective on the same boat bound for Matamoros. However, unfortunately his ship ran aground in the port, and since it was in such bad condition it broke up. Things were so bad that General Terán would have been lost if his luck had not been such that the American schooner *Topaz*, which was in those waters, had not come to his aid. They took aboard the crew of the *Constante* and carried them all to Brazo de Santiago where they arrived about the middle of December to continue their voyage.

But this was not to produce the effect that the general had

hoped for because fate was against him. A few days after his return to Brazo de Santiago, he again received information from Anáhuac that informed him of new attempts on the part of the colonists and some ships' captains of the United States; the latter weighed anchor and left the port by stealth without paying the tonnage and other established levies. Their arrogance even went to the point of firing cannon shots at the troops of the port that tried to prevent their departure. With all this, in addition to insulting in a most unworthy manner the national flag, they caused difficulties among the employees and the troops who were trying to uphold the laws and their obligations.

General Terán, however, urged moderation and prudence on both sides, but he did not fail at the same time to keep the general government informed of these events. Since there were complaints of officers and employees against Colonel Davis, he directed that Lieutenant Colonel Don Domingo Ugartechea, acting as second in command and accompanied by troops, employees and the necessary instructions, should set out to establish a maritime customs office at the mouth of the Brazos River. This is a short distance from the western end of San Luis Island that is in communication with Galveston by means of a lagoon that facilitates transportation by boats from one point to the other for aid to the customs and collection office.

As General Terán moved by way of Brazo de Santiago, he was occupied in reinforcing Galveston with troops, and indeed he contracted their transport with the captain of the schooner *Topaz* itself. This was carried out in January of 1832, with one hundred thirteen persons — eighty soldiers and the other officers, employees and their families — with five thousand pesos aid for the Anáhuac detachment, which fortunately were not lost. The supercargo of that boat, whose name was Robinson or Robertson, a ferocious and cruel man, conceived the infamous plan of stealing the money and sacrificing all the unfortunate people aboard, and even the boat itself.

With this evil intention, on one of the nights during the passage — and not one of the best — with the aid of two other sailors who were helping him he gave all those on deck to understand that the weather was going to be bad, and that it was better that they should get down into the hold. When he had accomplished this, he closed and battened down the hatches, thus leaving on deck only the ship's captain in the binnacle, a Mexican soldier as sentinel, Robertson himself, two sailors and a black cook. The officers and even Seaman First Class Don Juan Añorga of the Mexican navy went into their cabins. After these precautions had been taken, suddenly when all were quiet, the brigands pounced upon the captain and the sentry by surprise and threw them into the sea.

Immediately they armed themselves with razors, went into the cabin and began to inflict terrible wounds on the officers sleeping in their bunks. One of the eleventh company, Second Lieutenant Don N. Pintado was wounded several times, once in the throat, and almost beheaded he yelled *treason* as loud as he could. He was heard by Seaman First Class Añorga, in spite of the fact that at the same time Robertson was falling on him to wound him, which caused him to redouble his efforts to defend himself. Since fortunately the cabin was very high, he managed to put his feet against the chest of the murderer and threw him back over several articles of furniture that were on the floor of the cabin; as he fell he also made a lot of noise and repeated the word *treason*. All of this confused Robertson's accomplices who came out of the cabin cunningly blending their yells with those of Añorga and also calling out treason. After them came Robertson threatening death to Añorga and would have killed him if the troops in the hold who heard the voices and the noise had not forced the hatch with their rifle butts and jumped out on the deck. This so frightened Robertson that he jumped on the rigging, climbed along it, and made his escape up one of the ship's masts.

When he couldn't find either the captain or the sentry Añorga had the sailors and the cook arrested, and these declared Robertson's intentions; he ordered him to come down. However, the rebel refused to do so and even dared to make threats with his weapons. With this reaction, the command was given to fire, and Robertson fell into the sea mortally wounded. When his accomplices were questioned at once, they confessed that what they had intended to do was to murder the captain and the officers or throw them into the water, take the money and put it together with provisions and water in a small boat, scuttle the ship so that it would go to the bottom with all those that remained in the hold, and afterward go out to sea.

Indeed, when they searched the ship, they found the instruments and equipment referred to. As a consequence of this occurrence, Seaman First Class Añorga took charge of the ship and continued for thirteen days more on his voyage to Galveston, using the same sailors, but with the greatest vigilance. In like manner attention was given to the wounded. However, with the greater difficulties and the scarcity of food and water, and because of the bad weather which made the circumstances even worse, they also tried to turn against him.

The ship finally arrived at its destination on February 27.

When he gave his detailed report of what had happened, Añorga according to law handed over the guilty ones. Their trial was begun at once, and meanwhile the boat with everything belonging to it remained in the port at Galveston until a higher decision should be made. This was received the following March, and it was ordered that the schooner with everything else that belonged to the deceased captain should be handed over to the American Woodbury, the administrator of the family of the dead man. Unfortunately this could not be done because the boat sank in the mouth of the Brazos River.

Such were the influences operating on the establishment of the North American colonies in our country. One might well attribute these to chance, but also worthy of attention are the concurrence and repetition of so many sad coincidences, which if they do not make frank declaration against the morality and politics of the government of the North American Republic and the lack of adherence to the treaty of January 12, 1828, signed with Mexico on the settling of boundaries as indicated above, they do denounce, nevertheless the character and the antipathy held by those people against those of our soil. They make evident the impossibility of a constant and cordial understanding as we had the right to expect, and which have been sought and have deserved justice for us. This is a truth which time shall make more evident, and fortunately just and true men of good heart are beginning to know this, have understood it, and have had the courage and the necessary dignity to defend it even in the United States.

[17]

Incidentally, and to make still more difficult the regulation of the Texas colonies, to which General Terán had devoted himself successfully and earnestly, there occurred at that time, which was the beginning of the year 1832, the uprising in Veracruz, brought on by the dissatisfaction of the personnel that made up the ministry of the vice-president of the republic, General Don Anastasio Bustamante. He was acting in the capacity of the supreme executive because of the fall and death of Don Vicente Guerrero, upon whose shoulders the presidency had fallen.

The manifest reason for that revolution was the restoration of the ministers, and since neither the government nor the congress would consent since it was demanded by force of arms, it ended up causing a disastrous war, which after the nation had toiled throughout the year 1832, and exhausted its resources, resulted in the famous Zavaleta Plan which also paved the way for the Cuernavaca revolution and the disturbances of 1834.

Thus it was that, either because of political convictions or influences at work in Veracruz, as soon as General Santa Anna's declaration was known in Tampico, Captain Don N. Rodríguez hastened to support it, together with the garrison there and the one at Pueblo Viejo, both of which immediately placed themselves under his orders.

When he became aware of this event, General Terán, who was still at Brazo de Santiago, embarked at once on a national packet boat with the purpose of restraining the progress of that movement. However, Colonel Paredes, whom he left in command, advised him almost at the same time that they had also noted in the troops in Matamoros who were under his command the most open symptoms of wishing to lend support to the revolutionaries. With this in mind, the general moved on that place, and giving up his trip in Matamoros on the night of February 25, just at the time that a declaration was issued by Majors Surbarán and Villasana, Lieutenant Palacios, and another artillery subordinate, together with the eleventh artillery battalion which was quartered there and which the general did not have sufficient forces to oppose.

Nevertheless, he attempted to hold back that attempt, and trusting in the protestations that Colonel Paredes had made to him that he would come to his aid under any circumstances he ordered the latter to go with some of the officers that would obey him to the quarters of the rebels to see if it was possible to bring them back to order. Since these people were in the grip of drunkenness and confusion such as usually go along with such disorderly and irregular excesses, they did not foresee, nor could they prevent the entry of the colonel, nor his taking over the major part of the troops who had been deceived and led astray by that uprising.

Thereby also he was able to apprehend the four principal instigators of the plot, and these were sent immediately to Galveston, Tenochtitlán and two other points in Texas. At that distance they could not exert a harmful influence, and in this manner calm was reestablished in Matamoros for the time being.

A few days later the general received news that Colonel Moctezuma had stationed himself in Altamira with a small force to observe the rebels at Tampico, this on orders from the general government. When he tried to reinforce it with one of the presidio companies — when he could have done it better otherwise — he found out to his surprise by way of Major Micheltorena, whom he had sent to parley with those who had made the declaration, that not only had they not abandoned their objective, but that they were persisting in it aided by Colonel Moctezuma himself who had just joined them with all the forces under his command.

With this state of affairs, the general decided to march at once on Tampico and left Matamoros April 18 of that year, taking with him all the infantry of the eleventh battalion, the presidio cavalry of Matamoros and two artillery pieces. He left the general command in the hands of Colonel Guerra Manzanares because his aim was to attend exclusively to putting down the rebels. But let us leave this worthy and honorable general to his destiny to turn our gaze on what was happening in Texas, which is the principal purpose of these MEMOIRS.

It is worthy of note that since Terán left Anáhuac for Matamoros in the month of December just passed, Madero and his secretary

Carbajal had already left for Monclova where they no doubt informed the governor of the state of all that had happened to them in their turbulent and ill thought out expedition. In order to forestall its consequences instructions had been given to Colonel Davis to transfer the council that Madero had installed in the town of Liberty to that of Anáhuac, although even for the existence of the first there was still lacking the approval of the general government. It should be noted that the mayor who presided over that corporation together with members of his staff obeyed without resistance and continued carrying out their duties without the least protest.

The general likewise ordered that they purchase two cannon that he knew that some private citizens had in Brazoria, and that they be placed immediately as a battery at the mouth of the Brazos, where he had located the maritime collection office and the detachment that was supposed to protect it. In case that measure could not be put into effect, the cannon referred to were to be taken to the town of Anáhuac so that by one means or another they would be out of the control of the colonists.

This precaution was most opportune since during those same days toward the end of December of 1831, and the beginning of January of 1832, several foreigners spread out among the colonies with purpose of sounding out their feelings with regard to making Texas independent of Mexico. Among these there was an adventurer named John Austin, who was no relation of Stephen, and who was noted for his unruly, quarrelsome and enterprising character. However, unfortunately the colonists had not yet decided upon open rebellion, and the emissaries had no success in what they proposed.

Nevertheless, Colonel Davis as the commanding general of Matamoros continued to receive news of the machinations of the many speculators who did not cease to agitate among the colonists for rebellion, and he even ascertained that on the American schooners, *Nelson, Williams, Ticson, Sabinas* and others that were heading for those ports arms and ammunitions were indeed being transported. What confirmed these items was that the schooner *Ticson*, and also the *Nelson* and the *Sabinas* quickly and boldly set sail for the mouth of the Brazos, the first of the fifteenth, and the others on the eighteenth of December, with the collusion of more than fifty colonists who witnessed the event, doubtless with the intention of protecting the departure of those ships should the need arise. Thus they left without paying the duties that they owed, and they fired upon the troops that tried to oppose their flight; this resulted in the wounding of some of the detachment.

Cunningly taking precautions against the effect that the occurrences were bound to produce, Stephen F. Austin believed it opportune to pretend that the colonies were being oppressed and that attempts were being made to insult his compatriots and those favoring them. With such intentions, he wrote a letter to General Terán on January 8, 1832, anticipating their judgmment against the preparations made by his subordinates in those cases. Since the general replied to this letter in terms that were so appropriate to his understanding, wisdom and patriotism, we believe that we will be doing our readers a favor by inserting it here, since fate has brought a copy of it into our hands.

Summary of letter from General Manuel de Mier Terrán to Stephen Austin, dated Matamoros, January 7, 1832, pp. 175–179:
This is relative to the new customs house at Galveston. Because of the lack of such customs the colonists have enjoyed free trade for more than a year past the seven indicated. Only congress can authorize another port, but a clerk will be placed at Brazoria. All ports from Hudson Bay to Cape Horn pay customs duties, so why do the Texans complain? Ships that sailed in violation of port rules shall pay the duties required. Some colonists have fired upon Mexican port officials and wounded a Mexican soldier.
General Terán who wrote the letter, later died; there was a question of suicide, but Filisola feels that he has valid proofs to the contrary.

[18]

The insolence and arrogance of the colonists of the Brazoria party were not limited to the attacks already mentioned, for the man in charge of collections who had been stationed at the south of the Brazos de Dios River because of the crimes committed by the schooners *Ticson, Nelson* and *Sabinas* had also informed General Terán that according to the testimony of the merchants there those attacks had been made under the pretext that it was very difficult for the ships' captains and for commerce to have to unload at the mouth of the river. At that place there was no building in which to place the merchandise for shelter against the weather, and after that they had to take their manifests to Anáhuac which was thirty leagues away.

Taking this into consideration, the administrator consented for the collection office to be transferred to Brazoria, and in charge of it he placed Second Lieutenant Don Juan Pacho. When the latter arrived there on the night of January 22, he found it necessary to remain on board the ship for some time, and from there he observed several groups of armed men.

Because of this, he sent an orderly of his to go and find out the reason. Since he was watching what was going on, he heard that they were asking for him, and that the soldier refused to tell them, saying that he did not know where the lieutenant was, whereupon the ones asking him became angry and beat him so badly that they left him for dead.

When this happened, the collector no longer thought it advisable or safe for him to remain in Brazoria or on the boat, and taking advantage of the darkness, he landed and made his way inland among the thickets and brush of those woods where he spent the night; the next day he went on to a safer spot. But the collusion between the smugglers and the colonists was such that in spite of General Terán's orders mentioned in the previous chapter, the schooner *Sabinas* created a commotion by coming into the port of Brazoria on January 29 loaded with goods and provisions and bringing two cannon aboard. Because of this and the small detachment there, these new assaults went unpunished also just as the previous ones.

With this state of affairs so fateful and contrary to Mexico's interests and since the attempts at rebellion by the colonists could no longer be glossed over, Stephen Austin feared that the government would dictate measures that were more serious and effective. In order to protect himself from the consequences his characteristic suspicious nature suggested to him the new idea of asking for an interview with Colonel Davis.

This meeting took place in *Harrisburg* on February 5, and in it Austin declared that he had the greatest anxiety and fear with regard to the political aspect of the colonies. He did this with such appearances of good faith that Colonel Davis did not come to suspect anything. But neither was it possible for him to conceal the very events to which Austin was referring simply in order to protect himself in case of the failure of his project. He carried on his treacherous dissimulation so that he could lull the suspicions and undertake the following month a new trip to Mexico City without the least difficulty. His true purpose was to get in touch with the revolutionaries there to see if he could bring about the repeal of Article 11 of the decree of April 6, 1830, which prohibited the granting of lands in Texas to natives of North America.

As a consequence of the later occurrences in Brazoria, as soon as Lieutenant Colonel Ugartechea, acting for Colonel Davis with the troops that General Terán had given him to reinforce that military post, arrived in *Anáhuac*, Davis ordered on the following April 2 that he go with one hundred ten men and one piece of eight caliber artillery to set up a fort at the mouth of the Brazos. With him located there it would be easier to observe and give news of the colonists who were the most dangerous because of their ideas and conduct. However, misfortune would have it that the instructions that were given to Ugartechea on these matters fell into the hands of the very ones with whom they dealt, and this disposed them so greatly against Davis and against Ugartechea himself that the position of both of them became daily more difficult in that country.

Meanwhile, new American emissaries and adventurers were going about among the Texas settlements inciting them to rebellion and encouraging them with the prospects of being able to do as they chose with the fertile lands of the country that they so coveted. With all this they were finally able to change the peaceful attitude of the colonists or to get them to continue to mask what they really felt. However, since they were treated with such unusual consideration on the part of the Mexican authorities as well as by private individuals, they still needed excuses to rationalize their uprising and to cover up their unheard of ingratitude and treachery with the semblance of justice although only for the moment. Unfortunately such excuses were not long in presenting themselves.

On a certain day in May of that year in the town of Anáhuac, a few of the presidio soldiers who were given time for relaxation as is usually done in their work, abused the privilege, and planned among themselves to spend that short time in the infamous pleasure of seducing or raping a woman who was near the vicinity of an American home. On the pretext that this man did not go out to defend her, without finding out whether he could or did not hear the cries for help, according to the custom in the United States immediately a large number of Americans living in that town gathered and conceived the plan of taking the unfortunate fellow from his home and parading him through the town *tarred and feathered*.

Indeed, that is what they did, and such were the commotion and hubbub which they raised that it attracted the attention of the military commander Lieutenant Ocampo, who was standing guard with a patrol of a corporal and four men. When they reached the place of the gathering, he commanded them to halt, but far from obeying him they answered with insulting words and a few pistol shots, and they even dared to attack the soldiers. Grabbing one of the latter by his belt they dragged him until they took the belt and his rifle, which they shortly threw away and boldly continued with the rioting and confusion which they had started.

In order to restrain them the military commander went to get more men, and with them he again moved on the troublemakers; when these saw that the situation was getting serious they abandoned their victim and scattered immediately. It had been impossible to apprehend more than four of the ones causing the trouble, and they were a certain Travis, Jark and two others whose names we do not recall, but one of them was a *member of the council*.

By order of Colonel Davis all of them were taken under arrest to the barracks so that charges might be filed against them according to the regulations. Later the general in command was informed of what was happening; in order to avoid the consequences that might result from any act of severity because of the state of haughtiness and insubordination on the part of the colonists, from Tampico on May 31, he ordered Colonel Don José de las Piedras, who was in charge in the town of Nacogdoches, that as he went on to Anáhuac he should try to put an end to so much unrest. To this effect he dictated measures that seemed to him most appropriate and according to justice. But the die was cast, and decisions of a different type were needed.

John Austin, *at that time mayor of Brazoria,* who for some time had been working for the independence of Texas, took advantage of the incident referred to in order to incite his friends to begin to tempt fate. He decided to attack the military post at Anáhuac under the pretense of taking back the prisoners that were going to be tried by the military court, and also the presidio soldiers who had insulted the woman. He was sure that they would not be handed over in that violent and illegal manner, so that he could take advantage of that negative to cover up in that way his true intentions, should his daring undertaking turn into misfortune.

In order to carry it out he gathered together about two hundred armed colonists in Brazoria, and on June 4, he set out for Anáhuac. As he passed through in the vicinity of Fort *Velasco* at the mouth of the Brazos, the commander of which was Colonel Don Domingo Ugartechea, the latter came out to the road and did all in his power to persuade him to give up that daring attempt. Ugartechea believed in good faith that he was acting entirely in favor of the arrested men.

Austin pretended to be persuaded and offered that he would seek his aid purely in terms of petition and friendship. He even asked him to join him in his request by making a recommendation that he could give to Colonel Davis. With this understanding, Ugartechea wrote to the chief and had his aide, Second Lieutenant Don N. Domínguez go with Austin. He was flattering himself with the satisfaction that in this manner he had avoided all disorder and the fatal consequences that could still arise from it.

On the ninth Davis had news of the approach of that band of thugs. In order better to assure himself of the number of men that made up that band and to know what they were up to he sent out a scouting group of cavalry along the road over which they were coming; this was under the command of Lieutenant Don Miguel Nieto. In spite of the fact that the latter made his march with due precautions, he was surprised by Austin's men at a place called *Verdura* and detained with his group as prisoners, and only one was able to flee; this one did not present himself at the point from which they had left, as was to have been expected.

83

On the tenth at eight o'clock in the morning Austin continued his march; he stopped the men that he was leading four miles from Anáhuac, and presented himself in that town to Colonel Davis accompanied by Second Lieutenant Domínguez. Both made known the claims of the colonists and Ugartechea's recommendation; Austin added that the decision of his associates was to take the criminals with them, with or without the consent of Colonel Davis. The latter as the only one responsible, could have given him his answer either granting or denying that insolent effort, but he made the mistake of calling the officers of the garrison together to give their opinion, no doubt confident that it could not be anything else but negative.

However, in addition, he tolerated the audacity and rudeness with which Austin demanded that while the official group was deliberating the colonel should leave the room where they were meeting on the pretext that he was partial in the discussion because of the personal animosity which he had for one of the prisoners. The decision of the officers could not have been other than what it was — that is that the prisoners must be tried by the military court in accordance with Article 26 and several others of Title 10, Eighth Treatise of the General Ordinances of the Army. They were not to be handed over; there was no way, without even considering the circumstances and the illegal and insolent manner in which they had been demanded.

Austin pretended to remain calm and convinced, and even offered to persuade his companions to give up that unjust demand so that they might disperse and return to their respective homes. However, at that very moment they were entering the town, as was learned by a message from a small group of the troops that were guarding the hospital which was located in the small plaza called *Malinche*. These had to withdraw to the fort according to the order that had been given for such a case. The revolutionaries immediately occupied the plaza, and from there they began to scatter throughout the town against the peaceful inhabitants who had not wished to take part in the uprising. They wounded some, apprehended others and abused every one with indignities and insults.

In view of so many attempts Colonel Davis ordered that they be notified to leave the town and that whatever request that they might wish to make should be made from outside the boundaries. However, the answer was the sending of a commission which presented itself in the post to go over again the same thing that Austin had said. Although they were made to see the crime that they had committed by attacking a fortified point and trying to remove from judgment criminals who were already under the verdict of the law, they made it clear that they were determined to carry out their effort and to take whatever consequences might result therefrom. They then retired to a place that they had selected as a support point. As soon as they got there they opened fire on the guards at the military post. Davis, in order to drive them away, sent out a small force against the most advanced ones; these when they saw that they were being fired upon fled to join the others. From time to time some of them moved forward to fire at the parapets and flee again until they were out of rifle range.

But since Davis had under his command no more than forty-one men he should not and did not venture to move outside the post against a number so superior and which was increasing with those who were joining them from the town and the vicinity. Thus the rebels continued harassing the garrison all that day and the next, although about that time the schooner *Marta* dropped anchor in Galveston Bay. Colonel Davis had sent it to the port of Matamoros for provisions and money for the garrison, and it carried on board Colonel Surbarán and the sergeant who because of the row which this chief had headed up in Matamoros had been ordered by the general to Fort Terán under the orders of Colonel Piedras. Although the colonists who were aware of his ideas tried to get him on their side, Davis had them disembark at once. He informed Colonel Surbarán of the state of affairs, and they gained nothing with that turn of events for the time being, neither was Surbarán able to be of any use to them in any way.

On the eleventh an official note was received from Mayor Williams, who in the role of mediator asked for an interview with Lieutenant Colonel Don Felix Surbarán, which Davis (now sure of him) granted in the home of the administrator of that port; asked to attend also were Don Juan Cortina, accompanied by the minor aide Don Juan María Pacho and the physicist Don Andrés Hurtado. The discussion was rather lengthy. Finally it was agreed that in the interests of good order and to avoid bloodshed, forty-eight hours after Austin and those with him had left the town they would hand over to the mayor of *Liberty* the criminals, together with the testimony in the case that had been brought against them, so that the trial might continue.

Williams withdrew to make known the results of the interview to the rebels, and Colonel Davis hoped that everything would be concluded the following day and that peace would be restored with their consent. However, just the opposite happened. The rebels did not cease firing on the post during the rest of the day of the eleventh and the night of the twelfth, and the moment that Mayor Williams left for Trinity, Austin presented himself declaring that nothing of what had been agreed to was valid.

In spite of that inconsistency and the new insult to the national arms the colonel still granted the rebels the request to name a new commission to work together again for a rational agreement, designating for the place the same house in which they had met before. At nine o'clock in the morning there were gathered on behalf of the garrison the same commissioners of the day before, and on behalf of the rebels those that they had newly elected, whose names we do not know. The discussion lasted until after sunset, and from it the result was to agree on the same thing that had been arrived at in the first interview, and it was signed with all formality. As a consequence the rebels set at liberty the detachment of cavalry that they had surprised on the ninth, and it was considered that everything was concluded, but that was not yet the case.

Since the first condition of the agreement required that the band of roughnecks should leave the town and that the members of the group should go to their houses, they pretended to do so during the night, but only half of them left and went to camp at the distance of about a mile. The rest of them remained hidden in the houses to see if the confidence of those at the post would give them an opportunity to take it over later that night or the next morning. However, their treacherous intention was upset by the vigilance which the garrison maintained during the night and by the watchfulness and care of the outposts.

The latter noted after dawn that some houses, and they were the ones in which the rebels were hiding, remained closed up longer than usual, which caused them to suspect what the enemy was planning. Because of this the guard held itself ready and armed.

Colonel Davis ordered them to warn John Austin that if they did not vacate the houses and go to their respective homes within two hours, he would find it necessary to make them do so by armed force. However, if they did as directed, as soon as he was sure of it he would send the criminals and the case that was being drawn up against them to the mayor of *Liberty* according to the requirements that the agreement imposed upon him.

When more than an hour had passed since Davis's message to the rebels, and he had received no reply nor noted any movement indicating that they were beginning to evacuate the town — on the contrary some signs of resistance were seen — he was convinced that the only thing to do in order that the national arms should not be scorned was to make use of them by punishing those bold and persistent rebels. To this end, he ordered that at three-thirty in the afternoon Lieutenant Colonel Don Félix Surbarán, with a number four cannon directed by the second aide Don Juan Cortina, thirty infantrymen of the permanent twelfth battalion, under the orders of Second Lieutenant Don Miguel Araiza and Lieutenant Don Manuel Montero, and eleven mounted dragoons, under the command of a sergeant, should make a sortie and launch a determined attack on the enemy.

This was not necessary because the latter, as soon as they saw the troops starting out, fled shamelessly to the nearby woods in frightful disarray and without waiting for a single shot. Surbarán took six prisoners and rounded up some horses with saddles that had been abandoned as well as some firearms of all calibers. He searched the nearby woods, and satisfied that all of them had fled, he returned to the fort to celebrate a victory that because of the caution of the armed Texas colonists had not left as all the rest the sorrow of burying the dead, tending the wounded, paying pensions nor supporting in the future those that were disabled.

Thus ended the first campaign of the new Normans in Texas. The peaceful people of *Anáhuac* that had been obliged to take refuge in the post or the nearby woods because of the stormy visit of such guests returned to their homes and normal occupations, and quiet was restored in that town.

[19]

After frustrating for the third time the treasonous intentions of the adventurers with regards to the Texas colonies, and in spite of the humiliation, as we have said, of the enterprising John Austin's attempt against Anáhuac, he did not give up trying it again and directed his plans against Fort Velasco, which prevented the entry of contraband for Brazoria. In order to do this he once more excited the greed of his compatriots and managed to muster up to two hundred armed men, using as his excuse the declaration for the Veracruz Plan in order to cover up for the time being his true intentions of taking from the Republic the rich colony of Texas.

To this end a revolutionary junta was organized — a provisional government was named, they armed the schooner *Brazoria* with the artillery pieces that had been left there by the *Sabinas*, and forthwith with premeditation the revolutionaries made their way by the Brazos River against Fort Velasco, under the command as has been stated of Lieutenant Colonel Don Domingo Ugartechea. His calmness and bravery were sufficient to punish that treasonous aggression in spite of the reserves and the surprise element with which it was carried out, and the scoundrels that planned it all paid for it dearly. Here is an extract from the account that Lieutenant Colonel Ugartechea sent to Colonel Davis of these occurrences, as is customary:

Summary of communication from Colonel Ugartechea to Colonel Davis, dated July 1832, pp. 194–204:

On June 23 four of the rebels approached with a flag of truce and said that they had declared for the Veracruz Plan, inviting the fort commander to do likewise. Ugartechea refused. Later forces approached by land. The next day the schooner moved closer. When the forces moved still closer on the twenty-sixth Ugartechea opened fire. After repeated volleys and sallies there was a suspension of hostilities. When Mexican officials saw the lack of ammunition and the superior numbers he ordered a flag of truce. After much argument the colonists agreed to allow Ugartechea to withdraw with all equipment and arms and honor intact. There was no other way out for the Mexicans without supplies, arms, munitions or means with which to care for the wounded, and especially without any hope of receiving aid from anywhere.

[20]

Colonel Don José de las Piedras, military commander of the town of Nacogdoches, had received orders from General Terán to go down to Anáhuac and restore however possible the order of things that had been so upset in that place, as we have stated above. To do this he set out with only two men to be there at the end of June, with absolutely no knowledge of what was going on at Fort Velasco during those same days.

In the vicinity of Anáhuac he met up with a party of rebel colonists who tried to stop him. In order to avoid any abuse of his dignity and person he told them that if the cause of their dissatisfaction was the fact that Travis and his companions under arrest had not been delivered to them in Anáhuac, or the fact that Davis was still in that place as commander, he would oblige them on both counts by handing over the prisoners to the mayor of *Liberty* and relieving Davis of his command. The rebels were satisfied with this offer, promising to continue on their way, and Piedras reached Anáhuac July 1. Since he understood that the insurrection had spread to all the colonies and that he had no time to lose there because of the need for his presence in Nacogdoches, that same day he sent to Colonel Davis the remarkable communication that we are including below:

"His Most Excellent Commander General, under date of May 31 just past, informs me of the following.—The dissensions in the new settlement of *Anáhuac* endanger that place, and in order to avoid the consequences, leaving the most trusted officer in this place where everything is quiet, you will go to Anáhuac to take whatever measures seem opportune to quell the disturbances.—God and Liberty. Anáhuac, July 1, 1832.—José de las Piedras.—Señor Military Commander of this post, Colonel Don Juan Davis Bradburn."

90

Colonel Piedras was scheduled as military commander of Aná-huac to explore on the second, and as soon as that was done he had the prisoners Travis, Jark and accomplices as well as the sailors from the crew of the schooner *Topaz* to go to *Liberty*. These were being tried there, and this was so that the mayor of that place could continue the proceedings, which reverted to the place where they were. Since he considered that Colonel Davis did not deserve that insult, and also that his return to Nacogdoches was as necessary and urgent as we have indicated also, as soon as he had taken the steps that seemed to him most conducive to the restoration of peace and order in that garrison, he sent to Davis this second communication.

Summary of letter from Colonel José de Piedras to John Davis Bradburn, Anáhuac, July 4, 1832, pp. 207–211:

Colonel Piedras feels that there is no doubt but that the Texas colonists have plans for separating from Mexico, promoted by Austin's colony and making excuses to prepare everyone for it. The writer sees the situation as critical for lack of finances because of the revolution, with no hope of aid. There is a lack of manpower, and resources are spread over long distances. Great tact is needed to restore order, and the authorities must punish the insolence of the colonists. Colonel Piedras has calmed the people and halted the uprising in some districts that favored rebellion. They are awaiting the results of the prisoners' petition.

The colonel has arranged to return to Nacogdoches and make use of the truce. Mayor Thompson has given strict orders to avoid any further inopportune break. The stockpiling of needed supplies will be the main purpose hoping to receive aid from the interior. Administrator Cortina is to make collections, and Colonel Piedras will try to send aid to Nacogdoches. Fortification works must continue. He begs Davis to prolong the truce. Mayor Thompson is popular with the people. The officers and troops of the post are in excellent condition, and Lieutenant Cortina has a good reputation and the respect of the people.

Davis has learned that there are generals and officers from the North who have offered to lead them in the struggle to make the country from the Río Grande independent of Mexico.

When Davis refused to take command again, Piedras gave it to Lieutenant Cortina, a person highly commendable for his knowledge, honesty and moderation. He returned to Nacogdoches, leaving orders for Lieutenant Colonel Félix Surbarán to follow him to that place as soon as it was possible for him to do so. He ordered

Colonel Davis, in case of a new attack on the part of the colonists, to take command of the post again. But let us learn from the pen of Colonel Don John Davis Bradburn himself what happened after Piedras' departure, and what Davis himself witnessed until he was able to escape the persecutions of those men.

Summary of letter from Colonel John Davis Bradburn to General Filisola, Matamoros, April 28, 1833, pp. 212–217:

Colonel Davis worked feverishly on the warehouses and fortifications, and he learned from Cortina that the troops were in rebellion in the plaza. During this time the prisoners returned with a few barrels of whiskey and succeeded in getting some to follow them. By the aid of friends, Davis — together with Ocampo, Cortina, Montero, Domínguez, Añorga and Nieto — fled from Anáhuac.

On his trip to the Mississippi, Davis met many people who said that they were on their way to help throw the Spaniards out of Texas.

In this situation it is necessary to use force to subdue the colonists and enforce Mexican law. Between the Nueces and the Sabine Rivers there are an estimated 2,000 inhabitants. Cotton, corn and wheat are cultivated with livestock and hogs in great numbers. By way of the Neches River products are exported and goods are brought in from New Orleans. The colonists hanged three lawyers in effigy and hanged the priest Muldorn.

There are some colonists who are on the side of the Mexicans, some remain neutral and some have followed the rebels. Davis believes that by way of Galveston Island, Anáhuac might be occupied. The mayor of Acosito is favorable to the general government.

Thus there is protection for a division of the best among the colonists, and their zeal makes one see well the necessity for obeying the Mexican federal government.

[21]

In the previous account of Colonel Davis he made mention incidentally of the arrival of Colonel Don José Antonio Mejía in Galveston Bay, and in this regard it seems proper to inform our readers concerning the purposes that took him to that port and of the events to which his presence gave rise, on account of the great influence which this had on the affairs in Texas.

Colonel Mejía had left the port of Tampico about the middle of June in 1832, with a small squadron composed of six or seven boats, of which two were warships and the rest transports that were carrying something like two hundred fifty or three hundred infantrymen of the civilian militia and a few regular and active soldiers. His first destination was Soto la Marina, no doubt with the objective of occupying that town and bar and seeing what there was in that maritime customs in order to take these resources away from General Terán who was operating in the interior of Tamaulipas. In this manner he could engage his attention while General Moctezuma was organizing an expedition to go into the interior to San Luis Potosí, Zacatecas, Guadalajara, etc. But when Mejía found out at the bar that Sergeant Major Micheltorena was in the town with a company of troops in good condition, and that he had thrown up a fortification near the riverbank, he put the few men who had been on land back on the boat and headed for Brazo de Santiago to see if an opportunity presented itself to take Matamoros. There he should be able to find greater resources and obtain better advantages than in Soto la Marina.

With this plan in mind he went on to the Brazo de Santiago bar with all his boats and from there was able to order the surrender of Captain Yhary, the commander of the post. Since the latter could

93

put up no resistance, he was taken prisoner with three or four men who served him as orderlies. Mejía had his men disembark and moved on *Boca Chica* which presented no obstacle either. However, he did not spend the night there because he noted that his actions were being observed by the Matamoros troops. But many of the people of the area came to him and encouraged him to continue with his undertaking, in the belief that he had won over all the troops of the garrison, and that the people and the authorities would declare in his favor.

Mejía was afraid and could not make up his mind, but finally at dawn on June 27, he set out with his column and marched with the greatest caution, exchanging shots along the way with a guerrilla band of presidio troops that seemed to attract him to a certain point. As he approached the village of *La Burrita*, in the houses along the left bank of the Río Bravo (Río Grande), from a small hill to his left, he saw a large group of cavalry of about seventy or eighty men in formation that were trying to attack him. His first order, before commanding the deployment of the column or the execution of any other maneuver, was that a gun they had on a carriage should be mounted on the hill; when this was done, he ordered them to open fire. As a matter of fact, the shot passed above the band of cavalry where they observed movements of confusion and disorder, with one part coming down on Mejía's column, while the others scattered.

Nevertheless, this also produced great confusion in Mejía's troops and in the people who were following him on horseback, to the extent that they were all on the point of running away, each one in his own direction, when a sergeant came forward. He told Mejía and his companion not to be afraid, that those men were coming to join his side and bringing their officers as prisoners. Although they were glad to hear this, there were still some who rose up in anger; there was one who went so far as to rush out of formation to meet the group that was approaching and to open fire with his pistol on one of the officers who was coming under arrest. This braggart was Don Agustín Mora Basadre, and the one attacked in such an infamous manner was Lieutenant Don Ignacio Rodríguez.

When the prisoners were presented to Mejía everything was joy and excitement with *vivas* and *mueras* (*long live* and *death to . . .*). In this manner they all crossed the Río Bravo at the point called *La Burrita* to the houses on the right bank, where there was also presented as a prisoner by his troops an officer of the twelfth infantry who commanded a small band of the eleventh battalion composed of fifteen men. The sergeant had caused his troops to rebel and captured the officer, whom he handed over to Mejía, while he and his fourteen men added to the latter's forces. With these and with the people who could come out to join him he made his triumphal entry into the city on June 29, without any resistance. Immediately he thought it necessary to raise more troops, encourage the towns of the north and other places, and finally to provide himself with financial resources at any cost.

For this purpose he planned to sell for fifteen thousand pesos the rights to three boats that had just come into port, and which surely would have brought to the public treasury close to fifty thousand pesos in their respective payments. This squandering of money gave evidence of how little he was interested in getting anything other than victory for his own party. But before going on with the affairs of Colonel Mejía, let us turn our attention towards those that were taking place at the same time in Matamoros with the colonists.

We have already said that Colonel Guerra Manzanares was in command at that point, in all of Northern Tamaulipas, and in the general area of Texas. The garrison which he had in Matamoros was composed of seventy men, most of them from the first presidio company of Tamaulipas, and some from the second. Thirty men were from the civilian cavalry of Nuevo León and fifty were recruits in training from the eleventh infantry battalion.

As soon as Colonel Guerra learned that John Austin had rebelled in Texas with two hundred colonists and that he was between the towns of Austin and Brazoria, he gave orders to the effect that the detachments should send out troops that all together should fall upon the rebels and attack them, thus forcing them to disband and to return peacefully to their colonies, at the same time to lay aside their arms, and punishing the instigators of the uprising with the full rigor of the law.

All this he intrusted to Colonel Piedras, making preparations for him to leave Nacogdoches and take command of the expedition. He decided immediately to send information on what had happened to General Terán, who was then at the Buena Vista Ranch, otherwise called *El Cojo*. By extraordinary efforts he arrived at the ranch within forty-eight hours in time for Don Stephen Austin to have presented himself on his return from Mexico City in company with one called General Mason. Austin came as the agent for the colonization undertakings in Texas and was going to discuss the matter with General Terán. The latter exercised his confidence and showed Austin the correspondence that he had just received from Colonel Guerra. As soon as Austin learned of the contents he broke into bitter complaints against the acts of violence that the colonists were suffering, accompanied by the greatest demonstrations of disapproval for the provisions set forth, which he said would cause total rebellion and the loss of Texas.

Finally, whether because he was coming from the interior which was the theater of the revolution, or to lull the general and obtain contradictory orders, he even told him that he would answer with his head for the security of Texas if the general would revoke the provision set forth by Colonel Guerra. Because of his insistence and the most unusual guarantee the general agreed. He gave instructions to Austin and commanded him to march at once to Matamoros to have an interview with Colonel Guerra — whom he informed concerning Austin's unusual mission. He directed that the provisions set forth against the colonists should be canceled. Indeed, as soon as Guerra received the new orders, he issued his own, contrary to the first ones tht he had given to the detachments, and waited for Austin, who was not long in arriving from Matamoros.

On the third or fourth day following his arrival, and after he had conferred with Colonel Guerra, he was fully informed of what was happening at that place and in Texas, and as a result he sent to General Terán the letter which we include here. This is so that our readers may be aware of the rude, presumptuous and haughty terms in which this man began to express himself from that time, as well as of the ideas that he had spread about and of those which he might harbor for future plans.

Summary of letter to General Manuel Terán from Stephen F. Austin, Matamoros, June 27, 1832; second paragraph p. 223 to p. 228:

Austin appreciates the extension of time for the introduction of certain products but deplores the inclusion of whiskey. Iron, steel, tools, wagons, etc., are much more vital. Whiskey is admitted because of industry, morale and harmony. In truth he feels it is a curse, and nothing was said about it by the Austin council.

Austin doubts the wisdom of keeping Fisher in customs in Galveston.

He said often that it is impossible to govern Texas by military means; the greater the army beyond the necessary guard units, the greater the danger to peace and tranquility. Austin points out that he has maintained order without a single soldier; two years before he planned to organize the police but feared that suspicions would have created false ideas.

Because of confrontations in various places there has been mistrust, and the colony feels there is no government. The only legitimate authority to handle these evils is the state government and not the military.

Things are going badly in Anáhuac, but the people will reestablish constitutional order. Davis is very military, and another misfortune is his lack of moral fortitude to scorn rebels from whatever side. He is suspect by some because he is not Mexican by birth. He should do his job without listening to spies, pretended friends, etc., or he will have the trust of no one. He is a good man but lacks tact.

Austin expresses hatred of any sort of militarism. Removal of the military and religious tolerance are two badly needed changes. He also feels that the party against the ministry should not be called the Santa Anna party but *the democratic republican federal* party to indicate a matter of principles without regard to persons.

He plans to go to Saltillo to escape the heat and will return to Texas in October. In April or May Austin plans to visit his native land after twelve years of absence.

The observations to which the preceding letter gives rise to shall include in the following Chapter.

[22]

If we did not know so well the author of this letter, it alone would be sufficient to prove his character, his systematic politics and the treacherous intentions that he harbored concerning Texas, as well as the ingratitude with which he responded to the generosity with which he was granted privileges for his colony that were not enjoyed by any other part of the Republic. In the first place we see as is indicated, instead of with gratitude, he repays the government with the gravest of insults because his colonists were permitted the free importation of whiskey. He complains of the evil that this drink could cause to those people, as if by prohibiting them these people would not have been given a more plausible pretext for creating trouble. If they had not received it free of all duty, could they not have said also that the levies even on the most necessary items were unbearable for them?

In the second place, he enumerates the articles the importation of which should have been free because he believed that the colonists were exempt from all types of taxes and took as an insult measures of just precaution that they themselves had made necessary by their previous abuse and exemptions.

In the third place he reproaches the government because it paid no attention to the city councils and threatens it with armed rebellion if it does not remove an employee whose only crime was to take care for the exact and faithful fulfillment of the laws which the colonists who were Austin's compatriots scorned and infringed upon at every moment with the greatest boldness.

He implies that Texas was governed by the military, when those rebellious men did not obey any laws of the Republic, with no other basis for such gratuitous imputation than the fact that in accordance with an existing article of army ordinance charges were being brought against those who had insolently breached the peace and made an armed attack on a patrol that tried to avoid, as it should have, the excesses and attempts of the colonists of Anáhuac.

He speaks of an army in Texas when there were scarcely one thousand men to guard a multitude of anchorages, two hundred leagues of coastline, and more than three hundred of frontiers, and to defend the inhabitants against the incursions of the barbarians. These same men had as enemies even more dangerous than the barbarians Austin's compatriots, who under his shadow and protection came to settle in Texas to live as they chose.

He boasts with an impudence difficult to analyze that he had maintained order in his colony since the year 1821, without the necessity of a single soldier when there were always available in that Department the presidio companies of Béxar, the Alamo, La Bahía del Espíritu Santo and Monclova. Furthermore, they could count on all the Mexican people of Nacogdoches and Béxar, who for the war against the Indians were as good or better than the regular soldiers themselves.

He did not consider that the opening of the ports of commerce, to which settlers flocked as the advantages were becoming known, necessitated more soldiers to keep all within their rights and to see that the laws of the country were followed. At the same time they protected people from any rash attempt either by the inhabitants themselves or by some outside nation. Furthermore, when Texas was not subject to any kind of duties, and consequently when there were no population, ports or frontiers to protect, troops were not sent because they were not needed. This was done when that state of affairs had to cease and when the insolent disobedience of the colonists with respect to the laws and the knowledge of their future plans absolutely required that such measures be taken.

He hypocritically pretends to confuse the need that the whole nation has for guarding its coasts and borders with troops with the establishment of a purely military government, and he insists that he alone with his civilians, the constitution in his hand and wise laws would answer with his head for the security of Texas. This fatuous boasting is all the more insolent and repugnant in that right in his colony never had they observed the constitution or any law of the general congress or particular ones of the state, and when under his protection were born all the disturbances that involved Texas through the effects of the subversive doctrines that he himself had spread among his colonists.

He says that he did not organize civilian militias in Texas as a colonel named for this purpose by the governor of the State because at that time a thousand suspicions were raised against him. But the results prove that never could they have been more just concerning his treasonous plans.

He adds that the situation in Texas was very unfortunate because of Article 11 of the law of April 6, 1830, and that it was very important to correct it in that respect. No doubt he did wish that to be done! This article did not permit the entry into Texas of the great number of his fellow countrymen that Austin considered necessary for the bold takeover that he was planning and later put into effect, when in Mexico in a regrettable surprise move this article was nullified, and the increase in Texas vagabonds from the United States gave Austin the opportunity that he was lacking as he wrote this letter.

He observed that because of attempts of those of the general government to prevent attacks on state employees against the general laws that were being undertaken in Trinity by the inhabitants of the east of his colony, they were saying that there was no government there other than that of the strongest. But he forgets that his own people never respected the general or the state laws and did nothing but their own will, taking advantage of the fact that there was no one there to make them fulfill their obligations. This was the kind of order that Stephen Austin wished to have all the time in his colony!

Then he adds that the only legitimate authorities for correcting those ills were those of the state and the military. No doubt he would like to have things that way since the state could do nothing to oppose the ulterior and treasonous motives of Austin, who wished to be able to carry them out with the least opposition.

The reflections that he ventures also concerning the character and condition of Colonel Don Juan Davis Bradburn, up to a certain point had some foundation. But Austin's objective was to have him removed from Anáhuac because of his strength of character and his loyalty to his adopted country, and more than anything else because of the fact that he understood English. This often made him aware of what the colonists were thinking since in their frequent drunken bouts they could not help making known their true designs, pending the time that some opportunity might present itself for carrying them out.

We are as much opposed to military despotism as is Austin, but was there or could there even be such in Texas? In that territory the whole population was scattered by families over great distances from each other in dwellings or farms that they were establishing. The troop detachments occupied only the ports and military posts that had just been located there for the security of the country and the protection of the new customs houses. Consequently, these places were isolated and some distance from the homes of the colonists and had nothing to do with them or any influence on them. Hence it is that the questions that arose with the state employees had only to do with enforcing the orders of the general government and the procedures of the employees of the federal treasury. The colonists were the ·first to ignore both of these, refusing to pay the import duties and protecting the escape of foreign merchant ships without paying what the laws specified, and scorning the national arms and flag.

They were the first to insult and attack the troops and to claim impunity for their crimes by removing the culprits from the power of the jurisdiction that according to express laws was supposed to judge them. They were the ones who wished to live according to their own free will, smuggling and attacking the treasury employees. They were the ones who made fun of our religion, customs, and generosity and the provisions under which they had come there to settle. They were the ones, in short, who formed armed bodies to attack military posts and treasury offices and then under the excuse of liberty and federation participated in a revolution in which they should have had no part when they ought to have been busy in their work and the development of their settlements.

When all this is known, as it could not then have been known by every one — even Austin himself, who certainly knew him better than the former would have liked — it will be easy to deduce how great was the suspicion with which Don Stephen Austin made the argument that we are here refuting. Even more clearly, since the military chief in Texas — as was their duty — were restraining with a strong hand the excesses of the colonists, Austin says that that was military despotism. This was, in Austin's opinion, the exercise of military despotism.

Finally, the other reflections that he permits himself concerning the army, its strength, the revolution of General Santa Anna, religious tolerance, etc., etc., are not worthy of worrying about. However, we cannot overlook the treasonous insinuation that he makes to General Terán that he should take part in and even head up the revolution that began in Veracruz, nor Austin's vague forgetfulness on the matter of his protests at the Hacienda *del Cojo* concerning the pacification of Texas, for which purpose he left Matamoros so precipitously, as has been said. Better informed there of the advantages that those bandits had acquired over the troops through lack of agreement between themselves and of unity in command, he changed his mind. Wishing to give the appearance of having been extraneous to those events so that he might later offer himself for intrigue, he had been careful to tell the general that he was on his way to Saltillo, in the opposite direction from that of his offer. Such were the maneuvers and the distinctive character of Stephen Austin.

[23]

We realize very well that the unburdening of our ideas that we have made in the chapter preceding Don Stephen Austin's letter could merit apology if we were not aware of the truth concerning the deeds which are the things that most clarify this material and which must serve as a basis for the statesmen and even private individuals who may be interested in discovering the truth and of taking advantage of the lessons that are set forth by this disjointed but scrupulous and conscientious outline of the history of the Texas Colonies. With this in mind, we will not be accused of the presumptuous childishness of wishing to enlighten our readers more than is necessary for them to understand the materials that we have thought fitting to include here. If we have deviated somewhat from the mere role of narrator, it has been only for the sake of conscientiously taking on that of witness for whatever weight our poor but humble testimony may be able to give in favor of the events upon which the judgment of future ages must rest.

Taking up again then the chain of events that we left interrupted in Chapter 21, it must be stated that Don Stephen Austin, betraying the offers made to General Terán, had changed his route and advised Colonel Guerra of having seen from Soto la Marina the squadron and troops of Colonel Mejía's ships. By virtue of this the colonel marched the seventy presidio men to oppose Mejía at *Boca Chica* or *La Burrita*, and to continue firing on them and making things difficult for them all the way to Matamoros where he intended to put up a resistance with the rest of his troops and those which were to come, as has been said, to reinforce them, although they were quite far away. He conferred in great detail and at length with Austin concerning the events in Texas, the preparations that had been ordered and countermanded as a consequence of an order from higher up, and finally concerning General Terán's commands for the carrying out of which the necessary orders were being issued.

It is worthy of note that among the complaints that Austin made to Colonel Guerra on behalf of the colonists, one of them was that of the naming of foreigners for the filling of the principal public posts of that territory, such as Father Muldoon for priest, Colonel Davis Bradburn as commander and Don George Fisher as maritime administrator. To this Colonel Guerra replied that precisely by doing this they had sought the good of the colonies since they were given individuals who knew well the language of the inhabitants and could explain to them clearly the laws of the country and the religious doctrines, the knowledge of which everywhere contributes to the tranquility and good order of the people.

Thus other observations and objections were made and prolonged the conference from seven until ten o'clock at night. As a result of what Austin indicated this time, what the colonists wanted exactly was not to have these people who understood what they were plotting, nor those who would keep watch on their operations because they only intended to get around the rights of import, and above all they proposed to take over that territory. In a word, they wished to have an excuse for justifying their rebellion as we shall see later.

With things in such a state news came of the debarkation carried out by Mejía at Brazo de Santiago on June 27. After having made the necessary preparations to strengthen the fort and other points Lieutenant Don Adeodato Rivero arrived with two or three presidio men and brought news of what had occurred that same morning of the 28th at *La Burrita* Hill. It was also learned at the same time what had happened on the right bank of the river at that hill to Lieutenant Noriega with his guerrilla band, which had been sent to serve as support for the cavalry.

Because of this, Colonel Guerra in Matamoros — who had only twenty-seven men of the thirty from Nuevo Leon with thirty-five of the recruits from the eleventh battalion and a few criminals from various groups that had been in the prison — decided to retreat in good order towards San Fernando de Presas. This was the point where most of the help was supposed to arrive with which the city and port of Matamoros might be repaired, according to the information which had been given to General Terán concerning the situation and the circumstances.

Actually, on his withdrawal from Matamoros he left at six

o'clock in the evening of June 28, and spent the night at the Rancho del Tigre about six leagues away. On the 29th he stopped in Santa Teresa, and on the 30th he arrived at San Fernando without any mishap to his troops or to any of the several families that accompanied him.

It should be pointed out that Mejía, after the occurrence at *La Burrita* Hill, invited Guerra to an interview, which the latter refused forthwith. However, while he remained in San Fernando with his small force, he busied himself only in training it in the handling of arms and in preparing for the defense. On the afternoon of July 4 he received a dispatch from Mejía in which he was informed that the former had taken over a packet boat that was on its way from Brazoria (in Texas). On it he had found a large amount of correspondence from Colonel Ugartechea in which he also informed Guerra that the rebellious colonists had attacked him at the fort on the bar named Velasco. When he had used up all his ammunition, he had found it necessary to surrender, leaving the fort with all the honors of war, and he was on his way overland to Matamoros. This event, Mejía added, was worthy of the greatest consideration, and as a consequence he urged him to forego any other attempt against the opposing troops. He concluded by summoning him to an interview at the Rancho del Tigre.

Colonel Guerra, fearing that it was all a lie and a trick, delayed answering, and at dawn of the following day he received by means of a sergeant the sad news that was sent to him from N. Santander that Colonel Paredes y Arrellaga, who was supposed to come to his aid with more than three hundred men and two artillery pieces, had been detained because General Terán had died in Padilla the morning of the third. They were called to await the orders of the new commander general who was to follow, and this was General Don Ignacio Mora. Colonel Guerra then in order to take advantage of the time before the revolutionaries could learn of the unfortunate death of General Terán, replied to Mejía that he was accepting the proposed meeting, and to that end he set out immediately for Rancho de Palo Blanco where he expected to find him. Both of them met there on the sixth at four thirty in the afternoon, and after a long conference they agreed on the following arrangement:

"Agreement entered into between Colonels Don José Mariano Guerra, chief commander of the Matamoros and the Texas Expedition, and Don José Antonio Mejía, commander of the forces of Tampico occupying the town of Matamoros and its ports.

"Inasmuch as Señor Colonel Mejía had disembarked in Brazo

de Santiago and taken possession of Matamoros and consequently of all branches of administration, he intercepted several pieces of correspondence that were sent from Fort Velasco and various other points in Texas to the said commander. By means of these communications His Lordship was informed that all the colonies of that Department were in rebellion and that large meetings were being held for the purpose of attacking the authorities and detachments at Anáhuac and Brazoria, and that the state of unrest in which all those establishments were could compromise the integrity of the territory for the Republic.

"Considering furthermore that as Mexicans it behooved us one and all to rally to the prompt relief, leaving aside the political question which is disturbing the Republic at the present time, consequently the said gentleman submits to whatever his immediate superior Señor General Moctezuma decides and does. Taking advantage of a memo sent to him by Señor Guerra from Santa Teresa accompanied by the suspension of hostilities by Generals Calderón and Santa Anna, and the invitation that was made to him at the same time by the Most Excellent Señor General Terán to Señor Moctezuma, in his reply he invited Señor Mejía for an interview for the purpose of informing him of the events in Texas that he judged to be of major consideration immediately.

"Motivated by the same sentiments as Señor Mejía, Señor Guerra agreed voluntarily and readily, and this was carried out at Rancho Palo Blanco at four thirty in the afternoon of this day. As a consequence they have agreed freely and spontaneously on the following articles.

Summary of agreement between Colonels José Mariano Guerra and José Antonio Mejía, Rancho de Palo Blanco, July 6, 1832, pp. 241–243:

Mejía takes possession of Matamoros and its administration and learns that the colonies were in rebellion with large meetings and much unrest that could jeopardize the Republic. Guerra agrees that whatever else happens Moctezuma should make the decisions. In view of the suspension of hostilities in the civil disturbance by Generals Calderón and Santa Anna, Moctezuma invited Mejía for an interview to discuss events in Texas. Articles of agreement were drawn up at Rancho Palo Alto on this date:

Article 1.   General Mejía is to render aid with all forces to chiefs and employees of Galveston, Brazoria, Anáhuac, etc.

Article 2.   General Guerra shall aid Mejía with all his resources.

Article 3.   Forces of Mejía shall embark when ready.

Article 4.   Until terms of truce are known forces of Calderón and Santa Anna shall not resume hostilities.

Article 5.   Since people of Matamoros may favor one or the other side, they are to be guaranteed in their persons, rights and properties.

Article 6.   If by chance afterwards General Mejía should have to return to Brazo de Santiago General Guerra pledges to help him as he can even if the truce should be at an end.

Article 7.   As for the troops who have placed themselves under General Mejía and prisoners he has taken, this shall be decided upon by the chiefs who of the agreement — likewise equipment, ammunition and other supplies.

"All of which they offered to fulfill faithfully and legally upon their word of honor and signed it at Rancho de Palo Blanco on July 6, 1832.–José Mariano Guerra.–José Antonio Mejía."

By virtue of these agreements and the state of affairs to which things had come because of the death of General Terán, Colonel Guerra advised the impresario Don Stephen Austin, who was still in Matamoros, that he should march with Colonel Mejía's expedition for the purpose of carrying out the instructions that had been given by General Terán at the Hacienda del Cojo for the pacification of Texas.

He also gave orders that the commissary and maritime administrator of Matamoros, Don Francisco Jujero, should accompany Mejía to that city so that in the first place he might provide aid for his troops and men. In the second place he was to cancel the contracts that were so ruinous for the treasury that had been entered into by Mejía with the merchants of that port with the pretext of obtaining quick provisions. According to what he himself had told Colonel Guerra verbally, he had asked fifteen thousand pesos of the owners and consignees of three boats loaded with merchandise that had arrived in the port during those days, on account for all the duties that they should pay, as has been said.

Finally, he was to order the departure with Mejía of First lieutenant of the national armada Don José María Jiménez, who because of the knowledge which he had of the Texas sand banks, could be very useful to him to the benefit of good results from the expedition which Guerra was to aid according to the said agreement. In the thinking of the colonel this concerned the complete pacification of Texas and the preservation of the integrity of the national territory, of so much importance to all the political parties into which unfortunately the Mexicans were divided.

Immediately Colonel Guerra withdrew towards San Fernando where he arrived on the third day after Colonel Paredes with the section under his command to continue on to Matamoros, ready to take over that city by force and to do battle with Colonel Mejía. However, the latter, as soon as he had signed the said agreements, returned to Matamoros and began to make ready to reembark his troops and to put into good shape the boats that he was to use and which still remained in Brazo de Santiago. For the same purpose he loaded provisions and all that was necessary. On July 8, he left Matamoros for Brazo de Santiago with all the infantry and ordered the cavalry that had joined his ranks and could not go on the ships to make their way by random roads to join him in Tampico. He set sail for that port on the tenth, still planning to head for Texas accompanied by Don Stephen F. Austin and First Lieutenant of the Navy Don José María Jiménez.

We think it fitting to record here a circumstance that we should not pass over in silence, and that is that when Colonel Mejía had joined General Moctezuma in Tampico, and placed himself and the troops that accompanied him under the latter's orders — since he was afraid of being attacked by General Terán who was threatening them with a strong force — Mejía was sent out to attract Terán's attention in the direction of Soto la Marina. With this purpose in mind he set out for this point accompanied by the governor of Tamaulipas, Don Francisco V. Fernández, who had come to Tampico in flight from Ciudad Victoria which had been taken in those days by Colonel Paredes y Arrillaga with no more force than a company of grenadiers notwithstanding the fact that the governor was defending it with more than one thousand civilians, artillery and good fortifications.

Thus V. Fernández and Mejía embarked together and made their way from Soto la Marina to Matamoros. However, since Fernández was highly displeased on account of the agreements entered into at *Palo Blanco* with Colonel Guerra by Mejía, and since he knew of the death of General Terán, he refused to accompany Mejía to Texas. Instead, when Mejía embarked in Matamoros, as we have said, Fernández asked that he be sent to Tampico. There he spread the most false ideas concerning the conduct and political ends that the colonel had proposed during that fatal expedition.

But returning to what was happening in the port of San Fernando, the fact is that after Colonel Paredes had trained his men sufficiently, he left at dawn on the twelfth for Matamoros in order to attack Mejía. However, as he set out he learned from Colonel Guerra

108

that on the tenth, Mejía had sailed with his expedition. Thus he continued his march slowly toward Matamoros, where he stopped to inform himself as to what was happening in Texas and in the interior of Tamaulipas, and of the progress that the revolution was making, especially since the death of General Terán, for as soon as this event was known in Zacatecas and Jalisco, those states joined the revolution and took a very active part in the triumph of the Veracruz Plan.

Meanwhile, General Moctezuma saw the way clear from Tampico where he was to go to San Luis Potosí and to the interior of the Republic (in that direction there were no other government troops than those which General Don Ignacio Mora had in Victoria, and these were made up of the remains of the brigade that General Terán had commanded in person). Moctezuma planned to organize a strong force which in due time he put under the command of an Italian citizen and merchant of that city named Don José Averzana, lieutenant colonel of the civilians. He was to march against General Mora and reinstate in Victoria the governor and the other authorities who had previously fled. These were to provide him along the way with communications with the other states already in rebellion and with those who had joined the movement for the success of the revolution.

Such then were the plans carried out and the advantages gained on August 7 by Lieutenant Colonel Averzana who attacked and captured Ciudad Victoria, not only because of the strength of the determination with which he managed his forces, but also because of the weakness of the defense since many of the defenders were won over, or basely took bribes. To these maneuvers were due in large part the victory and the fact that General Mora, the commanding general of the Eastern States, his staff and all those who were resisting were taken prisoners. These were sent at once under the corresponding security to Tampico. Later the governor and the deposed authorities were restored to their positions. They continued to function there and to contribute to the success of the objectives which we shall explain later on. For now we shall again turn our attention to what was happening in Texas at the same time.

[24]

The following matters are closely linked together: 1. the events that led to the Veracruz Declaration; 2.   Colonel Mejía's expedition to the Eastern States to lend support to the cause invoked in that declaration; 3.   the onward march of the Texas colonists toward a distant and difficult goal, but one that was determined and unchanging, upon the success of which they agreed and hastened to take advantage of all those circumstances. We could not fail to concern ourselves with all these topics, although to bring them in it would be necessary to break up our narrative. We would have to turn the attention of our readers first to one set of events and then another, because otherwise it would be very difficult for us to follow the chronology or to give a less imperfect idea of the totality of our task.

It must therefore be stated that when Colonel Mejía arrived at the bar of the Brazos River with all his troops and accompanied by Don Stephen Austin, John Austin and the forces that this rebel was leading had already captured Fort Velasco as a consequence of the surrender of Ugartechea, who had carried it out with the loyalty that characterized him. During that same time Austin continued his march to Brazoria with the forces under his command. He found Colonel Mejía still on the road, and the latter tried to inform him of everything that had occurred in Matamoros and to reinforce his decision to proceed to that port in accordance with the *Velasco* conditions. In all of this he had a design that we did not understand, but which could later be understood very clearly.

Mejía and Austin were received and feted by the people of Brazoria with illuminations, serenades, parties, balls, etc. Likewise, so many pressures were brought to bear to turn Mejía aside from the main objective that he had declared had taken him to that port, that

110

instead of quelling the rebellion and obliging its instigators to return to order, he set himself up as its director, which gave a certain image to the proceedings which would make them appear less altered and to be results of a political opinion.

Indeed, solemn minutes were drawn up, as was the custom, in which they declared the adherence of those forces to the Veracruz Plan as modified by General Santa Anna. In this they no longer demanded the removal of the ministry, but the return of General Don Manuel Gómes Pedrazas, who was in exile, and that he should be placed as the first magistrate of the nation.

Mejía had done this and had visited Brazoria and other nearby new establishments of the colonists, to whom it was suspected that he offered the departure of those troops. Afterwards he left Austin in his villa at San Felipe and took ship again in Brazoria for Galveston. As he was crossing the bar into this port he met two or three boats that were leaving there carrying on board the troops who made up the Anáhuac detachment under the orders of Sergeant Major Don Féliz Surbarán. At that place he was informed that Colonel Davis had fled overland afterwards for the United States of the North. He was also told that Surbarán had gone over to the Veracruz Plan and that he was going about promoting it in the interior of the Republic with the troops of the detachment that had been put under him by the general of the Eastern States, as has been related in the previous chapter. For this purpose the rebellious colonists provided him with boats and all that he needed to withdraw from that fortified point, as indeed had happened. It is worth mentioning that the only ones who remained voluntarily were Lieutenants Don Juan Cortina, Don Carlos Ocampo and Don Manuel Montero, and Midshipman Don Juan Añorga. These refused to join the revolution and believed it to be their duty to guard the materials that belonged to the nation and that had been left in the fort. They had to rely completely on their own resources since they had been left with no other means of subsisting.

With this information Mejía did an about face with his expedition and headed for Tampico without taking into account in any manner the troops that were leaving Galveston, or of giving them convoy, and much less money or other resources that he could have given them and that he had gotten for those detachments with the greatest of sacrifices on the part of the national treasury, as has been related.

Major Don Ignacio Villasana and Second Lieutenant Palacios started out to join the detachment on Lavaca Creek at the extreme eastern end of Matagorda Bay. After they were taken prisoners in Tenoxtitlán, they had the opportunity to flee and to begin the undertaking of winning over those troops, who had already been invited by Mejía to abandon the country and to leave and join the forces of the revolution. When they had succeeded in this, on August 4, they loaded the necessary ships and sailed for Matamoros to learn in the first place what was happening, and to disembark there, if it seemed the thing to do, or to proceed on to Tampico to do so there together with the garrison that had declared. But the consequences of all these defections of many military men were much greater and more harmful to the nation than the promoters could ever have thought.

As soon as the rebels under the command of John Austin saw the troops that were occupying the military post of Anáhuac embark and disappear from Galveston, and knew that Ugartechea who was leaving also by land was some days' march away, they began to reinforce themselves with a considerable number of armed colonists. They prepared to attack Nacogdoches, the only point in the interior of Texas where Mexican troops remained. Although the opinion of the citizens of that town was divided, some for the revolution and others against it, the merchants, who were the most influential, were for it, and furthermore, against the person of Colonel Piedras because of commercial interests. This chief had unwisely monopolized almost all the lines that had the best trade and were the most lucrative. He had these come from New Orleans on his own account and took the benefit therefrom away from many. They wanted to get him out of there, hoping that he would be followed in the command by Colonel Don Elías Beau [*Ellis Bean?*], a North American and a resident of the town for many years.

On the other hand, they were also taking into account that the officers and Mexican troops likewise were unhappy because of the monopoly that Piedras had over their property and were desirous of an opportunity to get rid of him. However, with this decision these cunning revolutionaries had no such luck because when the occasion came the Mexican soldiers conducted themselves in a worthy manner that was not expected. This came on about August 2, when the rebels arrived at Nacogdoches and with the greatest vigor and confidence began the attack on the presidio.

Although Colonel Piedras counted scarcely three hundred infantrymen and fifty presidio soldiers from the Monclova company in the forces that he commanded, and they were of course many more than the number of rebels since they were more than double, they

112

accomplished nothing and were completely driven back without any loss on our part other than a captain named Ortega and a few of the troops. They had caused such damage to the ranks of the rebels with that brave defense that the latter began to put into action all means possible to win our troops over. This effort became such and so obvious that it caused fear in Colonel Piedras. As a precaution he decided to withdraw that same night to Béxar, Matamoros or some other point in the interior where he could find government troops and resources.

But as in war no hasty act or error fails to be harmful, Colonel Piedras soon had cause to be sorry for his excessive caution. It is true that he undertook his withdrawal in the best order. However, as he did not have resources, provision or means of transportation necessary for it, and even had to abandon the baggage and the company warehouse, when the officers saw the difficulties that they had to overcome and the privations that they would have to undergo on so long a march, they with all the troops rebelled at the creek called *Angelinas.* They declared in favor of the Veracruz Plan which had been circulated to them in Nacogdoches by the colonists who had attacked that port of entry and had just occupied it. When the latter became aware of their declaration, they went at once to join the troops and to take Colonel Piedras prisoner.

Immediately command and control of those forces were taken over by a certain Bony, a citizen of Béxar, who was with the rebel colonists, and he took charge of providing the troops with the supplies necessary for continuing on the road to Béxar. However, when they became aware that over there also the men had declared in favor of the Veracruz Plan, and that there were no supplies on which to subsist, they agreed to march to Matamoros to join the others who were there. Indeed, that is what they did, with the forces of the colonists going as rearguard and scouts as far as the vicinity of La Bahía del Espíritu Santo. Some of them acting as an escort took Colonel Piedras to Brazoria where they put him on a ship for New Orleans.

As soon as Bony arrived at the bay, he again provided aid for the troops, and from there he arranged for them to continue on to Matamoros under the orders of Captain Medina. Information concerning these events came to the commander of the detachment of presidio cavalry of about one hundred men at *Tenoxtitlán,* a military post on the Brazos River forty leagues above San Felipe de Austin. He with his troops doubled back to Béxar, unaware that certain signs of revolution were noted there also. However, their spirits had risen in such manner that various groups of them began to separate from that garrison, and most of them joined the troops that left Nacogdoches and were marching to Matamoros.

In this city which was being occupied by the group under the command of Colonel Paredes, as they received news of what was going on in Texas, and finally of what happened in Ciudad Victoria to Commander General Don Ignacio Mora, their spirits rose day by day. Finally at dawn on August 19, all the sergeants and their respective squads rebelled and placed themselves under the orders of sergeant major of the eleventh battalion Don José Garduño. They placed Colonel Paredes under arrest at his home, as well as the rest of the leaders and officers, and after some debate on the matter they elected as their chief Sergeant Major Don Manuel Micheltorena.

The latter, when he accepted, convinced the troops of the need that they had for their officers, and on the second day those who wished to take part in the revolution were accepted. Next they ordered the departure of Paredes, Guerra and the other leaders and officers who were not in favor of the Veracruz Plan, and they awaited the arrival of the troops that were in Texas and at other points in order to combine the movements of all of these with Colonel Moctezuma. He had already left Tampico for the interior of the Republic for the purpose of bringing about the adoption of that plan without exception in every part of the nation.

During that same time those forces were joined by those whom Major Surbarán had taken out of Galveston. However, after having suffered many setbacks and a great scarcity of provisions and water before being able to reach Soto la Marina, the leader himself died at the moment of debarkation. Because of this and since they found nothing on which to subsist, the soldiers had decided to continue on to Matamoros and to disembark in Tampico, as indeed they did two or three days later.

The troops that Major Villasana had taken out of Lavaca arrived in Matamoros also, but only a few officers got off the ship there, and the soldiers continued on to Tampico because of the mistrust which they felt.

Likewise Colonel Ugartechea arrived in Matamoros by land around September 20. Although as one who had capitulated he had greater reason not to take part in the revolution, at last he was persuaded by the rebels and went over to their side, placing himself under the orders of Major Micheltorena who was the one chosen to command.

Finally, at the end of September, the troops that had evacuated

Nacogdoches and come on to Béxar arrived in Matamoros, thus increasing Micheltorena's contingent up to more than two thousand men. They left immediately by way of Ciudad Victoria for San Luis Potosí. However, they had learned there of how unfortunate for their cause and for General Moctezuma had been the famous action of the Gallinero and the march of General Bustamante, who was the one who won out, to go with his troops to the aid of the capital of Mexico which was threatened by General Santa Anna, who was directing the attack in person. Under these circumstances there was time to repair the damages done to General Moctezuma's forces and to attack the city of San Luis Potosí again.

This they decided to do, and finally took possession of the city in the following month of November of 1832. As a result of this all the interior states of the East were removed from adherence to Vice-President Bustamante, as will be made evident in the following chapter.

[25]

Now that the cities, presidios and military detachments of Texas no longer had support because of the defection of the military leaders who had succumbed to the persuasion or the force of the rebels, there was no longer anything that stood in the way of the colonists in the carrying out of their undertakings. In Béxar there remained only a small number of presidio troops under the orders of the principal commander, Colonel Don Antonio Elozúa. These were scarcely sufficient to hold back the Indian raids in their immediate vicinity. In Tamaulipas not a single soldier remained, and on the Coahuila border there were only a small number of presidio soldiers whom the citizens supported at their own expense in order to defend themselves from the raids of the savages who were laying waste that department and those of Nuevo León and Tamaulipas, the frontiers of which they attacked with impunity.

Thus these three states and their respective borders — where with such disorders not only was the authority of the comandancy general nullified, but all military forces were displaced from their respective posts — were left to the decisions of interior and exterior enemies. This was harmful to the administration of justice, the integrity of the treasury and the security of the borders themselves, which should have been defended by the military forces.

The colonists realized their desires even beyond what they had dared to hope for because under such circumstances the actions of the government of Mexico could not reach out across such immense distances. Spread thin as they were in those vast States, the few loyal troops left there and lacking all sorts of resources and communications with the capital and the states were reduced to nothing by the spirit of revolution which divided them either for or against the Ve-

116

racruz Plan. There was also a lack of a center of unity in the command, which therefore made completely impossible the good services of all the detachments, and the attention of these to their principal objectives of defending the frontiers, and maintaining throughout the country the authority of the general laws of the Republic, the special ones of the respective States, and the repression and punishment of the colonists who upset or attacked the public order.

As soon as the secret directors of the uprisings in Texas and the land speculators that lived in that Department and in New York and New Orleans had knowledge of so sad a situation, they considered their prime objective already in hand. They had already achieved the expulsion from there of the troops that were guarding the borders and the coastline, as well as the customs employees, so as not to have to pay any of the duties established by the laws. Neither would there be any power sufficient to stop them from smuggling or to force them to fulfill their contracts. This encouraged them to move all the more rapidly and openly toward the achievement of independence and the taking over of those far flung territories, and they put this into execution.

They even persuaded themselves that they could do so with all the appearance of popular support and backed by legal opinion, which they could not have in their favor as is proved by the unceasing and heated claims on the clear thinking part of the population. These implored the government, which had just been placed in the hands of President Pedraza at the end of 1832, for the necessary aid in the reestablishment of order and the defense of the country against all the enemies that surrounded them. The latter would no doubt have carried out their aims if this aid had not been provided as a consequence of the restoration of peace that came about, although for only a short time, by the treaty of Zavaleta.

But as the aid that they were supposed to send from Mexico City could not arrive soon enough to hold back the ambitious projects and the indefatigable activity of the partisans of Texas independence, the latter had time to carry forward their schemes during the first days of the year 1833. One of the first things was that the council of the Town of Austin should send its proclamations to all the population centers of Texas proposing the idea of celebrating a *convention* that *they said* was to concern itself only with a petition that would be sent to the government for the better organization and well being of the Department.

This meeting took place in the Town of San Felipe toward the end of October. After they had set forth a form for the elections and various measures relative to putting them into effect, the meeting was adjourned, leaving a permanent commission of the participants to circulate those decisions to the different areas and towns of the Department. If opportune, the elections of representatives were to be held March 1, 1833, and those elected were to gather the following April 1, in the Town of Austin where they would organize themselves into a legislature and form a separate constitution which was to be in force in Texas, with independence from the State of Coahuila.

All these decisions were realized in Texas in spite of the formal and repeated disapproval with which the mayor of Béxar attempted to prevent them by his messages from November 7 to November 22. Far from honoring these, the members of the convention on the contrary sent emissaries to go to all the towns and places of the territory charging them not only to indoctrinate them and persuade them to petition for their separation from the State of Coahuila, but also from the Mexican nation, the name and government of which they attempted to make look odious by every means that their treachery might suggest to them.

We wish to point out to what extent they succeeded by such means in leading astray public opinion in Texas, even among the Mexicans themselves, and how the latter, careless, indiscreet or blinded, worked to bring about their own ruin and in the interests of the rebels and speculators. For this we think it opportune to give space here to a message from the council of Béxar, either basely surprised or laboring under a delusion, made to the State legislature, and the note with which it was circulated to all the other councils in times that were so critical and endangered for the Republic.

Summary of Circular Letter from the Council of Béxar to the city councils of the Department, Béxar, December 21, 1832, pp. 261–281:

A commission of two members from the group and four from outside has drawn up a petition to the state legislature. This had been approved by the council and citizens' meeting, and copies are to be circulated to all the city councils of the Department so that if they approve they may so advise the legislature.

Petition sent to the city council of Austin, December 21, 1832: Since Béxar five other towns have been founded plus three additional military establishments in over a century. Only three remain, and this is because of savages, hunger and pestilence. Neglect by those who govern are in large part responsible. Since 1821, ninety-seven men have been killed by Indians in addition to those killed in campaign. Other places have suffered even more.

With civil war there has been little help, and in Texas there are only seventy men under arms, and they must support themselves.

There is much evidence to support these statements, and there are several other annoyances since Texas has been a part of the State of Coahuila and Texas. Settlers have six years to cultivate and occupy allotted lands, but cannot dispose of them until they are in total cultivation. If they were granted in any other legal manner, they could sell or transfer by other means.

There is no single inducement to provide settlement of Mexicans. A parcel of land is set at 300 pesos in Texas and 15 in Coahuila; because of resistance to emigration to Texas from fear of living there with limited capital there would be few who could pay. Also one fourth of the amount is demanded immediately.

The law prohibits the immigration of North Americans, but there are no troops to watch over it. Honorable men with capital and industry are stopped because of the law, but adventurers and felons have come in any way. Likewise, many Indians expelled from the U.S. have crossed the Sabine with no one to stop them. It is difficult to dislodge them or to bring them under our laws.

Those who came before this law have within seven or eight years been provided with a comfortable living. We regret to say that blankets, hats and even shoes have been begged from the interior, but with the North American colonists these resources have been provided. Also they furnish the best means of controlling the Indians. This can only be accomplished by bringing in enthusiastic men who are skilled in dealing with Indians. These advantages are not possessed by any other of the European nations who wish to colonize.

The opening of direct roads from Texas ports to New Mexico and even Chihuahua would bring enormous benefit. It would give direct communication from all northern Mexico to the state of Missouri in the U.S. They could also easily achieve a prosperous good fortune with the fertile lands, pleasant climate, abundant game and beautiful pelts and fishing.

There is no question but that the lack of a concerned government with the necessary measures has been and will continue to be the source of our sufferings. During two legislatures in four years nothing has been done to give Texas some separate government. It must be noted that this lack of action is due to sectionalism in the capital against all the towns they characterize as "frontier."

This municipality speaks for a free people that resents the end-

119

less vexations. It asks for a part in reworking the laws since the most informed persons cannot have more knowledge than the people of Texas because of their topographical knowledge and eight years or more of practice. The complete implementation should be delayed for from four to six months for the careful examination by the city councils.

The pact between Coahuila and Texas should never have been made. There is not, nor has there ever been, a government in Texas. Educated men of the frontier lack even books for study. Nacogdoches is 350 leagues from the capital, and the nearest adviser is 200 leagues distant. There are often involuntary delays. The tasks of the alcalde are very onerous, and those who can, refuse them. Those selected are of mediocre quality. There should be judges of record and public notaries and also interpreters for Spanish, and English criminal trials and civil ones where possible should be decided by juries.

The commanding general of these States stopped the functioning of the commission given to Francisco Madero by the supreme government in order to gain control of the people between the San Jacinto and the Trinity Rivers. He even passed sentence on Madero in Anáhuac. The Anáhuac commander Colonel Davis Bradburn had caused the formation of another council in Anáhuac itself.

After an exchange of communications with the minister of relations the Texas representatives were expelled from the assembly without cause against the will of all the towns of the Department and almost all the others of the State. The constitution was violated, and the towns of Texas were insulted.

The failure to appoint an inspector for the civilian militia of the State is impossible to assess. Whenever these men leave their homes they should receive a decent wage, but this has not been so.

The State has provided no funds for school construction but has only passed laws. The councils are expected to pay out of the school allowance. The people of Béxar have had to provide the miserly sum of twenty-five pesos for a primary teacher. This is what is supposed to provide a foundation for the best civil and moral virtues.

The prohibition of retail trade to non native Mexicans was not made for Coahuila-Texans by adoption. According to the latest statistics on population Texas should have four representatives. These towns have never been able to achieve anything with only two deputies.

Texas was granted the right to divide itself into two districts, but the legislature near its close has not deigned to resolve this matter. Also Texas was given seven years of exemption from duties, but

120

with all the delays only a few months remained for those to be in force. Foreign merchants and some Mexicans have discontinued trade to Texas, and this has meant a loss in population and resources.

The new settlements of Anáhuac and others have been lost to the federation; not one Mexican has remained.

Delays granted to Powers and Hewitson have not been able to bring in a single family. The legislature alone is responsible for this delay, and this should be remedied.

This petition deserves attention and foresight. The following articles sum up this point of view:

Article 1. The organization of a civilian militia.

Article 2. A new colonization law should be drawn up granting land free to each Mexican family born in Texas.

Article 3. Grant permission for the immigration of industrious North Americans with capital in order to prevent entry of adventurers and criminals.

Article 4. Better conditions for public employees and the naming of properly qualified judges of record and public notaries.

Article 5. Some reward for those with council duties.

6. Bring to the supreme government's attention the scandalous proceedings of the military in Texas.

Article 7. Satisfy demands for personal representation.

Article 8. Adequate payment by the State for primary school salaries.

Article 9. The prohibition against foreign born merchants should be repealed.

Article 10. The number of representatives for Texas should be increased according to population.

Article 11. A District chief of this department should be named at once.

Article 12. The exemption of duties should be granted for ten years through ports of Galveston, Aransas, and Río de Los Brazos in Texas for local consumption.

Article 13. Annul the delays granted to impresarios Powers and Hewitson.

Article 14. Let the legislature busy itself with these points as prime and necessary matters.

"Béxar, December 19, 1832.–José Antonio de la Garza.–Angel Navarro.–José Casiano.–Manuel Jiménez.–Juan Angel Seguín.–José María Sambrano.–Ignacio Arocha, secretary."

The foregoing events have indeed proven, and in a very bitter manner, how ill thought out and absurd were the reasons that were alleged in the above petition by the Béxar council, how unfounded and tactless were the provisions that were requested, and how malicious and evil were the objectives that they disguised. An attempt was also made to lead the congress* in this direction because of a fatal error into which the councilmen had been led by cunning men who had treacherously taken advantage of their good faith and lack of experience.

They had no other purpose than to implicate them in their cause through the infamous trick of finding themselves delinquent, or at least suspicious in the eyes of the higher authorities of the State and even of the nation, and dragging the others down through the same necessity of escaping punishment. This leads them later little by little into the pain of rebellion as happened afterwards, with the notable circumstances that they were some of the first victims, as must generally happen, and the lesson of which should never be forgotten in similar cases.

But since those of Texas had never had occasion to learn it, and day by day the maneuvers of the plotters were more calculated and more venturesome, opinion generalized in their favor among many of the natives of the country and among the honorable and industrious colonies that were among the rest, and particularly in the districts of Nacogdoches, Liberty, González, Goliad and Béxar. If indeed they did desire that the territory be organized as an independent State, they wished to bring it about by the rules laid down by the Constitution, and in no way by means of a revolution, just as there did not enter into their innocent aspirations that of separating from the nation, whose protection and support they wanted because it was beneficial, more advantageous and absolutely neces-

[* This same declaration, or another in its place, was also sent to the general congress, asking that the territory of Texas be organized into a State in the federation since it had the eighty thousand inhabitants required by the constitution, since its interests were in absolute opposition to those of the State of Coahuila, and were ill provided for because of the large number of Coahuilans of which it was made up; because Texas itself needed to provide for its necessary and urgent defense against the savages who were constantly attacking them, and they demanded for their better well being to have their own energetic government. But the general congress, seeing through the true aims of this petition, and finding it devoid of foundation and false in the data that were cited in it, disallowed it to the despair of their authors and of Don Stephen Austin, who for the purpose of supporting it had been back in the capital from the end of 1832 to the beginning of 1833. — TRANS.]

sary to have on their part in order to assure their welfare and future happiness.

Thus it was that from that time on those settlements remained in a state of absolute independence, although those in charge pretended a respect and loyalty that they never felt toward the central government. This ridiculous fiction must have been all the more insulting and criminal in that they did not again permit the stationing there, much less the existence, of any public office. Rather they destroyed and burned those that there were and the forts and quarters, stealing at the same time all the materials that belonged to the nation and to its troops. They carried their insolent boldness to such an extent that they *beat and tarred and feathered* officers of the army, treasury employees, and some private citizens, as well as any Mexicans that had the misfortune to remain among them, either because of their interests, illness or other similar reasons. In addition to harming them in every way possible, they treated them with grossly insulting scorn as if they were dealing with their slaves. They did not govern themselves otherwise than by the laws of the United States of North America or those of their own fancy. To perpetuate these and to exercise them to the fullest, they tried to attract there all the adventurers that came their way and to provide themselves with arms and ammunition in order to be prepared to commit all kinds of aggression against the country and to continue their smuggling in the most open and insolent manner. With their own people they infiltrated all the departments of the frontier and of the interior of the Republic, even to the extreme of the barbarians' taking part in the traffic of Negro slaves, in spite of the fact that this was prohibited by the general congress and disapproved of by the generous and compassionate nature of the whole Mexican nation. Such for the Texans was the period that came to an end with year 1832.

[26]

The government which as a consequence of the Zavaleta peace replaced that of General Bustamante on December 26, 1832, as soon as it was organized in Mexico and had a perfect awareness of the condition of the frontier area and of the political and military situation in the Texas colonies, thought seriously of doing something about the evils that the recently ended revolution had produced and made worse in that interesting part of the Republic.

With this in mind in January of 1833, it named Brigadier General Don Vicente Filisola as commanding general of the Interior Eastern States, and with the necessary instructions he was ordered to proceed there. Under his direction were placed the first and seventh permanent infantry battalions, the fifth cavalry regiment of the same class, a company of mounted artillerymen with six pieces, the pickets of the presidio companies of that part of the frontier, who during the revolution had come to Mexico City, and in addition the tenth permanent battalion which was being organized in San Luis Potosí, a detachment of which was located at Brazo de Santiago, and the remaining pickets of all types that because of the lack of support from our forces were scattered about in that or adjoining states. For the aid of these forces and to provide them with some uniforms ten thousand pesos were allotted, and this money the general invested and distributed with the care and economy corresponding to the objective and as circumstances demanded.

One of the greatest difficulties against which it was necessary to struggle was that the majority of the troops mentioned had remained more loyal to the administration of Vice-President Bustamante. Evil minded people took occasion from this to cause it to be believed that that assignment had as its only objective their punishment with political exile and the removal from the capital of the troops that had not wished to take part in the revolution, and concerning whose loyalty the new government did not feel sufficiently secure.

General Filisola, who had grasped the situation, was not unaware of these fateful inclinations and presented the matter to the government immediately. However, the answer that he received was that since these were a fact, the best thing was to remove from the capital those who harbored such feelings and to busy them in places where the national interest would cause them to forget their partisan feelings and the resentments of the moment. Thus it was recommended to the general that he should exhort them continually on the matters of obedience, order and love of country, which were without doubt preferable to all those inclinations and attachments of the Mexican army.

The departure of these troops was ordered at once, and this was carried out in the following terms.

The first and seventh battalions went to Veracruz to embark for the port of Matamoros, and General Filisola, with the rest of the forces took the road to San Luis Potosí from where he set out with the artillery and the presidio pickets for Saltillo, arriving there on March 20. There he stopped as long as it was necessary to give time to be joined by the fifth regiment, which because of the poor condition of their horses caused by the rigors of the previous campaign could not keep up at the same pace. Likewise he had arranged for Colonel Don Manuel de Andrade to lead it with short and comfortable marches so that they might recover in the best manner possible.

While General Filisola remained in Saltillo, he carefully informed himself of the political and military situation in the states that he was going to command and the resources upon which he could count in order to cause all of them, and especially the Texas colonies, to return to constitutional order and tranquility as had been recommended by the supreme government, and as he himself so effectively desired. To such end he took care also to put himself in communication with the governors, military commmanders and other authorities and persons of respect and influence that resided in those parts, and to provide himself with their replies before going there, in order to choose better the line of conduct that it would be necessary for him to adopt with his first actions.

In this manner he had the opportunity to receive communications from the military commander of Anáhuac, Second Adjutant Don Juan Cortina; from the adjutant inspector of Coahuila and Texas, a resident of Béxar, Colonel Don Antonio Elozúa; from the military commander of the port of Matamoros, and from the lieutenant governor of the state of Coahuila. These letters almost without exception contained most unpleasant and alarming news because of the disorder, anarchy and poor intelligence that held sway among those people and which presaged an open rebellion on the part of the colonists which would not be easy to repress because of the absolute lack of all kinds of aid for the bare subsistence of the few troops that there were in those states. On this subject it is worthy of note that the Second Adjutant Cortina had written to the governor of Coahuila and which this official had sent on to General Filisola. Here it is:

Summary of letter written by Second Adjutant Cortina to the governor of Coahuila, who then sent it on to Filisola:

A declaration was made giving allegiance to the Veracruz Plan on July 9; there had been no way of doing so before. Since then the colonists have moved on to emancipation. The Brazos collector and Second Lieutenant Ignacio Domínguez left for New Orleans on September 29, no longer able to bear the temper of the Brazoria people who refused payment of duties. Much of the national property is in the hands of the colonists and cannot be reclaimed.

On the night of November 29, they burned the quarters at Hidalgo and the fortifications at this point. San Felipe de Austin has formed its own government and has elected representatives for a Texas congress. They get their militia ready for their support. Many North Americans are crossing the border. Colonists from New York are expected momentarily. As he sees it, the state of Texas will be lost soon if something is not done. Moreno and Astorga are still with him, but with only three men boats come and go without any formalities of customs.

The situation is sad, and only honor keeps them there. Cortina has ordered Añorga to get this information to the governor.

Inspector Don Antonio Elozúa, also an adherent of the Veracruz Plan, has added more.

Frontier and coasts of the department have been abandoned with only the presidio companies of Béxar, Alamo, Monclova and La Bahía del Espíritu Santo. Many have very limited forces and lack provisions. Many have had to neglect the service to provide subsistence. Río Grande, Agua Verde and Bahía on the Coahuila frontier are in about the same situation. Of six thousand pesos due monthly, very little has come for four years. The frontiers and coasts of Texas are exposed and abandoned.

Many people are coming in from the North, and Austin colonists are making very advanced claims. A convention has been called in Sal Felipe de Austin, ostensibly to arrange claims. This convention, which has been disapproved by higher ups, has set up a permanent junta. On March 1 they are to name delegates to meet in San Felipe to set up a constitution. They want Texas to be a separate state. This will likely be unpleasant.

The Tehuacana and Comanche Indians are still at war with the Mexicans, go as far as Matamoros and the Río Grande. Presidio troops, although in poor condition, have attacked some of them during last November. Three companies have just returned from the Coahuila frontier.

This will make aware the ills that beset Coahuila and Texas, the dangers threatened and what needs to be done.

And finally, the military commander of the port of Matamoros, stating that in that area there were many judges who had not received their salaries, added that they were in the direst poverty and in a state of desperation, and that this situation was weighing down upon the people of that city.

When General Filisola's attention was so strongly called by these communications, and he had informed himself through responsible people who had confirmed the deplorable situation of the states that he had under his command, he immediately advised the minister of war of it on March 25, so that the supreme government might be informed of the needs of the troops that were occupying Matamoros.

He had also informed them of the pressing needs of the presidio companies when they had not had sufficient supplies so that matters had reached the point where the assistant inspector for the states of Nuevo León and Tamaulipas had permitted the soldiers to go out in search of sustenance, neglecting in this manner the security of the country which had been commended to their care. This was a most dangerous step, as the military commander of Anáhuac had indicated in the remarkable terms that we have seen in the official communication inserted above.

This also gave information to the governor of the state, who had transferred to Monclova, and the general asked to be informed of everything that he knew about the matter so that he might make provisions that he considered opportune and consult with the general authority concerning those matters that did not fall under his jurisdiction. He added that in order for the troops to continue their march, he the general had decided to enlist private protection since he feared that difficulties might increase, if on their arrival in Matamoros they did not find supplies. He charged him with the considerable increase of troops of the first, seventh and twelfth battalions that were perhaps already on the way.

With the same objective he also set out for Tampico so that he might render whatever aid was possible. He had decided in case he did not find money at this place, or if they refused to give it to him on some pretext, thus making his situation more difficult, to adopt whatever measures might be necessary to solve the problem, although it might not be within his power. These then were the difficult circumstances that surrounded the general, which did not give cause for any hope that any resolve from their superiors might bring them the remedies that were needed.

In the midst of so many troubles there was the good fortune that the pickets from the presidio companies and the artillery had arrived without anything going wrong. Although the fifth regiment of Colonel Andrade was delayed some days because of their late start from San Luis, they did leave on the twenty-seventh of that month so that the general could march the following morning for Monterrey and Matamoros without worrying about them. He considered it indispensable that he be there at the earliest possible moment, and he had not been able to get away because of having to attend to the arrangements of some other things relative to the march as well as the presidio companies, and because of the delay of the fifth regiment beyond the time that he had calculated.

When the general left Saltillo, he left orders with that leader to continue on to the city of Monterrey where he was going to await that body, and where the general arrived on March 31.

He was greatly relieved and much satisfied because he was well received by the authorities and people of that city, and because they made it clear that they wished to see order reestablished by him and the peace of that vast country assured. He was also pleased that as soon as he arrived in that city there was distributed among the presidio companies the sum of ten thousand pesos that had been sent from Mexico City when he was confirmed in the command, and that he had been sent from Mexico City when he was confirmed in the command, and that he had thought would be impossible to hold on to with all the delay along the way. He had planned to use it for the purchase of material for capes, and this could not be done except for a small amount. The result was that most of it was available to give that aid to the troops, thus avoiding an increase in their discontent and desertion that he had feared so much since they had left Mexico City.

128

[27]

Joined in a few days by the fifth regiment which had remained in Saltillo since it could not proceed at the same pace as the presidio soldiers, the general also took care to aid and look out for it in order to avoid all complaint and any reason for anxiety or jealousy. When that body arrived in Monterrey the governor of Nuevo León provided all the supplies that were at his disposal, demonstrating thereby and in every manner possible the kindly disposition and patriotism that motivated him.

It is quite true that this aid was not sufficient when compared with what the division needed to fulfill its requirements under the circumstances in which those departments and border areas found themselves. They might expect greater aid if the national government on its part did not make an effort to help out in the general's difficulties and those in which the troops might find themselves.

In addition, because of lack of resources the assistant inspector for Nuevo León and Tamaulipas had found it necessary to allow the individuals of the presidio companies under him, as has been said, to go out to look for subsistence as best they could. Those of Coahuila and Texas was cared for no better, and the Matamoros garrison also was in dire need. In short, there was no hope that they would receive aid from anywhere.

To make this sad situation worse, the lieutenant governor of Coahuila and Texas, in the exercise of his executive power, when he answered the plea that the general had sent him from Saltillo trying to persuade him that the situation of that state was even more difficult than that of the troops, explained his position in these terms:

Summary of note from Saltillo from lieutenant governor of Coahuila and Texas to Filisola:
The lieutenant governor of Coahuila believes that the removal
of powers to this capital and a gentle manner will calm the malcontents. Attention is called again to the lack of supplies and the sufferings of the troops.

The two communications from the perfect of Béxar to which the
lieutenant governor referred contained: the first one, news from a
citizen of Nacogdoches about the events in that city concerning
Colonel Don José de Las Piedras and his battalion, and those of the
port of Galveston, the towns of Anáhuac, Liberty, Fort Velasco, etc.,
etc., at the end of last year, which we have put down in detail in the
previous chapters; and the second an extract of the notes from the
same prefecture to the city councils of San Felipe, González and Liberty, disapproving the meeting of the *Constitutional* Assembly, which
had been set for the first day of April.
However, since the terms in which that official expressed himself have seemed to us most remarkable, we shall transcribe this part
of the document that revealed truths, which if they were no mystery
in those parts at the time they were written, have nevertheless been
so for the rest of the Republic where the scandalous events of that
period in Texas are still unknown.

Summary of communication from the prefecture of Béxar to
Governor Ramón Músquiz of Coahuila and Texas, Béxar, March
11, 1833:
There are a considerable number of North Americans who realize that the time has not yet come to set Texas up as a state. It may
be inferred that there are not sufficient informed people for this, nor
do they have the resources.
It is not believed that they will make an attempt to set up a territory as they are averse to any military government. Even more remote is the inference of independence because of lack of resources.
There seems to be an eagerness on the part of the southern states for
their own separation, and the acquisition of Texas would be helpful
because of added territory and wealth.
Chargé d'affaires Butler of the U.S. indicated purpose of trip to
Mexico was to contract for the purchase of Texas. He wished to de-
termine the revolutionary movements of the colonists.
The possible idea of a separation of the southern states seems
unlikely but should be noted.

All right, if as we have just seen the prefecture of Béxar was certain that the rebellious colonists were not aware nor could they deny that the time had not yet arrived when Texas could be organized as a state, it is clear that such pretense was nothing more than an excuse to deceive the unwary or to openly mock the dignity of the government from which they wished to withdraw. Nevertheless, neither the prefect who wrote the letter, nor the government which sent it on to the general command, showed any hesitation in still affirming with a candor and boldness equally surprising that the movements put into action up to that time were not aimed at just the thought of making Texas into a state, because it did not have the necessary and indispensable elements according to the constitution to organize itself on this scale. Neither was it reasonable to think that it would wish to be organized as a territory because the disadvantages that would accrue under such a regimen were too well known, in addition to the hatred and dislike which the colonists naturally had towards any kind of military government. Even more remote was the idea that they might try to rebel against the country in order to establish any sort of government independent of the Mexican Republic, for which they plainly counted on even less resources than for existence as a state in the Federation.

Consequently, since none of these suppositions could be taken as the proposed fruit of the war that they were undertaking with the rest of the nation, it was necessary to seek some other more likely motive which would more clearly explain the current state of affairs in that beautiful country. That motive seemed to be spelled out in the long manifested desires on the part of the government of the United States of acquiring Texas by any means possible, as well as in the tendencies that two of the Southern States of that republic likewise manifested to secede and form another nation independent of the United States of the North. For this purpose the acquisition of Texas was much to their interest, as much for its vast territory as for its quality and wealth.

Finally, Señor Butler, chargé d'affaires from the United States to Mexico, as he passed through that state at the end of 1829, had stated that he was taking to Mexico City the commission for the purchase of Texas, and his return from the capital overland to San Felipe de Austin in July of 1832, had no other purpose than to urge the colonists to rebellion, and they did so at once. Until that time not only had they kept the peace but had protested that they were taking no part in the declaration that General Santa Anna had made in Veracruz in January of that year.

131

Hence, nothing is more natural than the conclusion reached by the prefect of Béxar, but nothing more insulting than to see it sent on by the governor of the state in so frank a manner to the general command, as if we were saying to the government of the Republic that in all the actions of the rebellious colonists a very positive influence had been exercised by the government in Washington, or at least by the Southern States of that Republic for the purpose of seceding from that nation and extending their boundaries to include the territory of Texas.

On the other hand, no less crafty was what the government of Coahuila and Texas was proposing in the communication that we cited previously relative to the transfer of the state's powers to the city of Monclova, recommending a more gentle and paternal treatment of the colonists. Just as if more gentleness and generosity were possible than there had been up to that time with them so that they might cease their protests of discontent and return to the order from which they had departed — in the concept of the governor, perhaps with *reasonable cause*.

Thus the commander general could not yet forget what Austin himself had told him. Contrary to the truth of the matter, he had said that the colonists had been handled in a military manner and removed from the jurisdiction of the authority which should judge them according to the constitution of the state.

Finally, it became painfully and irritatingly clear to General Filisola that he should be well advised not to continue with his troops on to Béxar unless he had with him the necessary supplies for their subsistence, at least for from four to six months, if he did not wish them to perish in poverty.

Aware of these facts and those which the council of Béxar threw out to him, which we have also included earlier, there could no longer be any doubt of the determined defection of those civil servants and the part they were taking in the treasonous designs of the Texas colonists. Thus the insistence upon excusing the attempts that the latter had made, attributing them to their being led astray, which had not been necessary, or to the outrages — also untrue — of the military authorities to whom was commended the security of that frontier and those coasts, together with the freehandedness with which the state authorities heedlessly and without treasure granted them vacant lands, made up the most irrefutable proof that the Mexicans themselves were encouraging the boldness of those adventurers. They were aiding them in their treasonous aims, when not out of malice, at least through lack of foresight and because of the

132

tolerance with which they permitted the excessive accumulation of those people in the colonies with the evident infraction of all the precautionary laws against a takeover, and granting so much and such extensive territory to all those who asked.

By virtue of this, how can it seem strange to thinking men that the prefect of Béxar should speak with such candor concerning the aims of the government of the United States on the matter of the acquisition of Texas and about the part that the uprising of the colonists might play? The strange thing for us was the indifference of our governments of that time concerning so well founded a denunciation as this, even though we might have had no other basis for making up our minds in the affirmative.* But the opinion of this civil servant and the governor of Texas about the administration and rule of the district and territories of the federation we cannot qualify otherwise than as an absurdity of the understanding of an unworthy dissimulation with which they were trying to cover up the antipathy that they had for the military class. For this they had no other basis than the displeasure caused the colonists and impresarios of Texas by the commission which the government of Mexico had given to General Terán for him to order the suspension of the great and frequent grants of lands that he was making in that state. The excesses of the colonists, the scandalous contraband that went on and the introduction into Texas of new North American settlers were all very much in line with the provisions of the Law of April 6, 1830.

Thus when General Filisola saw such opinions in the very authorities in whose untarnished zeal and reliable cooperation he should have based his hopes of supporting the reestablishment of order and for making effective the force of laws in Texas, he could not help but foresee from then on that very far from achieving the objective of his mission and patriotic desires, he could expect from such antecedents consequences very much to the detriment of the integrity of the Republic, to its honor, and even to the well being and security of the very ones who were so carried away by the theories of those ungrateful adventurers. These considerations had to be all the more painful, so sad and fatal were the difficult circumstances in which the general found himself because of the lack of supplies and the discontent that, since the departure from Mexico City, had spread among the chiefs, officers and troops upon whom he would have to depend for the campaign.

In addition it must be noted that these difficulties were increased because of the poor intelligence of the parties of Saltillo and

---

[* This was written in the year 1840. — TRANS.]

133

Monclova who were respectively interested in carrying forward the campaign and in opposing the plan for the removal of the powers of the state from one city to another. Some declared that this could contribute to the reestablishment of peace and order in Texas, and those of the other party said that such action not only would not succeed in pacifying Texas, but that it would give rise to fatal discord with Coahuila, and there would be an increase in the difficulties of putting down the rebellious members of the colonies.

Under such difficult circumstances General Filisola received a message from the ministry of war with which was inclosed another from the treasury relative to the fact that the government had received warning that the Texas colonists had established commercial relations with some houses in the island of Cuba which had as their purpose the sending of expeditions directly from that island to the ports of Coahuila and Texas. He was charged to be on guard and to try to prevent such traffic, which in addition to being prejudicial to the public treasury was likewise against the national honor. But Filisola could not carry out such orders nor avoid that fradulent trade, which was so much against the interests of the treasury, because he did not have at his disposal a single warship to guard the coasts, in spite of the fact that he had repeatedly requested them from the government. He had foreseen that the occasion and need for them would arise, either for this purpose, or for the transport of supplies to the Texas ports, or for other various necessary services if the campaign was finally opened.

With this in mind he repeated his request on April 3, 1833, and received only evasive answers, as had been the case with other petitions regarding troops, money, arms and munitions. Nevertheless, he received orders dated March 5, that he should reestablish the customs, collection offices and treasuries at Galveston, Brazos, Matagorda and Nacogdoches when money was so scarce that he did not know how he would be able to continue his march to Matamoros.

In truth he would not have been able to do so without the aid extended to him by Don Julián del Llano and especially by Doctor Don Pascual Constanza Napolitano, both of whom had been influenced by their feelings for a hometown friend. They let him have on his personal responsibility six thousand pesos in hard coin, with which he was able finally to leave Monterrey for Matamoros at the end of April of that year.

When we arrived at that port on May 4, instead of finding supplies, he came upon nothing but poverty, complaints and dissatisfaction. But what increased his troubles even more was a communication from the ministry of war in which was enclosed another from the ministry of internal affairs, drawn up on behalf of the military commander of Anáhuac, dated the previous January 5, which we have already included. In this note the minister stated by order of His Excellency the Vice-President:

"From previous information that has come into the secretary of communications it appears that in the Department of Texas there was a move to separate it from the government of Coahuila and set it up as an independent state or territory, for which purpose they counted on elements that were promoting the belief that with time this reform would be suitable in order to give those colonies the organization for which they were ready. With this in mind, His Excellency advised him to recommend to the minister of war that in the instructions which were to be given to General Filisola concerning military preparations on that frontier, he should be advised that while he should not oppose the public feelings concerning the separation in question, he should make the colonists understand that this could be promoted by legal steps without giving cause for outbreaks and unrest.

"He should instruct the supreme government as to what was happening in this respect and the means of correction that in his opinion the supreme government should take. He should above all, as the principal aim of his commmission, be on guard for the integrity of the territory and for preventing any disturbance that could break the peace, as well as the frauds that were being committed to the harm of the public treasury."

Such was the order that was sent to General Filisola in the name of His Excellency the Vice-President in his exercise of the supreme executive power. The general was commanded furthermore that he should move the troops under his command towards those important objectives, hastening his marches with this same objective in mind. With respect to this, according to the information that had been given to the secretary of war the government considered the matter of Nuevo León to be concluded. However, in case it was not, His Excellency ordered that in accord with the Most Excellent governor of that state he should likewise commend the fulfillment of that to the special commander, while he continued on to Texas without a moment's delay. He should count on the fact that the troops that had embarked in Veracruz should be in Matamoros.

Thus the minister of war continued as follows:

"If the intent of the inhabitants mentioned in the enclosed communication were only to change their political situation by making these settlements into a territory or perhaps a state in the Mexican federation, Your Excellency will make it clear to them that they have at hand the legal resources provided by the constitution. However, if it is a matter of trampling upon that constitution, of breaking the laws, of detaching one handsbreadth of territory, the entire army will violate the orders of Your Excellency. The government's last effort will be in an attempt to avoid your jealousy as well as the valor and discipline of the military men who follow it. It is certain that the last Mexican will sacrifice himself rather than permit the slightest insult to the Mexican nation."

Here we have two irrefutable witnesses to how little the cabinet in Mexico City understood the demands of the territory of Texas, the dangers that beset it and the measures that the high command would have to take in those circumstances in order to salvage respect for the laws, the authority of the government, the national integrity and the private interests of Mexicans, either native born or residents there. And here we have also a sketch on our part at the same time of the situation of the troops and of General Filisola in the Eastern States. There they were not provided with aid, nor could they count on the sympathies of the local authorities because the latter had decided in favor of the colonists.

In the following chapters we shall continue to point out how the indicated obstacles, with which the ministry did not bother itself, were on the increase from the first part of May of 1833. Finally they became so insuperable that they prevented the opening of the campaign which was to have reestablished order and the submission of the rebels in Texas. Toward this main objective the government should have dedicated all its purposes and resources so that later it would not have had to go all out in exhausting them in order to defend the nation from the blow directed at it by the neighboring republic, and for which it should have been preparing even then.

[28]

General Filisola observed that the objectives of the leaders of the Texas uprising were not to set that land up as a separate state from Coahuila, and even less as a territory in the Mexican confederation, but rather that their aims were much more advanced, although they were trying to hide the fact. They were pretending that they only wished for an organization more in line with their social needs, without breaking the ties of nationality that bound them to Mexico. He declared, and rightly so, that force of arms was the only thing that could bring them back to the orbit of their obligations. However, he lacked absolutely the indispensable elements in order to accomplish this, and the government, as we have seen, contented itself with sending out orders, never speaking of the supplies that were needed to carry them out. Therefore, he decided to give to the government the frankest and most exact declaration possible of the true aims of the Texas rebels, of the resources upon which they were counting, of what were needed on our part to bring them back to obedience, and what we had that were effective in those circumstances.

With this information the ministry should be able to take the corresponding steps opportunely and with certainty, which they could not have done if they lacked such indispensable knowledge which nobody possessed on the subject with greater perfection and assuredness than the late General Terán. Since in this document he gives data on the topography, situation, boundaries, population, etc., etc., of the Texas territory, it has seemed most proper to us to preserve it in his own words and give it a place in these MEMOIRS, lest at some later time it be confused and mingled with diverse accounts that have multiplied concerning that country *since that time*, and to which we cannot give the same credence as to the present one.

Summary of communication from General Filisola to the Secretary of War and the Navy, Matamoros, May 9, 1833:

In this document General Filisola relates information that the late General Terán gives data on the topography, situation, boundaries, population, etc., of Texas as he has seen it. No one could have possessed greater knowledge than Terán on the matter according to Filisola.

Attention is called to Indian raids with occasional thefts and abuse of a few people with the Indians returning to the wilderness. On the other hand the purposes of the Texas colonists in his opinion show a desire eventually to separate Texas from Mexico beyond the left banks of the Río Grande.

If their purpose is only to form a territory or a new state then they have at hand legal resources that the constitution provides. However, at any attempt to separate an inch of Mexican territory the army will be ready. Every soldier is ready to defend against this.

Whatever the pretext for the mobs and uprisings of the colonists, there seems to be no doubt that their aim was independence from Mexico. The Plan of Veracruz and Zacatecas has only made their plans easier. This belief is held for these reasons: they have run off all federal employees; they have refused to pay rightful duties or to allow troops on the frontier: the scorn of our laws and the aversion to everything Mexican; the destruction of federal fortifications; the haste to organize the militia with foreign leaders and their all out effort to acquire artillery and ammunition.

Even if their intentions were proper, they should obey the constitution and general laws. It is felt then that war is inevitable. This brings the need for positive instructions as well as troops, munitions and supplies.

The part of Texas in rebellion is drained by the San Antonio, Guadalupe, Lavaca, Navidad, Colorado, Brazos, San Jacinto, Trinity and Neches Rivers, most of which cannot be forded because of melting snows or heavy rains at certain seasons. These rivers afford the ports of Matagorda, Brazoria and Galveston. The temperature is very hot or very cold, and there are numerous lagoons and swamps.

Occupation is difficult and defense easy. There are about 15,000 inhabitants who were not born there. Hence at least half are capable of bearing arms; this they know well since they are mostly hunters. They also have the friendship of the Indians of the Red River of the North: Cherokees, Shawnees, Delawares, Yeganís, Caddos, Cioreapuz, Coushattas. They wish to settle in Texas to escape persecution from the U.S.

The Texans do not build towns generally but settle separately. The town of San Felipe de Austin is the capital and focal point for the colonists. General Terán has ordered the occupation of this and El Paso del Caballo, Lavaca or Barranco Colorado, Fort Velasco, Galveston, Anáhuac, Fort Terán, Harrisburg, Nacogdoches, Tenoxtitlán and some others.

It is said that the colonists have an armed militia of 4,000 men with six artillery pieces and much ammunition. It is probable that armed boats have provided food and war materiel. There is a company in New York for the colonization of Texas. The colonists are probably attempting fierce resistance because they fear the loss of their settlements and their future. Means for bringing back constitutional order must be proportionate. San Felipe de Austin is about 130 leagues from Matamoros with no other settlement except La Bahía del Espíritu Santo, which is small and about thirty leagues from San Felipe and more than eighty from Béxar. This latter town is seventy leagues from San Felipe and west of La Bahía.

Everything must be brought from Béxar to La Bahía for supplies and provisional hospital. Matamoros, Brazo de Santiago and Soto La Marina or Tampico must not be left without garrisons.

But needs far exceed what is at hand. There are only six artillery pieces that can be used in a campaign, but the horses are exhausted. Four reserve gun carriages are needed. There is no carpenter, gunsmith, carriage maker, blacksmith or harness maker, and ammunition has not come from Veracruz. There is a shortage of men, and the horses they have are useless. Presidio companies are six months behind in salaries. Quarters are in shambles with no hospital or medical facilities.

All services are in complete abandonment and anarchy, and many things need to be done at great expense. There is not enough money for the budget of the past month, even with a 20,000 peso draft against the Tampico customs. After all due consideration there are needed: 2,400 infantrymen, 600 horses, three companies of foot artillerymen and one mounted, armory, a company of sappers with tools, six engineers, three medicos, a frigate, three schooners, cannon and ammunition, as well as the establishment of a commissary general with a capable and honest leader.

The best season for the invasion of Texas is from the present time to October. All forces should be dispatched via Tula and Victoria to Matamoros with an additional 800 men with arms, 300 mounts, 300,000 cartridges, 20,000 flints, and ten cannon with ammunition. Various artisans are needed for harness, forge, etc., also sappers and medicos for other units. The proceeds from customs at Tampico, Soto la Marina and Matamoros should be dedicated to this division to the exclusion of all other purposes.

Urgent messages to governors of Tamaulipas, Nuevo León and Coahuila and Texas should be sent with orders for aid by civil authorities with mules and saddle bags for transport. Communications are being set up with Brazoria, Galveston, Anáhuac, Nacogdoches and other places. Filisola is ordering the construction of quarters and a fortress at Brazo de Santiago and is going to occupy La Bahía del Espíritu Santo, hoping to put an end to the contraband at that point.

[29]

We recall at this point that among the principles of the best criticism that we know is found in the following: in order for any history not to become an unbearable burden and consequently useless for scholars, most particularly one should find in it truth and economy. This is because only the first should be respected by men of all times, of all parties and of all the countries of the world, even if there should be some who are interested in covering it up, refusing to recognize it or wishing to contradict it. Also because with the second one avoids the danger that the narration may turn into a history of the private opinions of the author, which in general are apt to be a part of the story of human errors, and those who wish to be instructed are relieved of or spared the tiresomeness of it.

Overlooking this wise precaution has the result that at the same time that there appears an increased number of histories of the same people so voluminous that not even the most diligent can read them in a life time, it is also noted that one looks in vain for a single page of the history of other countries which we never get to know and which we cannot judge accurately and with certainty. Since there is no doubt that the checking of truth should be the preferred objective of our attention, all the more gladly have we adopted the second extreme of the principle which we have just invoked, so that without making it an invariable system, we are spared in great part the responsibility that we would of necessity have to submit ourselves to in the presentation of our own ideas. In the first place this is because of a justified lack of trust in our capacity. In the second place it is because of the pressure under which we are obliged to revise our materials. Nor are we permitted the leisure and the calm that we would need to edit what has been written or to correct opportunely the repeated typographical errors that our readers have probably observed in the preceding pages.

Returning then to our principal objective, and for the reasons that we have just mentioned, we shall give space in this chapter to the correspondence that was exchanged by General Filisola and Colonel Don Stephen Austin in the month of May of 1833, which is the period at which we have arrived in these MEMOIRS.

From these documents it can be seen that if the treachery and bad faith with which the colonizers of Texas concealed their designs could not be hidden from the general, neither were they able to cover them up in such manner that they were not made clear by the conduct that was observed from every angle that they might be considered. Thus it is that only through fate or because of an inconceivable error could it be possible that they were not understood by the administrations that have ruled the Republic up to this time, and that those men could even create sympathy for themselves in other countries, and even among our own people, who from other points of view are very commendable and worthy of our respect.

In confirmation of this truth we can record here also one of the most explicit and insistent communications that General Filisola addressed to the minister of war about the middle of May of that year, as if he had a feeling that the one that he had sent a few days earlier and which is included in the preceding chapter had not been sufficient to get the attention of the cabinet. He pointed out there the bringing in of numerous cargoes that had just been effected along those coasts, defrauding the public treasury of the duties. He pointed out also that the colonists openly interfered with the customs officers in their duties and have opposed their decisions. Such disorder could not be stopped by the General's course of ordering that two hundred men should move to station themselves at La Bahía del Espíritu Santo (a point nine leagues from the port, halfway between Aransas and Matagorda, on the right bank of the San Antonio River, and which was protected by a fortress that dominated the river crossing and the road). Notwithstanding the fact that the force referred to could be enough to prevent smuggling, the supplies that the general could count on were not even sufficient to cover the budget for that month.

Also brought to the attention of the government are the dispatches that the military commander at Anáhuac had transmitted to Matamoros concerning the events that took place in that town upon the election of delegates for the *Convention* in Brazoria. These were of such nature that peaceful citizens had to absent themselves there for the space of the three days duration of the drunkenness and other excesses with which the colonists celebrated the election. And finally the general did not fail to put into the dispatch to the government the very important item that on the twenty-third of last April he had received from Tampico and which was that upon the arrival of Lieutenant Colonel Yhari from New York the colonists had been informed concerning the organization of a company enterprise in said city to send men, arms and ammunition with which to reinforce the Texas colonists.

The documents upon which the general relied for his new revelations left no room for doubt, and the one from the administrator of customs at Matagorda must have made a deep impression, considering the scandalous attempts of the colonists which were denounced in it, and also because of the lack of means which could be counted upon to correct them. However, the general without stating this and doing what he could, continued in person to carry out the reconnaissance of the mouth of the Río Grande, Brazo de Santiago, and the other points along the coast. At the same time he issued the most forceful orders for the establishment of hospitals, quarters and lodgings, for the best arrangement for the offices of the treasury and for saving as much as possible in behalf of the national interests.

He was careful especially to bolster morale, which he found at a very low ebb in the presidio companies, and to bring about the observation of the best discipline in all the troops that were under his command. He did this because his main purpose was to march against Texas as soon as he received from the general government the supplies that he needed so that he might do so in good order, and to obtain the results which were the objective of such an expedition.

Such was the state of affairs on May 21 when Colonel Don Stephen Austin presented himself in Matamoros, and declared to the general that he was going as a delegate for the Texas *Convention* to present to the general congress the rights of those inhabitants to set themselves up as a state independent of Coahuila, and other matters that will be seen in the following communications which he delivered with his own hand.

Immediately the general advised the supreme government of the matter, adding that this was no reason for him to be persuaded that the need no longer existed for them to send the supplies necessary for the campaign. Even if that might no longer be the main purpose for which it was planned to be undertaken, there would be, nonetheless, the matter of obstructing the repetition of the attempts at rebellion and the scandalous smuggling by which the colonists continued to defraud the interests of the Republic. After this, the savage Indians that continued to attack the country would be brought to respect the authority, and they would put a stop to the introduction of the Indians from North America who were settling on the left bank of the Río Grande without the consent of the government, with grave danger to the integrity and security of those borders.

Summary of note from Stephen Austin to General Filisola, Matamoros, May 24, 1833:

Austin is on his way to the national capital as a delegate from the Texas convention to petition that Texas be made a state. There is scarcely a judicial system, and there is a lack of order and system in the administration of justice. Hence this proposal for a state government.

The proposal was made at a convention of delegates from all parts except Béxar and Goliad. If there was a mistake in method, it is because of customs and with no desire to proceed violently. This is a daily practice in the U.S. and shows no lack of respect. The convention was called to calm the fears of Indian raids. It is the wish of the colonists to cement the union with Mexico.

There is no interest in Texas separating itself, and the basic interest of Mexico is agriculture and mining. The rich lands of Texas are suited for products such as sugar, cotton, etc. With the proper proportion of such products there would no longer be the need for the extraction of metals. It cannot be presumed that Texas would wish to separate itself form a nation so richly endowed.

During the present year 750,000 pounds of cotton have been ginned and cleaned. There are thirty gins, two steam sawmills and several run by water. This progress will be lost with the anarchy resulting from the lack of adequate local government. The statement is repeated that if the *method* was in error, the people of Texas will correct any mistake that has been made. Austin again gives his assurance of unalterable loyalty of the people of Texas to the constitution and to the integrity of the territory of the Republic of Mexico.

When he had made himself aware of the contents of this note, General Filisola could do no less than observe to Colonel Austin orally that even overlooking the attempts committed by the Texans the year before, either by attacking the artillery garrisons that had been placed on the frontier and coasts of the State of Coahuila and Texas, and by destroying the redoubts and quarters built for the account of the federation, or by persecuting and mistreating the Mexicans and openly opposing the authority of the treasury employees and boldly

144

insulting the officers of the army, the conduct that they were showing in every respect, according to reports that were continually being
received, the contraband goods that they were bringing in, and the
insulting scorn which they continued to show toward all Mexicans,
their laws, etc., not only indicated insubordination and disrespect,
but also a true rebellion on the part of any harmony, any working together with the Mexicans, and even any social organization among
those populations. But Austin's reply was only silence. However,
General Filisola sent him the following on the twenty-seventh of that
month:

Summary of General Filisola's letter to Austin, Matamoros,
May 27, 1833:

Filisola acknowledges Austin's declaration of loyalty and of his
petition of reorganization. The claims should not exceed legal limits.
If things should go to the extremes, no Mexican would hesitate to
make the necessary sacrifice.

On the third day after this answer had been received Colonel
Austin sent a second note to General Filisola, the import of which is
as follows:

Summary:
Austin acknowledges Filisola's note, and he repeats that the
Texans do not wish to go outside the laws. The constitution of the
State of Coahuila and Texas states that its object is the happiness of
the people. The petitions do not believe that this can be achieved in
the political society that exists in that state at present. The reasons
have been set forth and believe that that society should be dissolved.
Texas resources are limited for a state, but this indicates the need.
With the close of the sessions of congress nothing would be gained
by continuing on to Mexico City.

Austin states that the rumors of rebellion are exaggerated and
have no foundation in truth. Similar events have occurred in all
parts of the Republic and have ended happily.

He is attaching a copy of the council of Béxar and the original
petition of the convention to be sent on to the Vice-President.

[30]

One would have to be overly prejudiced in favor of the author of the notes which we have just included in order not to have realized, as did General Filisola, as much in his context as in the allegation* of the bold colonists that they dared to call their rebellious conventicles a convention, which they addressed to the congress. It is true that on the surface they were only contracting for a decree for the erection of Texas into a State in the Mexican federation, but in reality this was nothing more than a pretext which should give no one any false ideas. The conduct of the colonists would allow none to judge that their desires were any other than to lull the general government in order to gain the time necessary for the arrival in the colonies of a greater number of adventurers, and for them to provide themselves with arms, munitions, and other plentiful supplies that they needed to carry out the treason which they had previously planned. At the same time they wished to continue without hindrance the contraband commerce that they had established, not only through the ports of Texas, but also in the adjoining states, as a means of defense. In this way they were ruining our trade in the interior, as well as the income of the public treasury.

With this background we will begin by observing the documents cited without other rules than those of good common sense. At first glance one will realize that the protests contained therein to the effect that the public peace of Texas was not disturbed, and that not a single foot of territory was in danger, were as much lies as their statement that the colonists were not inclined to resist the presence

[* See the one that has been included in Chapter 25 and the note that we have given there. — TRANS.]

146

of Mexican troops and that there was not among them any sentiment in favor of the separation of Texas.

Likewise, when they stated that they only wished for that territory to be erected into a state in order that they themselves might see to the administration of justice and other matters hitherto neglected by the government of Coahuila, they wanted not only to be heard, but that all hostile preparations against the colonists be suspended. It is enough for the Mexicans to be better informed of the intentions which motivated them. The end result was no doubt sufficient so that afterwards nothing could bring them back to order.

In proof of the justice that supported them in such pretensions, and of the good intentions that motivated them, the *conventioneers* and their representative Austin alleged that through their efforts and hard work the desert had been reclaimed from the power of the savages. They spoke as if such reclamation of the desert, for which they took so much credit, was not a natural consequence of the population which occupied it and was increasing under the protection of our arms as well as of the national sovereignty which had dictated the law that permitted and systematized the colonization, not limiting itself to the concession of lands, but also extending privileges and assistance to the colonizers. The latter had not only taken advantage of what was offered but had abused it to the burden and injury of the very nation that had so generously accorded them these benefits, and had even extended them for two more years.

Add to this the fact that when the colonists went to that country, they carried with them the most perfect knowledge of the fact that it was a wilderness frequented by savages, where consequently it was necessary to defend themselves against these people and expel them from the territory in order to make the lands productive and to take advantage of the other benefits that they would produce with work and industry. If these lands had been inhabited and cultivated by industrious men, it would not have been necessary to colonize them in the manner that was done.

No less without foundation is the argument that they also made to the effect that what they accomplished in that territory was done for themselves, because if they had not worked the land, neither would they have been able to live. If the nation had given them lands that were secure and cultivated and with fruits in season so that they would have come only to reap and to enjoy, it would have been rather a purchase by the settlers and not a cession of lands in order for them to have been owners and not slaves on the land.

To our greater astonishment, these baseless allegations were produced by three or four individuals of the council of Béxar who were not colonists, nor could they call themselves such. They were nothing more than the mouthpieces for the ideas of the rebels, and thus we may consider those who made the representation to which we here refer; that is, the accomplices of the rebels, duped by the latter with the hope that caused them to believe that once they managed to have Texas erected into a state, to them would fall a large part of the benefits of the monopoly which they would continue more freely than up to that time.

When we know these mysteries, then we have an explanation of the fact that it should naturally be suspected that the authorities of the State of Coahuila, far from having placed obstacles in the way of the accumulation of adventurers and suspicious people in the colonies, and promoting the productivity of the Mexican establishments and the progress of commerce, industry and the arts, had shown a major lack of concern with regards to these problems. Also they showed excessive tolerance towards the colonists while at the same time they hastened to make them concessions beyond the purview of the laws and what prudence prescribed. This is confirmed by facts as notorious as those of having distributed lands to them without any precaution whatsoever, not having demanded the fulfillment of their contracts, and instead of this having permitted them — against the most express intent of our laws — to introduce and maintain slaves.

As for the administration of justice, it may also be observed that the colonists had through the State constituion, just the same as the Mexicans, the right to name their judges, and had at hand the resources for achieving justice in all those instances where judgment might be passed. In view of this, what they were really asking for was a decision to allow them to withdraw from the formalities and rules of our legislation in order to continue to observe that of the United States which they were used to following. But even if this had not been so, it was not fair to grant to them what was not permitted to the rest of the people.

And this consideration has all the more foundation since the colonists had come to Texas with the idea that they would not be governed by the institutions of the country of their birth, but by those in force at that time in the new country which they were adopting, or those which time and circumstances should make necessary or fitting to establish in the exercise of national sovereignty. Thus Moses Austin, the first colonist of Texas, submitted and swore obedience to the laws of Spain, his son Stephen to those of the Mexican

148

Empire, and the colonists who came after the fall of the Empire to those of the Republic. Nothing was more natural than this because it is inconceivable that a few newcomers should in any way have the right to subordinate the will of seven million Mexicans to their opinion, instead of the obligation under which they were to accept and respect that of those already there.

It is equally true that if they complained about the lack of administration of justice and said that the colonies were in a state of anarchy, disorder and insecurity, it was only another example of deceit on their part, because it was all the result of their machinations, unruliness and lack of faith, which because of the weakness of our forces could not be remedied as was in the best interests of the nation; the government recognized this. Hence they took occasion to attribute it all to the lack of adequate organization for their needs; therefore, they pretended to petition so strongly that Texas should be constituted as a new State in the Mexican Federation.

Granting this desire, on the surface so innocent, would have been nothing more than to fall into the most treacherous and stupid of traps into which the Mexican government could put itself with respect to the colonists. In the shadow of the sovereignty to which they aspired to elevate Texas they would only have prepared the final blow which they had planned in advance for separating themselves. Meanwhile they would have increased their means of carrying it out by monopolizing and systematizing in their own way the alienation of lands, protecting the infamous and shameful slave traffic, increasing and favoring the introduction of North American vagabonds, delaying the reestablishment of the maritime customs as well as the military garrisons, so necessary for the defense of those frontiers, for the prosecution of smuggling, for carrying out the annulling of titles to occupied lands acquired without the established requirements, and finally for the fulfillment and observance of national laws, which the colonists not only had evaded, but looked upon with the utmost scorn and contempt. What then were the just and legal reasons that could aid them in such pretensions, and what were the guarantees that they were presenting so that one would not rightly be fearful of their abuse?

The truth of the matter was exactly the opposite. Texas lacked the number of inhabitants fixed by the federal constitution to be erected into an independent state, and it lacked all the indispensable means for subsisting as such. Don Stephen Austin admits this himself in his preceding notes, and the conduct that the colonists of Texas had observed in all cases must cause a justified suspicion that

149

would still be there when they should be elevated to such a political rank that would give them greater means of resistance and the trappings of legality with which they would take care to gild their intentions, which would always expose the general government to serious and continuous embarrassment. Since the weakness and bad character of their trumped up reasons could not help but be evident to them, they feared therefore that they would not succeed in persuading the national congress, and that they would receive a negative answer to the representation which they advanced.

But this negative itself entered into their plans in order to give an appearance of justice to their premeditated rebellion and to attract to their cause in this manner the sympathies of those who were not fully aware of their true directions. Thus in their combination for this purpose they set up a dilemma for the national government. If they were granted the formation of a state, they would take advantage of this break in order to provide themselves with all the advantages that such position and character could give them in order in due time to declare themselves incorporated into the United States of the North. But if their pretension were denied, by the same token they would declare the right to proclaim for themselves absolute independence of Mexico and of any other nation of the globe.

But such plans and such treacherous deceits were recognized; their petitions were denied; and although they hypocritically pretended to accept, they continued their traitorous preparations waiting for a better occasion to realize their treachery, as in due time we shall relate, because the time that corresponds to it has not yet come. We must turn back to the year 1833, whose events we were recording up to the previous chapter.

[31]

After the success, or rather the impunity that Don Stephen Austin had gained with the artifice with which he surprised General Terán's loyalty by failing to keep the promises that he had made to him at the Hacienda del *Cojo* as related in Chapters 21 and 22, he again made use of the same reprehensible craftiness with General Filisola in Matamoros. He feared that the latter, who had let him know how he felt about his plans, might place some obstacles in the way of his carrying out his activities to put them into effect. Thus it is that, although in one of the communications that are included in Chapter 24 he had announced to the general that he was heading for Texas, he left Matamoros before the end of the month of May and took the road to Saltillo, and from there he went on to Mexico City. He was always intent upon taking the government by surprise and lulling it to sleep so that they would suspend the preparations that were being made for the campaigns upon which the general was so insistent, and for lack of which preparations he had not yet begun his operations.

Meanwhile, General Filisola not only hastened to inform Mexico City of Austin's communications and the answer that he had given him, but he also set forth to the minister of war in a note of the 30th of that month and year all that Austin had said to him in the meetings that he had just had with the general, the protests that he had made, and the line of conduct that he proposed to follow. General Filisola firmly believed that all of this could not fail to get the attention of the cabinet in Mexico City and when it saw, as it must, that Ausitn was going the opposite of what he said, there could be no doubt of the faithlessness with which he was proceeding. Perhaps it was due to these circumstances that the congress of the Union had not fallen into the net by acceding to the Texans' petition. In order that what we saw about Austin may be confirmed more clearly and may be judged and compared with what he said in Matamoros and what he continued to do in Mexico City, we shall give in order the account of each of them.

And while we are waiting for the time to come to set forth what Austin was doing in Mexico City, we shall give our readers information concerning what General Filisola was thinking back in Matamoros, as the chief sent it on to the minister of war after the departure of Austin from Matamoros. Here is what the general had to say to the government in the note already mentioned concerning the conduct that he expected in the future from Don Stephen Austin, and to which the attention of the ministry should be duly turned:

"The authority there will see also that Austin intends to return to Texas first because if he continues on to Mexico City his trip will be fruitless since he will find the sessions of congress closed at the time of his arrival. In the second place, because the government of the state has named commissioners to enter into discussions with those colonists, providing them with what is necessary, although in accordance with the instructions that have been intrusted to them. Austin's return then seems wise to me for the reasons set forth, and furthermore it is proper, taking note of the prestige and influence that he enjoys among the new settlers and of the fact that he can co-operate effectively and with rational and just agreement that will bring advantages to the colonists and avoid expense for the state and the federation.

"The repetitious Señor Austin has assured me that the troops under my command can go into that territory in any number with the assurance that there are no intentions to resist. If there was formerly opposition, this was caused by the circumstances of that time, by the conduct of some officers. However, he has had the opportunity to observe that of those who are there today, which is in no wise similar. In short, I can come to no other conclusion than that which is the result of his offers and his words, so much so that in the case of his falling down the government has abundant resources to bring to order those who might not be on its side, especially when it is a matter of a cause so clearly national. Will Your Excellency be so kind as to convey the knowledge of these matters to the Most Excellent Señor Vice-President, bearing in mind that not because of this do I think unnecessary the aid which I have asked for in my communication Number 107, the ninth of this month. Without it I cannot move from this point because of the absolute lack of everything."

Weary of having related up to this point only the intrigues and the crimes of the Texas colonists with the indignation that they must inspire in us and with the shame of the fact that many Mexicans were accomplices or careless helpers in their treachery, we have true consolation and relief in mingling among such disagreeable accounts that of the event described in the communication which the governor of Coahuila and Texas received during the time of the residency of General Filisola in Matamoros.

Summary of note to the governor of Coahuila and Texas from Filisola to be dispatched to the Vice-President of Mexico, Monclova, May 20, 1833:

The Vice-President is to be informed of the unpleasant events occurring recently in the Department of Beẋar. He is asked to issue orders not to use arms against the rebels until the government advises that the commission for constitutional order has not achieved its purpose.

It is true that we should wish to have a great deal of testimony similar to that which precedes in order to prove in these MEMOIRS the honorable conduct of the Mexican authorities who were doing their duty in the State of Coahuila and Texas during the time to which we refer. Neither can we make mention of that of the council of González, although it came to deserve the approbation of the supreme government because it indicated its loyalty and obedience and a firm resistance to the ignoble suggestions of the malcontents when later they put in evidence their treachery and dissimulation with the uprising of that town in order to prevent the recovery of an artillery piece that was there with no purpose in the national service.

We can, however, remove with satisfaction the consequences which awaited the council of Beẋar, who sent out the communication to which we have referred when invited by Don Stephen Austin, as were all the authorities of Texas, by means of a circular which he sent to them from Mexico City, dated October 2 of that year of 1833, for them to decide to organize an independent government, although it might be resisted by the supreme authority of the Republic. The council of Beẋar not only answered making known their disapproval, but were indignant and offended by such boldness. They brought it to the attention of the ministry, who as a consequence issued on December 21 the order for arrest, which was not carried out against the person of Austin until January 2 in the following year of 1834. But we have wandered astray. It is proper that we should continue relating what happened in Matamoros during the second half of the year 1833, and whether the campaign that was being prepared against the rebellious colonists was effective or not.

[32]

People still have not forgotten that the year 1833 was for our country one of the harshest and most disastrous. Conspired against by revolutions and the horrible epidemic of *cholera morbus*, the former decimated the population, and the latter decimated again those who remained alive. How many reasons thousands of families must have had to remember constantly and bitterly that fateful period! We shall not point them out because it is impossible to name them all. However, we have no doubt that one of the most grievous that could be pointed out was the manifesto made in Morelia on May 26 of that year by Lieutenant Colonel Don Ignacio Escalada with two hundred men of the active battalion of that capital.

In it he declared support of the Apostolic Roman Catholic religion and of its ministers, together with the continuation of ecclesiastical and military privileges and a general reform in the government of the nation. At the same time he honored the President-General Don Antonio López de Santa Anna, recognizing him as supreme chief of the Republic for life. He did not hesitate to make attempts to dissolve the state legislatures, to make prisoners of the governor and the commanding general and to abolish the powers of each in order to dictate and put into effect other decrees. These, in addition to being within themselves the least skillful, carried even in their outward appearance the most repugnant and undisguised character of the inability and the capricious whim of their author.

However, this absurd and injudicious plan was immediately taken up by Generals Don Gabriel Durán and Don Mariano Arista, the former in Chalco, and the latter on the road to Cuernavaca with the same force that had left Mexico City to pursue the rebels, under the command of General Santa Anna. The latter because of his resistance to accepting the dictatorship was placed in prison, from which a few days later he was able to escape to place himself at the head of new forces with which he continued to do battle against the rebels until he defeated them and pacified them completely in the month of October following in Guanajuato, as every one knows. For this reason we do not think it is necessary for us to go into the details of these events here.

But for our purposes it is indeed proper to recall that the news of these reached Matamoros almost at the same time that cholera invaded the coast and had made its horrors felt in Tampico. It filled the people with fear because of the terrible ideas that for a long time had haunted them concerning the ravages that that epidemic was producing in all areas through which it spread.

On the other hand, since the news of Escalada's manifesto, the adherence of Generals Arista, Durán and other chiefs with the forces that they commanded, and of the imprisonment of the president-general, and the news that these events had as their author this same person, that his imprisonment and all that was being done publicly was only for the purpose of saving appearances, and that the truth would not be brought out until the leader himself considered it fitting to his purposes, these items were unfortunately received among the greater part of the leaders and troops of Matamoros with the enthusiasm of men who were not only unwary but were willing and disposed to promote them. They were anxious for an opportunity to be able to avenge the humiliations that they said that they had suffered at the hands of the civilians for infractions of Zavaleta Plan, and the confinement that had been imposed upon them by sending them to Texas.

To circumstances so painful for the commanding general of those states was added the other no less disturbing of the lack of money and resources to attend to their needs. To meet those most necessary and of little importance General Filisola had found it necessary to pledge his personal credit at the bank and with the wealthy citizens; otherwise the troops under his command would not have been able to subsist. But even this lone expedient would disappear in the face of the fears inspired by the news of the progress of the revolutionaries. The principles proclaimed by their followers were sufficient to upset everything forthwith from top to bottom and to leave standing nothing at all that had been done since the year 1821 up to that time.

Then to make the general's situation even more painful he was attacked first by a malignant fever that degenerated at once into a bloody dysentery that deprived him of all movement. However, from his bed he tried to take the measures that he considered useful to the preservation of the fortifications and of the order of the troops as well as in the city.

But meanwhile the garrison leaders met daily in the home of Colonel Don José de las Piedras in order to consolidate their defection and to join the ranks of the rebels. This was an undertaking that certainly must not have been very difficult because of the opinions held by all of them and by some of the leading individuals of the town, and also because these had become general throughout the army where it seemed to be very difficult to find a single person who had not taken part in the uprising. The only thing that held some of them back was simply the very exaggerated nature of the principles proclaimed by the movement. But just as there was no doubt on the part of those men, neither was it feared by the general masses that this would reach its fulfillment and that everything would be upset.

In the midst of these circumstances that General Filisola understood perfectly, to which must be added his lack of good health, it would have been impossible for him to calm the tempest by direct means. In order to attenuate or at least delay the effects of that effervescent situation he called a meeting of all the leaders in his own lodgings. He began by dispelling the idea of personal grievances that they said they resented. He pointed out to them that although these were true, for noble souls who loved their country they should never be sufficient reason for attacking its institutions and plunging it into blood and misfortune such as war always brings. Much less should there be any thought of upsetting things in such a manner that the country would find itself desolated by a formidable plague such as cholera.

In spite of the fact that the opinion of the rebels seemed to be widespread in the army, the general for his part did not think so, and rather expected that many officers, leaders and generals would oppose it with abundant support from the civilian militia and among the people. These viewed such ideas with the horror and disapproval with which they would look upon the announcement of the return of privileges that attacked liberty, the rights of man and of the citizen, and the independence of the states guaranteed by the constitution. Upon these ruins there could only be raised up a tyranny that as the end result would bring to naught the fruits of the sacrifices of all kinds that the nation had made to free and organize itself, and would end up by wiping out the pleasant hopes that still remained for a future of happiness and prosperity.

157

With this in mind he invited them to organize their thinking in favor of the institutions of the fatherland and of the preservation of the small number of individuals that the political upheavals had left in the army. This was to give the greatest proofs of their morale and discipline, with no other purposes in mind than the glory that they would achieve by defending the integrity of the nation which was threatened by the ambitious colonists and adventurers of Texas. This noble undertaking was commended to their honor and determination, and the redeeming of this pledge, at the same time that it afforded them the most plausible occasion for avenging in a most generous manner the insults that they had received, as well as those against the country. Bringing respect to the Mexican name and valor would be far better than staining their hands with the blood of their fellow citizens, friends, relatives and brothers, as is always the case with civil wars.

To this they should also add that whoever might be the party that won out in the present unrest, their efforts and services would always be esteemed for these were rendered not to one or the other of the contending parties, but to the entire country, independent of the system of government which might be finally adopted by it. There was an example of this magnanimous attitude in the French fighters at the time when they were witnessing the greatest horrors of the past century. These, in order not to involve themselves in the civil war flew as volunteers to swell the ranks of the armies on the frontiers to resist and punish the foreign enemies of France.

They all seemed to be touched by these just reflections, and in proof of it each one on his part and for the troops that he had under his immediate command offered to maintain and to see that others did so too the greatest loyalty to the government, and the most exacting discipline and fulfillment of their obligations. With this the meeting ended.

However, these gatherings continued in the home of Colonel Piedras without the knowledge of the general who was in bed gravely ill, and who did not have even enough strength to turn from one side to the other. In spite of all this he could meditate and mull over in his mind how he might turn these men from so dangerous a step in which they might find themselves compromised and ruined. He also considered that many of them had in their time rendered important services to the country.

There was then another means that he might adopt, if not to eliminate completely the movement within the garrison, at least to delay it, upon the chance that meantime they would receive from the

158

capital news more favorable than the last, in which case they could bend the minds of their subordinates to quiet, obedience and the carrying out of their respective duties. This means, which the general indeed adopted, was to disperse the bodies of his division to several different points, removing their respective leaders, officers and troops from immediate contact with the rest, and especially from the presidio companies, who on the other hand were definitely needed in their respective localities, and it was wise to preserve them from the contagion and the evil of the declarations.

With this double objective he commanded that they be equipped for the march, giving preference to all the other troops that were to set out at the same time as the former, under the reasonable excuse of the harm that might be caused by the *cholera* in a town where they were all gathered together. He persuaded them that by separating there should be fewer and less frequent cases of the epidemic where there were less considerable numbers of men who were together at each point. It would also be all the easier to obtain the necessary help to attend properly to those who might be taken ill.

But there remained one more grave difficulty for carrying out that plan with the troops that were not from the presidio. This difficulty consisted of the lack of money for supporting them for the march to their respective destinations. Since at that time the general expected the arrival of twenty thousand pesos from the port of Tampico, he thought also that with this aid the way was clear and his noble purposes achieved.

Meanwhile there was also promise that he could frustrate completely the purposes of Colonel Piedras and his collaborators with this other plan. There were in Brazo de Santiago and Boca del Río one hundred twenty infantrymen of the forty-second permanent battalion, whose officers, and especially the commander Captain Don Manuel Sabariego, were completely reliable. There was also in Reynosa a civilian cavalry company of one hundred twenty men, the same in Camargo, Mier and Revilla, and one hundred fifty infantrymen in Matamoros. Although in order to muster them there was also the problem of money, the general proposed to overcome it because as we have said he expected the twenty thousand pesos that they were to send him from Tampico. Furthermore, he knew that several boats that had been announced were due to arrive there from New Orleans and could produce something like thirty thousand pesos in duties.

Consequently he had resolved to have march immediately to the town of Reynosa, one hundred men of the Fifth cavalry regiment (who his chief General Don Manuel de Andrade had assured him were as loyal as his excellent officers) and cross the Río Bravo at that point, going down the left bank and locating themselves in the pass of that river opposite Matamoros. The one hundred fifty infantry militiamen of the latter city were to do the same thing, taking with them two artillery pieces from the city, and taking two eight caliber guns to set them up in the same pass.

While these operations were being carried out the militia companies of Camargo, Mier and Revilla were to meet to take the same position and establish the customs at once at that point also. The general was to set up his residence there in order in this manner to have more under his control and under his immediate disposition all the resources and means sufficient to assure the obedience of the leaders who may have tried to withdraw from them. These would not have been able to undertake anything without supplies or money with which to buy them in order to be able to cross that wilderness devoid of all types of resources with the exception of meat.

However, since the people were all loyal to the system in force he could easily deprive the troops of that means of subsistence by a simple cordon directed at the ranches situated in the direction of the only two roads that lead to the interior; these are the one from Matamoros to Monterrey and the one that from the same place leads to San Fernando de Presa, Soto la Marina, Etc. The carrying out of this other part of the plan indicated could not be so difficult. With this accomplished he thought it would also be easy to have the rest of the troops cross the river in groups and direct them in the same manner to Bahía del Espíritu Santo or Goliad where the general had planned to locate his general quarters, while he was receiving supplies and replacements to fill in his troops.

But unfortunately the money that was supposed to come from Tampico did not appear; a storm had delayed the arrival of the boats that were expected. The one hundred dragoons of the Fifth regiment whose horses were grazing in the field at a considerable distance from the town (the only means known in those parts for keeping them) delayed longer than they should have. For another fateful event the presidio companies did not leave for their respective posts because Lieutenant Don Ignacio Rodríguez of the one from Laredo had led off a great part of them, and each day they had some new excuse for postponing their march, giving them time for the uprising to be carried out. To complete the difficulties the general himself fell ill again with his troubles to the point that he could not even get out of bed.

Meanwhile the conspirators who were meeting daily took advantage of these circumstances to carry out their plans for rebellion, and they thought that the time had come to realize them. They began on June 17 by ordering Lieutenant Rodríguez named above, and the one of the same rank from the Fifth regiment Don Angel Miramón to surprise on the road to San Fernando a special dispatch which the general was sending to the government in order to inform it of his difficult situation.

From here they made an excuse to give the troops to understand that the general wished to arrest the leaders, put them on a ship for Veracruz and to have the other ranks continue on to Texas where they told them they were destined to go. With this and by offering the troops that they would return to Mexico City, the rebels succeeded in winning them over to all they wanted, and on the night of the nineteenth they declared for the Plan of Escalada putting it into words that seemed to them most conducive to their ulterior motives.

When this happened the city was thrown into the greatest consternation, and several individuals among the most prominent and well-to-do left to go to their ranches or to the mountains. The rebels immediately collected the arms of the civilians and committed outrages against those who were marked as being more in favor of the federal system, and broke out in shouts of "Long live . . ." and "Death to . . .," as one might say is unfortunately the custom under these circumstances.

General Andrade was forbidden to enter his corps headquarters; second assistant Don Julián Miracle was threatened with death and persecuted. Colonel Don José Stáboli, Assistant Inspector Don José Juan Sánchez, Captain Don Manuel Sabariego and those of his rank Sans and Don Juan Cuevas, were arrested the following day. Messages were sent with invitations to all the presidio companies of the three states and to various civil authorities for them to support the declaration, and the home of General Filisola was surrounded by troops.

Then Colonel Cortina and the third chief Don Juan Rondero was commissioned to invite the general to take part in the rebellion, but the latter answered them that his inability to move because of his illness incapacitated him for everything. But he said that even if he were in perfect health his oath of loyalty to the nation and his own conviction in particular would not permit him to take such a step because he believed that it was a retreat and going contrary to the liberty and prosperity of the country. Under these circumstances he

161

begged them at least to respect his opinion as they should respect the others without trampling upon any one for the ideas that he held and making it possible for the troops to keep order. And he asked them to take away not only the guard that they had placed around his house, but even the orderlies for which he had no need at all.

These leaders replied that the following day they would withdraw the guard but not the orderlies because they considered them necessary for his service as well as to the decorum of his position. However, the general again insisted that they were in no way necessary, and certainly not because of the decorum of rank when at that very moment they had just overrun and disobeyed it. Bringing an end to the conference the men of the group immediately withdrew the troops surrounding the house, and they were careful also to take away with them the records, seals, maps, etc., etc., of the general command, which were turned over to them by the assistant inspector Don José Joan Sánchez, and the secretary who was Lieutenant Colonel Don Vicente Luna.

The next day the general informed the government of this unpleasant event, and Filisola added that bedfast as he was he viewed with greater pain the evils that the authors of the rebellion were going to bring upon themsleves and upon those departments responsible than the ills which kept him physically prostrated at the present, and that it was not in his hands easily to avoid this because he had neither health nor liberty. However, he turned over in his mind the things that he might do to extricate himself from that position and get himself to Monterrey to prevent, if such were possible, the projection into that state and that of Coahuila the ills and unrest that were being experienced in Matamoros. Perhaps he would be able to bring to obedience to the government those leaders and ill advised troops who had recently rebelled.

Since, in spite of all that he did he could not accomplish this, from that time on he doubted that in the future they would see the colonists any better held in check or returned to obedience to the laws of the federation. Quite disillusioned as to what extent those events could influence the fate of the colonies, he must likewise visualize the things that would come as a consequence, and with time would prevent the general government from taking the forces and resources necessary for an undertaking that was already beginning to show itself quite superior to the government's power.

Meanwhile, one morning Acting General Don Lina José Alcorta presented himself to the general asking for a passport to the capital of the Republic. However, since the day before the order had been given by Colonel Piedras that all those who promoted among the troops any rumors that might move them to a lack of unity, discontent, desertion or lack of trust would be treated with all the force of the ordinance, the general feared to compromise his dignity. He limited himself to explaining to Alcorta that his situation at the moment would not permit him to grant this passport to him because such a step might result in sad consequences for both of them. Alcorta was so convinced that the following day he came back to visit him and to tell him that the leaders of the garrison wished to ask him to take command of it. Filisola encouraged him to do this so that by restoring order and discipline he might avoid persecutions, calm the spirits of the people, now quite upset, and see in the end the services that in those circumstances it might be possible to render to humanity and to the cause of civilization.

Two or three days after this event General Filisola, from his bed, heard the sound of war drums in the direction of the roads to Reynosa and San Fernando. He had them call Colonel Don José Stáboli to ask him what was going on, and the latter told him that it was Colonels Piedras and Cortina who were marching with their troops, the first heading for Tampico by way of San Fernando and Victoria, and the second through the towns of Reynosa and Camargo to the State of Nuevo León to occupy Monterrey its capital. The rest of the garrison was remaining in Matamoros under the orders of General Alcorta.

Filisola understood at once that that plan of action must cause the ruin of the three sections because no one of them had sufficient strength to carry out the objectives that they had. They were marching in divergent directions to put great distances between themselves without being able to count on the resources necessary for subsistence because the lack of loyalty felt towards them by the inhabitants would be injurious to them. Just by hiding the little that they must have in the small towns and settlements of territory that they did not know would be enough to destroy those forces. If all of them together had undertaken the march to Monterrey and Saltillo, they would have been able to obtain supplies, increase their forces to nearly two thousand men with the presidio companies of Coahuila and Nuevo León and march from there on Zacatecas, etc.

However, he kept these ideas to himself without permitting Stáboli or any one else to know about them, and he only busied himself by bringing these thoughts to maturity as will be told later.

[33]

As the reader is probably already aware, nothing upset General Filisola more than the desire to escape the violent situation in which he had been placed by the events that had just taken place around him. And indeed one of his first objectives was to anticipate the arrival of Cortina at the city of Monterrey in order to prepare the defenses of the city and oppose the progress of the revolutionaries, who in his opionion not only threatened the peace and tranquility of that city, but would likely continue by invading Saltillo and all the places that were included in the general command of the Eastern States. But since his health did not permit him to put this into execution as soon as he needed to, he waited anxiously to have a moment of relief in order to undertake the movement that the situation and the determination of the rebels were marking out for him.

In the midst of these ideas he was awakened at twelve o'clock at night on July 1 by the captain of the cavalry Don Juan Cuevas, his aide, who presented himself at that hour to deliver a dispatch from the minister of war in which he was advised that President Don Antonio López de Santa Anna had managed to free himself from the arrest under which he was being held by Generals Arista and Durán and to flee to Puebla.

Taking advantage of this circumstance, as unexpected as it was credible, he deemed it fitting to send the message without a moment's delay to General Don Lino José Alcorta because the garrison was led to believe as certain at that time that General Santa Anna was the one who was directing the revolutionary movements, and that the arrest and all else that had been done to him had as its only purpose to save appearances. With the publication of that document the general hoped to derive a great advantage in order to divert

164

many of the rebels who had in good faith believed the things that had been used to win them over. But as the hour was very late for a sick man such as the general, he did not consider it convenient for Alcorta to come to see him immediately when he received the dispatch, and he sent word to tell him to wait until the next day.

In fact that is what he did, and the first thing that he said to the general was how doubtful it seemed to him concerning the facts of the matter referred to in the communication. But the general insisted upon trying to change his mind, and after doing so he continued to presume upon the affection and authority which he had with the colonel [sic] until he persuaded him to undertake on his part the opportune and noble act of bringing the rebels back to order by disillusioning them concerning the freedom of President Santa Anna and his opposition to the ideas of the revolutionaries.

Although Alcorta replied that he did not feel himself so favored by the circumstances that he could promise such fortuitous success as was to be desired because the leaders and the troops were enthusiastic to the point that they not only believed themselves capable of giving impetus in general to the movement of the revolutionaries, but that they could take an active part in their triumph. The general, however, pointed out to him that that was folly because Piedras's movement would be restricted by General Don Estevan Moctezuma who was already on his way from San Luis to Victoria with a sizeable division, and that Cortina would do the same for Colonel Ugartechea, commander general of Nuevo León, who had placed the active militia of that state under arms. The rebels at Matamoros would be brought back to order right there by the forces from the states of Tamaulipas and Nuevo León since nothing could stand in their way after defeating and subjecting Piedras and Cortina's troops. They should march upon that port concentrically while these three sections could not find cover against all that number since they were eighty leagues one from the other, and each one alone was respectively inferior to the government troops. They had neither the time nor the resources to be able to regroup effectively in any one place.

These observations finally convinced Alcorta, and consequently he offered the general to begin work, although with the caution that the circumstances demanded, in order to penetrate the plans of the influential leaders and officers, as well as of the troops, so as to influence them to a counter movement. With this purpose in mind, it was decided in that friendly meeting that the general through Colonel Guerra would ask for a passport to Monterrey in

165

order to warn that city of Cortina's arrival and to prevent its occupation, as we have said that the general was planning.

A few moments later as luck would have it Colonel Guerra presented himself in the general's lodgings, and the latter, taking advantage of the opportunity, indicated excitedly how interested he
was in moving from that city to Monterrey in order to regain his
health. Indeed, he asked the colonel to obtain for him the necessary
passport from the leader of the rebels. Although the colonel excused
himself pointing to the small amount of influence that he had with the
leaders of the garrison, and even less with General Alcorta in order to
obtain the permission desired by the general, at the latter's renewed insistence, he agreed to ask for the passport. But since they only wanted
a middle man as had been agreed so that Alcorta would not be suspected by the rebels, the passport was issued that same day.

Consequently General Filisola began his march on July 3 for
the Rancho de Guadalupe, three leagues away on the road to Reynosa, and there he spent the night, accompanied then by his secretary Lieutenant Colonel Don Vicente Luna and the Neopolitans
Don Luis Pierro and Don Vicente Constanza. However, before setting out he had planned with General Alcorta, and the latter with
Colonel Don Manuel de Andrade, Colonel Stáboli, Lieutenant Colonels Don Constantino Ternova and Don Luciano Muñoz, Assistant
Inspector Don José Juan Sanchez, Captains Don Manuel Sabariego
and Don Juan Cuevas, other lower ranking officers, and the clerk
Don Andrés Zenteno, that as soon as Filisola was some days' journey on his way to Monterrey, they would attempt to reverse the
opinion of that garrison. Those referred to would previously arrive
at an agreement with various influential private citizens of the town
who were disposed to help so that the movement would not come to
naught and might bring about the desired results.

Likewise it is worthy of mention that the general also had in
mind that with Piedras's group there were also Captain Sans, Lieutenant Miracle and other subordinates also who were disposed to
join with their troops the first detachments of the supreme government that they might meet, so that all this combination of circumstances gave him hope that the return to order by the rebel forces
would be carried out very quickly, and perhaps without any misfortunes.

Consoled by these ideas the general eased the pains of the situation during the night that he spent in Guadalupe. However, since
at two o'clock in the morning he had seen from there a party of cavalry pass by along the road that goes from the Rancho de Santo

Domingo, from Matamoros to Monterrey, and fearing that it might be in search of him because of the discovery or bad luck of the plans of Alcorta and his companions, in spite of how bad he felt, right then he left the place for Reynosa. The seriousness of his illness caused him to remain at the Rancho de la Mesa, from where Don Vincente Constanza returned to Matamoros for medicines, catching up with him the following day in Reynosa, where the general had managed to get to that same day.

There the general was informed that in Matamoros Constanza had learned that on the third and fourth Alcorta had tried to get the garrison to change its mind. For this purpose he had called a meeting of all the leaders and officers, who after hearing all that Alcorta thought fit to explain to them showed themselves convinced, deferring to his ideas to the point of supporting them, using their influence with the troops to bring them back to obedience to the supreme government and other constitutional authorities.

But as soon as they left the meeting, several of these same officers went to the various barracks where the troops were located to denounce the ideas put forth by General Alcorta and those of Andrade, Stáboli, and other leaders who had shown more inclination for retracting and disavowing the pronunciamiento. From these maneuvers there resulted, as the insubordination of those military men reached the ultimate extreme, that the sergeants of the companies decided to order the taking up of arms and that a group of the Number 7 of the infantry, under the command of a sergeant, should proceed to Alcorta's home with the purpose of arresting and shooting him. The same thing had been proposed for carrying out against Don José María Girón and several other private citizens who were suspected of being in opposition to them.

No doubt this would have happened had it not been for the good offices of Colonel Guerra to prevent these attempts, who at the same time that he tried to persuade and calm them down, sent word to those threatened to get to a place of safety, which they did with some of them hiding and others saving themselves by flight. Among those also were General Don Manuel de Andrade and Don Andrés Zenteno, who took ship for Veracruz.

Finally, since the rebels were directed by inspirations higher than they possessed, they also had presence of mind enough to dispatch a detachment in pursuit of General Filisola. This was the same one that he saw pass by the Rancho de Guadalupe the morning of the day before. When they had not been successful in finding the general, they had marched away to Santo Domingo.

General Filisola, who never had any reason to doubt the truth of the news that Constanza had just given him, and after he had confirmed it in a much more positive manner, knew at once the great importance that he should give to it, and that as a consequence there was no time left to come to the aid of such a situation. Since he knew that Colonel Cortina was in the town of Camargo, he took the road by Zacate Pass in order to avoid an encounter and to see if he could get there before the other one. Thus he decided to leave for Monterrey from Reynosa at twelve o'clock on the night of the fifth to the sixth, and although the state of his health was worse every day, he was able to arrive at the Rancho de la Noria with all those accompanying him in the span of fifteen hours on the road. From there he wrote to the governor of Nuevo León, Don Manuel María del Llano, and to the head commander Don Domingo de Ugartechea, informing them of his march and urging them to preserve constitutional order in that city and state.

These communications arrived most opportunely since Governor Llano was getting ready to leave the city, and on the other hand a detachment of cavalry that Ugartechea had sent to reconnoiter the vicinity of Mier and Serralvo had just joined Cortina's section. Both authorities were heartened by the receipt of these messages and commanded bells to be rung, rockets fired, etc., and since the rebels were not aware of how far away General Filisola was and whether he had sufficient forces to do battle with them, they became intimidated and gave Ugartechea an opportunity to show force and presence of mind that will do him honor.

This was the way that he did it. He placed himself at the head of a small number of loyal soldiers and going directly to the barracks he placed the rebels in the guardhouse. This was enough to restore order and confidence to the city and for the governor to have time to put eighty militia infantrymen under arms to secure the people against any new insult.

Immediately they gave orders to send a small body of troops to Filisola to escort him so that he might make the rest of the journey with greater security and honor. This general continued his march on the seventh, although his illness was getting worse than it had been the previous days, and he spent the night at the Rancho del Zacate. There he learned that Cortina with a detachment had marched the day before from Camargo to Mier, and then he had no doubt that he could reach Monterrey first. With this in mind he moved on to spend the night of the eighth at the Rancho de la *Manteca* as his illness would not allow him to proceed farther.

But on the ninth on his way to *El Capadero* he met the courier who was bringing him the answers from Governor Llano and from Commander Ugartechea. In these dispatches he was informed of the things that had happened in Monterrey, and they congratulated him on his approaching arrival in that city. When he arrived at El Capadero where he was to spend the night, he was met by the escort which had been sent from Monterrey under the command of the presidio captain Don Anastasio de Ugartechea.

Late on the night of the same day, he also received a second communication from Governor Llano in which he was told that the mayor of *María* had informed him on that same date from that place that there would arrive there at any moment the rebel troops that Colonel Cortina was commanding. On the following day, the tenth, these were to march by way of *Cadereita Jiménez* to Monterrey. He gave him this information so that he might hasten his march and avoid falling into the hands of the dissidents.

Because of this, in spite of his illness, Filisola continued the next day, the tenth, on to Cadereita where he arrived quite ill at nine o'clock at night. But he took care to inform Llano and Ugartechea of everything at once so that they might be guided by it. Early on the morning of the eleventh he continued his march to Monterrey. He arrived there at noon and was received with all formalities and honors by the troops and the civilians that were under arms there, and with the greatest cordiality by Governor Llano, Commander-in-chief Ugartechea and the other constituted authorities.

The state of the general's health at that time was so grave that as Llano embraced him he said to him with his genial good nature: "Man, instead of coming to defend us you have rather come for us to take care of you. But that doesn't matter; your name and your prestige will be worth more to us than any number of troops that you might bring with you." They lodged him without loss of time in the home of the honorable and esteemed Licenciado Guimbarda, where they showered upon him all manner of care and attention. Thanks to all this he was able immediately to make the necessary preparations for putting the main streets of the city in an attitude of defense. In these they constructed fortifications and parapets, and also upon the flat roofs of the barracks and some of the principal houses that seemed to be adapted to this.

In all these tasks the commander-in-chief Ugartechea and Filisola's secretary Lieutenant Colonel Don Vicente Luna were untiring. The general became so helpless that they moved him to the home of the Illustrious Señor Bishop Belaunzarán where they gave him the sacrament and the last rites because they did not think that the general would live longer than three days. However, either because of the care that they gave him, or because of a change in his physical condition, the illness passed the crisis, and in a few days there was no doubt as to his recovery.

[34]

All this was happening while Cortina, filled with doubt and confusion over what he should do as soon as he learned of Filisola's return to Monterrey, could not make up his mind to march on that city, nor, as he might have done, by way of Revilla de Laredo (where the company commanded by Captain La Fuente had gone over to his side, as well as those of Río Grande and Monclova), where he could have gathered all the rebels to march on Saltillo, in which city where there was no garrison at all they could find means of subsistence with which to continue their undertaking. However, it seemed to him more prudent to go by the road along the Pilón and linares with Colonel Piedras, who should be in the vicinity of Victoria with his detachment, towards which place, as we have said, he had gone by way of San Fernando de Presas.

With this in mind, Cortina took up his march from *Mier* by way of *Los Aldamas,* and *China* to El *Pilón,* and before arriving at the latter point he received news that Victoria and vicinity were being invaded by the terrible *cholera morbus.* Also that there was no other doctor than the one who was practicing in those parts, and he was a frightful foreign professor.

If Cortina was indecisive concerning what line of conduct he should observe before receiving this terrifying news, afterwards his perplexity and that of the other officers with him reached the greatest extremes. In fact, his situation was very bad, even without the new circumstances which made it worse. Evidently General Filisola understood this and proposed to take advantage of it for the benefit of Cortina himself, those who followed him and the cause of restoration of order.

With this noble intention he sent the Neapolitan Don Luis

Pierro, who presented himself to that leader on July 20 with a long communication in which he exhorted him as well as his companions to return to their loyalty to the government. He informed him for what it might be worth to him that he had received official notices from General Don Francisco Vital Fernández, governor of the State of Tamaulipas, informing him of the capitulation of Colonel José de las Piedras with all his troops. Also that the towns of that area, ravaged by *cholera* did not want war either, and that everywhere they were looking forward from one day to the next to the arrival of General Moctezuma with a strong force. He said that Filisola himself was on his way with his troops to the port of Matamoros to restore order to the garrison there.

He said that in view of all that had been exposed Cortina and his men were compromised and that his ruin would be inevitable because it was impossible for them to continue on to Victoria, either because of the ravages of the pestilence or because the towns of Pilón and Linares through which they had to pass were up in arms and disposed to fight them. Neither could they rejoin those in Matamoros because they would probably arrive much ahead of General Fernández since his men were more than eighty leagues away. Besides this, the towns and settlements along the route, Mier, Serralvo, Camargo, Los Aldamas, Reynosa, etc., etc., had decided in favor of the national institutions, and there was no way that they would provide the rebels with any sort of help, without which it would be impossible for them to travel. To join the companies from Laredo, Río Grande and Monclova, in addition to the existence of the same difficulties, they must count on the fact of that being at a greater distance than Matamoros. Even less could Cortina head for Saltillo because he would have to pass through the outskirts of Monterrey, where his men would be battered, and even before they got there, since for this all that was necessary was for some men to come out in front of them (in the direction of Saltillo), and others behind them (in the direction of Monterrey) as soon as they were on the road from one city to the other. This road is a narrow boxed in pass between two mountain ranges of extremely high rocks that has no exit in any direction except towards one of the two cities mentioned.

Don Luis concluded by saying that in consideration of their past services they were offering to recommend for them to the supreme government that it look with consideration upon them and overlook their actions. But this was on the necessary condition that they submit without delay.

Cortina was convinced of the correctness of the general's defections, and trusting in his good will he spoke to the officers, and these in turn to their troops, and immediately they turned away from their ill considered resolve, marching forthwith to Monterrey to present themselves to General Filisola. The latter received them courteously and kindly, satisfied with the sincerity of the majority of the officers and troops, and that they had proceeded under false conceptions that had been put into their minds by treasonous betrayers, who were really the guilty ones.

Since there were in the city no other troops than the civilians who had taken up arms, and since because of the scarcity of financial resources they could not continue to have them as a burden on public funds, they were ordered to return to their homes. From that day on the few men who remained of the seventh and twelfth permanent infantry battalions were the ones in service, together with the Fifth cavalry regiment that had come with Cortina, a small number of the presidio company of Lampazos and the company of active cavalry of Nuevo León. Here then was the simple and happy manner by which was achieved the restoration to order of Colonel Cortina's troops.

Since what we have made known at the end of the previous chapter was one of the most interesting events upon which rested the realization of General Filisola's plans, we had skipped ahead without remembering the scheme to which we should limit our reminiscences. It is time then to step back. Let us see what was going on during those same days with the troops commanded by Colonel Piedras, and with those left behind in Matamoros under the order of Praga following the day when General Alcorta found it necessary to abandon them because of the *Sergeants'* rebellion.

We have already said that Colonel Piedras had taken the road to San Fernando to make his way by there to Ciudad Victoria. But it must be said that his troops did not fail to commit outrages along the way, and they traveled with great difficulty because of the reluctance with which they met on the part of the people to provide them with what they needed. This feeling reached such an extreme that most of the settlements were abandoned by their owners in order not to provide any resources for those troops. Nevertheless, they passed San Fernando and were on the road toward Güemes. However, on the march they were deserted by Saens, captain of the presidio troops, and the second assistant of the infantry, Don Pedro Miracle with some troops. They presented themselves to the governor of the State of Tamaulipas, General Don Francisco Vital Fernández. The latter had gotten together some of the civilians of Victoria and other points and was in those parts for the purpose of stopping the passage of Piedras's men on to the capital of the state.

In fact, on July 11 the two forces sighted each other at twelve o'clock noon in the *old pass of the Pilón River*. Since the guerrillas of General Fernández's troops under the command of the aide Miracle, without a moment's hesitation opened fire on those of Piedras, these not expecting the encounter, withdrew after a little more than half an hour of fire. With night coming on, Piedras ordered them to make camp at a short distance from the river. He could not do otherwise in view of the fact that that same day his soldiers had been attacked, as were those of Fernández also, by the terrible *cholera morbus* epidemic. It was in a different manner than what had been known, but very violent and fatal.

Thus it was that at dawn on the twelfth a number of dead bodies were stretched out in the camp, and most of those who remained alive were also attacked by the sickness and incapable of moving, with the troops consequently reduced to a small number of men. Terror and confusion reigned among all of them; because of it they could not understand what part they must take in those circumstances. Thus they received as a stroke of fortune the communication that in the early hours of the day was sent to them by General Fernández, and they made immediate reply. They agreed to surrender with some conditions that Colonels Piedras and Morales did not wish to accept, and because of which they tried to run away. However, they were apprehended and had to accept the same fate as the rest of them.

General Fernández, in spite of the terrible condition of the troops, lost no time in sending advices of those events to General Filisola and to the general government, making his way at once in the direction of Matamoros. As he passed through San Fernando he was joined by General Alcorta who had been a fugitive since the day when the garrison in Matamoros rose against him. From that moment he made up his mind to lodge a formal complaint with Colonel Praga who was commanding the third section to which we have made reference.

Praga recognized that he could not resist and called a meeting of the leaders and officers. There he made a presentation of the events in Piedras's section, his recent capitulation, and the need for all of them to return to their loyalty to the government, or at least protect themselves from new consequences in any untoward and unexpected event that might overtake them.

The results of that meeting held on July 18 were very similar to those of the one that took place with Cortina's section. It was unanimously resolved to get in touch with General Filisola and indicate to him that from then on they were under his orders and only awaited some supplies in order to join him. They made the mistake, however, of giving space in that communication to excessive praise of the discipline, patriotism and honor of those who made up that section. Praga did not note that his previous conduct was in direct contradiction to what he was saying about it.

But the truth of the matter was that, not knowing yet what was happening to Colonel Cortina's section, with those demonstrations he was only trying to put off General Fernández in order to gain the favor of the treasury employees, and likewise to delude the rich men so that they would provide him with the supplies that he needed and was asking for to make the march that he was planning to Monterrey to join Cortina. In case they could not gain anything there, they were going to present themselves in that city to General Filisola since he inspired them with more confidence than did General Fernández.

In fact, by these double maneuvers they were able to provide themselves with considerable quantities that they collected in Matamoros from the offices and from private citizens, and they set out for the Rancho de Guadalupe on their way to the town of Reynosa. They were very proud of the advantages that they had just gained. These were principally the satisfaction of not having submitted, as they said, to the militia commanded by General Don Francisco Vital Fernández, and in the second place of fleeing from the cholera that was getting closer to Matamoros.

But since bad faith never remains unpunished, neither was it on this occasion because the shame that they might be discovered as a result of these actions must always have followed the ill advised officers who played a major role in that uprising. One of them named Romero was so indiscreet as to write on the twenty-first in the name of Praga and of the artillery command Captain Don Onofre Díez, to Colonel Cortina urging him to stand fast in his ideas and assuring him that they would soon have the satisfaction of finding themselves together again. But when on the twenty-third at the *Rancho de la Entenada* they received the news of Cortina's submission to obedience to the government, those of Praga's section lost any hope that they might have held and hastened to draw up a declaration by which they placed themselves at the disposition of the government under the following ridiculous conditions:

"Article 1. This section places itself at the disposition of the su-

175

preme government which they beseech that it not be included in the laws issued against the rebels of bad faith since the men have not taken up arms or committed any outrages in the place where they were garrisoned, and consequently the section is on its way to Monterrey to place itself under the orders of the Most Excellent Señor General of the Division Don Vicente Filisola.

"Article 2. It begs the same supreme government to initiate the laws that it deems fitting that will guarantee to the army its existence and other enjoyments to the end that the enemies of the country not touch this fabric of their adolescence."

But let us return to the communication from Romero to Colonel Cortina. The latter leader, as soon as he received it, put it into the hands of Colonel Don Domingo Ugartechea who was the commander *ad interim* because of the grave illness of General Filisola. Immediately precautions were taken such as were dictated by circumstances to take Praga's section by force, and even disarm it if necessary.

Furthermore, the word was passed on to the governors of Tamaulipas and Coahuila so that they might guard their borders, and also to General Moctezuma, who had already passed Victoria, so that he might hasten his march towards Cadereita Jiménez. Also Ugartechea took care to send orders to Captain Don Manuel Sabariego, who after his escape from Matamoros on the night of the Sergeants' uprising had joined seventy militia cavalrymen from the towns of Reynosa and Camargo, that he should proceed and observe Praga's forces in the area opposite the Río Grande. All this had as a necessary consequence that although the message referred to was received in Monterrey two days later, it was not believed, and rather it was taken as a confirmation of the bad faith by which that leader and the section with him operated.

Meanwhile, somewhat recovered from his illness, General Filisola had resumed command. In order to give time for the arrival of Moctezuma and to satisfy himself as to the true disposition of the rebels commanded by Praga, he commanded him to stay in the town of Mier until he received new orders and to remove from the section with various pretexts Captains Padilla, Alvis, Díez, and Romero himself, who were the most influential in the group. However, he realized that all these measures as well as what had been previously announced would not have been sufficient to stop Praga if he had in his case taken the same resolve that Cortina had been able to adopt in his similar circumstances.

That would have been to head for Laredo, Lampazos Point and

176

Monclova, incorporating into his section the presidio companies of these three points and that of the Río Grande, who had rebelled. He would have then marched immediately with all these forces into the interior by way of Parras or Saltillo, since in Monterrey there were only the one hundred twenty men of the same unit and one hundred thirty of the fifth cavalry with fifteen artillerymen of the brigade with horses all belonging to Cortina's section. Besides this there were about fifty men who could join those of the presidio company of Lampazos and the active units of cavalry from Nuevo León, but almost all of these on foot.

On the other hand, Praga was in Mier at a distance of fifty leagues from Monterrey and only thirty from Laredo, which is eighty leagues from the city. Thus in addition to the fact that it was impossible to stop him, it was very impractical and risky to go in search of him with only forces composed of his same rebel companions when Moctezuma was still more than seventy leagues from Monterrey and almost as far from Mier and was marching with all the hindrance of several artillery pieces, equipment and a large number of sick men of the section, which had already been attacked by *cholera*. And, although we cannot believe that Praga did not know all this, he did nothing because he was simple and honorable in his heart, and if he had become involved in the rebellion, he himself could not explain it, and neither could many others much more knowledgable. It could only be attributed to the force of circumstances.

Thus he not only obeyed all the orders of General Filisola that we have mentioned without showing the least resistance, but also all those given to him later by Moctezuma when he could no longer have had the least doubt that they were about to order disarmament and arrest him with all his companions and followers.

All this happened in the first days of the month of August, and on the seventh of that month Moctezuma finally arrived in *Cadereita Jiménez* and with him the cholera. It is truly doubtful whether those people had more horror of the one than of the other. Both had been preceded by a reputation as foreboding as it was well deserved — the first because of the attacks and outrages that he was committing along the way in all the towns that he passed through against all the people of any distinction and affluence, without distinction as to sex, condition or party and the second because of the ravages that it was also causing everywhere that it passed through. What is certain is that after Moctezuma and the pestilence brought relief to those departments by their absence every one said that in the case of the return of one or the other of those plagues they would prefer the second to the first.

177

This man, in addition to his natural boorishness, was ill-advised by three or four of the officers of his staff, and they caused him to commit the most horrible of his attacks. His conduct was rather comparable to that of some of those barbarians who invaded the Roman Empire from the fifth to the eighth centuries, and to that of a general of an American republic.

He answered the protests of honest citizens which unfortunately they had the need to make, and there were a considerable number every day, with the threats of tying them up and carrying them off or of ordering them to be shot on the spot. There were several who instead of indemnity or release received from him buffetings and kicks, without consideration for their circumstances, for indeed there were several cases in which even those attacked by cholera received no better treatment. This was the fate of the leaders and officers of Colonel Piedras's section, who had been turned over in Ciudad Victoria for the disposition of Don Francisco V. Fernández.

General Filisola was unaware of all this, and if he could have had any suspicion of it, he would have made every effort to take care of it opportunely out of respect for his duty and because he was deeply interested in the reuniting and preservation of the remnants of Cortina's and Praga's sections. This in spite of the fact that he knew that they could no longer be of use to him in those departments because all the people and authorities mistrusted them and begged him to return them to the interior of the Republic.

Otherwise, he would not have thought, as he did, of incorporating those military personnel into General Moctezuma's division on his way to Monterrey. He was in such haste to put this into effect that as soon as he learned of Moctezuma's arrival in Cadereita he informed him of that determination and ordered him with that objective to put on the march the ones who were left from the twelfth battalion of the artillery and the Fifth cavalry regiment, leaving only those of the Seventh infantry. But what was his surprise when he learned that as soon as they arrived in Cadereita Moctezuma commanded that all of them be disarmed, that the soldiers be incorporated with the militia and that all the officers, sergeants and corporals be put in prison!

[35]

Any other leader besides Moctezuma would have blushed at such absurdities, but he was as far from recognizing them as he was from doing anything about them because both things were beyond his comprehension and that of his advisers. Thus it was that the following day, August 9, he had no qualms about ordering one of those, and one of the highest rank that accompanied him as an aide, Captain Don Ramón Parres, to set out for Monterrey to investigate the attitude of the political and military authorities concerning the levying of a forced loan of ten thousand pesos, which without any consideration whatsoever for the straightened circumstances of the times he was trying to extract from those suffering people. Also he recommended to his emissary that he observe as best he could the opinions and the political conduct of government employees and persons that could be seen there.

When these actions became known by General Filisola, and taking care as far as possible that Moctezuma should not understand that he was trying to go contrary to him, the former did all in his power to send Moctezuma only five thousand nine hundred pesos that the people had agreed to advance Filisola in the form of a voluntary loan for the aid of Moctezuma's division.

The tyrannical and distrustful procedure of the latter at once caused Filisola to perceive the unpleasantness that Moctezuma was preparing for him for the time when the latter no longer needed his aid, and that the presence of such a person rather served as a new danger of discord and inflamed opinions when he should be thinking only of calming them with prudent and conciliatory conduct that was in accord with the law. But since on the one hand the commanding general did not have the forces at his disposal with which to

179

make Moctezuma respect his decisions should the occasion arise, and on the other hand It seemed to him that any show of disagreement between the two generals and their respective forces would have been fatal and would have had the gravest consequences, he concealed his just indignation as best he could.

This effort was no doubt so strenuous that it brought about a relapse for him, bringing him to his bed again and leaving him unconscious for a period of eighteen hours. As soon as he regained consciousness, in order to avoid all disagreement, he resigned for the duration of his illness, turning the command of those states over to Moctezuma himself.

General Filisola would not have taken this step could he have foreseen that General Moctezuma would be so insensitive to the honor and confidence shown in him, and even less to the decorum and responsibility of the duties that were intrusted to him. But unfortunately Filisola was also mistaken in this because that madman, as soon as he took over the command, was changed into a brutal tyrant and thought of nothing else than acts of the blackest vengeance. As one of the least of the proofs of this procedure we shall include here the two following documents that make clear in an unmistakable manner the fury and the stupid animosity with which the general and his imbecil advisers were filled.

Summary of two letters from Estevan Moctezuma to Colonel José Domingo Ugartechea, Cadereita; first letter, August 14, 1833:

Colonel José Mariano Guerra Manzanares and Lieutenant Colonel Francisco Lojero are to be taken prisoners and brought to that city without delay.

Second letter, August 15, 1833:

Moctezuma is greatly disturbed over the escape of Guerra Manzanares and others and orders an all out search to bring them in as criminals. No expense is to be spared, and any house may be searched. The judge who pardoned them is to be arrested and put in prison to explain his act. The supreme government will name a replacement. The commissary general and the auditor are to be arrested and brought in also. Ugartechea is to put behind bars all those in similar circumstances. He is also responsible for the person of Colonel Ramón Cortina. Second Lieutenant Jesús Cuéllar has brought in under arrest six officers referred to.

The accumulation of arbitrary and outrageous decisions that are contained in these two notes are sufficient proof of the character and limited awareness of their author. But so that you may judge more precisely the deeds to which they refer, in the first place it should be known that Colonel Guerra and Lieutenant Colonel Lojero had been absolved by the general command, and as long as they had not been guilty of any crime, in no way could it be just or legal to bring a new judgment against them or to bother them with punishment of any sort.

In the second place, the threat or proposal to order shot all those who may aid in the hiding of those unfortunate men was no less tyrannical than dangerous in the results for many innocent people and for the prestige and respect for authority itself, in whose name and abuse General Moctezuma wished to proceed. In the third place, the arrest of the district judge was as illegal and as much an assault upon social guarantees as was also prejudicial to the national interests that of the commissary general and the auditor, whose innocence was proclaimed by all who knew them and who had absolutely nothing to do with the revolution.

Finally, since the freedom of Colonel Cortina had been guaranteed by a solemn capitulation, it was unworthy of the good faith and honor of General Moctezuma to break that guarantee as was inhuman the prosecution of that leader at the time when he was attacked by *cholera*, of which illness he died that same day.

Thus it is that the rumors that as we have stated previously preceded and were spread throughout all those towns upon the arrival of General Moctezuma and his subordinates or followers greatly exceeded what they justly deserved every day in various ways wherever they went. The ease, lack of discretion and the popular credulity with which he gave acceptance to all that he was told against the most outstanding and respectable people, without stopping to see whether those who said these things were motivated by personal enmity or partisan spirit, decided him to proceed frivolously and indiscriminately in the most hateful and detestable manner. He himself would beat the accused ones, whatever might be their class and condition, having them bound and taken with armed escort to the place of their imprisonment.

The result of this was that when they found out that General Filisola had temporarily handed over the command to Moctezuma, the individuals that Moctezuma was demanding in the note to the commander-in-chief of Nuevo León, Colonel Don Domingo Ugartechea fled immediately, as did others who are not mentioned in it. Filled with fear and horror caused by the idea of the treatment that he dealt out to all those whom he counted as his adversaries, and who had the misfortune to fall into his hands, even many of the prominent citizens of Monterrey fled.

Thus Lieutenant Colonel Praga and his whole section who arrived in Cadereita on July 18 could not have gotten more attention and were treated in as unworthy a manner as those that General Filisola had mistakenly sent him a few days earlier from Monterrey to be incorporated into the forces under his command.

On the twenty-first Moctezuma finally arrived in Monterrey, and from the moment that he appeared upon the streets of that city he filled it with terror, consternation and hatred for that personage who was followed at his entry by a multitude of unfortunate men that he led bound like the captives of an ancient barbarian conqueror. The disorderly conduct indulged in by his subordinates confirmed this repulsive similarity; their lack of discipline made them undeserving of the honorable title of military men. To this sad picture were added the fearful ravages caused by the cholera, which in those days had put in its appearance and was at its worst.

Then after having afflicted that city with all these horrors and having demanded of its desolate inhabitants various levies and contributions, General Moctezuma was kind enough to relieve them of his presence on the twenty-third. He set out for Saltillo, taking with him all the artillery pieces and munitions of war that were there and that had cost considerable sums of money and a great deal of effort to have them brought to Monterrey. Neither the arguments of Colonel Ugartechea, the governor or even the commander General Filisola were sufficient to sway him from this determination. He denied to Filisola the courteous deference that should have been his, apparently thinking that he had done enough by visiting him on his sickbed, to which he himself had brought the general with his outrages, complaints of which were coming in daily, and which Filisola could not avoid in his deplorable situation.

In addition to this Moctezuma left in prison all the sergeants and the militia that had rebelled and that had later renounced their action. After that the governor found it necessary to muster these soldiers out with a complete discharge for them to leave there to beg along the roads, or perhaps to do other things worse in order to survive. He ordered that the leaders and officers should be taken with him, but bound and closely guarded by the civilians of his *division*, as he called it. Despite this high sounding title there could be noted in it a mile away the most terrible disorder and confusion.

Infantry, cavalry, artillery, prisoners, the sick, munitions, women, baggage and the kitchen brigade — everyone marched mixed together without any order, organization or distinction whatsoever. As a necessary consequence the armament, munitions, pack animals, horses, officers' baggage, the supplies of everything that belonged to the troops, and especially to the rebels, everything went astray, everything was being lost.

As with generals of this character, with procedures of this nature, with troops with such lack of discipline, without supplies, without the means of waging war and maintaining respect in the people and tribes of the frontier, was there any possibility of putting down and punishing the Texas colonists? And the general government, what provisions was it making in those circumstances? Of what use was its power?

[36]

Answers will be found to the questions that we have just posed in the official communication which we are including just following this, as well as the reasonable observations that the reading of them suggests concerning the attention that the administration at that time had directed towards the preservation of our frontiers, the subjugation and establishment of order in Texas and even to the fate in general of the Eastern Interior States. Likewise they will make clear the principles that they set up and the knowledge with which they issued the most important decrees for the attainment and assurance of those great objectives. Such is the reason why the archives preserve these documents and why the historian must always consult them. The communication reads as follows:

"Most Excellent Señor: The Most Excellent Señor Minister of War and Navy with the date of August 10 last has seen fit to inform me as follows:

"By the message from Your Excellency dated July 31 last, and copies accompanying it, His Most Excellent Señor Vice-President has been made aware of all that you said. Informed of everything, he instructs me to tell Your Excellency that he approves all the provisions that you have ordered. Furthermore, he instructs you that those leaders and officers who have given proof that they were involved in the revolution, and recognizing their error have withdrawn their declaration placing themselves in good faith at the disposal of the supreme government, let them be in this command. Those who are not in this situation, Your Excellency will send to Texas relieved of their duties, and there they will be given lands so that they may return to being useful citizens."

Summary of letter from Colonel Domingo de Ugartechea to General Filisola, Monterrey, September 2, 1833:

The Vice-President approves Filisola's provisions and instructs that those who are in good faith now be placed in the command. Those who are not are to be relieved of their duties and will be given lands to return to being good citizens.

Guerra Manzanares, Praga, María Romero, Onofre Díaz, Padilla, Alviz Aspeitia, assistant inspector Morales and Juan Morales are to be relieved of their duties and banished for six years. José de las Piedras has been advised likewise. It is believed that Guerra Manzanares has fled this capital before the arrival of Moctezuma.

In this supreme order the first thing we see is that the general government approves all that had been done by the commander in charge of Nuevo León, Don Domingo Ugartechea, and consequently what has been ordered by the commanding general of those states, under whose orders the former had followed his line of conduct in the various points which the ministry refers to. But in the next line it orders the dismissal from their duties and imposes exile for the leaders and officers whom it designates by name, and they are the same ones whom the general command and Ugartechea, in the name of that same government, had just offered a complete overlooking of the same mistakes because the general government was trying to punish them in the manner indicated in this same communication. Thus it is clear that either the government was not completely aware of the course of events and of the people who made these decisions, or that the decisions prove nothing more than the lack of seriousness or inconsistency, both characteristic of times of revolution, and how little one can trust the promises that are made in such times by persons who are elevated to positions of power.

On the other hand those leaders and officers in our opinion could no longer be subjected to such treatment, even by the government itself. If Filisola and Ugartechea had exceeded their authority, they were the ones who should have been punished, and in no way should they have failed to keep the promises that those officers had made in the name of the government. But let us examine the reasons that they might have for doing so and thus might merit the forebearance of the ministry in those circumstances, even if they had exceeded their authority.

Those commanders were three hundred leagues distant from the government, with the knowledge that it could not send them aid or sufficient resources for continuing the campaign, nor operate in any manner against the dissidents because the entire Republic was in a state of revolution; those towns were invaded by cholera, and they had no other means of adjudication at their command for bringing the rebellious forces back into line than that of pardon and overlooking the mistakes or crimes that they could not punish with the full rigor of the law. This is a devise used in all ages, and much too frequently among us, even in favor of the most guilty of men, and in circumstances less pressing than those in which Filisola and Ugartechea found themselves, for salvaging those departments from the scourge of war, since it was not within their power to free them from the hunger and the pestilence that afflicted and ravaged them at the same time. This was a device in short that corresponded to the former good services of those military men, in the continuation of which the well being and security of the people themselves of the frontier were at stake; these towns would be the theater of the battles that they were avoiding. Above all, there was the honor of the government itself, obligated by the guarantees that had been given to the rebels to cause them to put aside all fear, and consequently the arms that they had taken up in support of their plan.

Although the greater part of the leaders and officers mentioned by the ministry had been carried off by Moctezuma as we have said, there had remained nevertheless some hidden in Monterrey because they did not have the same belief as the others over how their surrender might be taken. Ugartechea, perplexed over what he should do, made the decision to await the restoration of Filisola so that he might decide what was proper. The latter general, who naturally knew the difficulties of the period, limited himself to making statements to the government in terms that those difficulties permitted, and he wrote especially to the minister of war in the most friendly and confidential manner, as will be seen in the copy of this letter which we include further on, as one of the best proofs of the truth of all that we have related concerning those unfortunate events:

Summary of letter to José Joaquín de Herrera from General Filisola, Monterrey, September 19, 1833:

Filisola confirms the acceptance of the retraction of those officers who rebelled, but he is at a loss as to how the sentence of exile against others is to be carried out. After two weeks he has no solution and asks for ideas. There were three groups of dissidents. Colonel Piedras marched on Victoria, Colonel Cortina set out for Monterrey and Captain Romero was the other. Peace was being restored when Romero indicated intentions of new outbreaks.

186

General Filisola became ill and resigned temporary command to General Moctezuma. The latter dissolved the corps and seized leaders and officers. They lost horses, arms and equipment and were obliged to march on foot with the cholera. Soldiers were put in with civilians. Many had to beg and steal. They were treated with great inhumanity, not distinguishing the good from the bad.

This was all based on the letter of one scoundrel Captain Romero. Those who rebelled were terribly wrong. However, without letting the principals go there would have been advantage in separating the most influential leaders, good or bad, and would have saved many good men, horses, arms, etc. Not everything would have been dumped into the pits.

This has been written out of compassion for the families of so many unfortunate families and consideration for past services of the men themselves.

[37]

We failed indeed to make known what happened to General Moctezuma after he left Monterrey. However, since we fear to make the reading of this history as painful to our readers as the writing is for us, we shall limit ourselves to giving only a very simple idea of that expedition which was as useless as it was onerous.

Moctezuma made this march hounded constantly by the fateful *cholera*, as if Providence had wished to associate the memories of this epidemic with the conduct of such an individual. Thus he arrived in Saltillo just at the time when they were beginning to experience the ravages of the pestilence, and there both arrivals are mentinoed with equal horror.

To the epidemic was due the orphaning of countless families, and to the general's arrival the debasement, the depredations and the most insulting outrages. He demanded new contributions, threatened, imprisoned and exiled almost all of the most outstanding people of the city. When he could no longer inflict greater injuries upon those inhabitants, after a very few days there, he set out on the march to Matehuala and Real de Catorce.

In these places Moctezuma's conduct was no less odious and arbitrary than it had been in Matamoros and Saltillo, just as it was in Linares, Villa del Pilón and everywhere else that he went. His memory will endure in those departments as long as there are people and tradition there. It could be said that that man alone caused more disaffection against the federation than all the rest of the enemies that might fight against it, and all the other reasons that they might lean upon for doing so with good success.

And as soon as those towns saw themselves free from the presence and tyranny of Moctezuma, they turned to the general command of the state, pointing out to him the treatment that the former had dealt them, and imploring at the same time the protection and aid of the laws in favor of prisoners and exiles. Consequently, General Filisola, although still in bed and seriously ill, saw the absolute necessity for him to take back the command. That is what he did, and his first acts were to examine and revoke all the arbitrary and unlawful decrees that General Moctezuma had issued. With the latter, after what has been said, we shall not have the unpleasantness of bothering ourselves concerning him in these notes again.

We shall replace him, and with the same objective interest that we have had in his regard, with the conduct of the governor of Tamaulipas, Don Francisco Vital Fernández, a general also. When he learned that Lieutenant Colonel Praga, after evacuating Matamoros, had set out for the towns of the north towards Monterrey, he discharged the few civilians that had remained with him, of the ones whom he had armed so that they might oppose the rebels, and he set out also for Matamoros where he arrived at the end of the month of July.

It is worth mentioning, for what in these circumstances can be gained of honor and profit for the people in the history of their great crises, that of those forces, between war and pestilence, there scarcely remained the fifth or sixth part of the men under arms who composed them. Nevertheless, they still held firm, patiently hoping that the government of the state would send them back to their homes rather than to forsake the cause that it was their place to support and defend with their arms in their hands.

If such noble sentiments were shown by the citizen soldiers who contributed so much to the honor of that general, it would be fair and natural to suppose that he would also protect them, and even to a greater degree of energy and power. However, unfortunately, this was not so, or else Praga was not persuasive enough, and his arrival in Matamoros was more harmful than favorable to the public cause. Immediately there was raised against him the idea that he was the arch enemy of the permanent and active troops. Rather it was thought that his conduct only demonstrated an extraordinary adherence to the cause of the Texans and an insatiable thirst for money.

So that it may in no way be supposed that we are giving our own opinion, we set down the following this a part of a letter in his own writing and other accounts of people who although they merited his confidence and friendship, nevertheless could not condone such conduct and censured it severely. Here are the thoughts of Señor Vital Fernández written in a private letter which he sent to General Filisola dated August 3, from said port of Matamoros:

Summaries of letters to General Filisola; from Vital Fernández, Monterrey, August 3, 1833:

Ugartechea did not wish Vital Fernández's troops to leave Matamoros, but the latter felt that to maintain men there would cause unrest. He does not want Ugartechea's men to return and sees them as vandals. The people of Tamaulipas do not want any force at all to remain in the state.

From Colonel Luciano Muñoz, August 12, 1833:

He is happy to see that Filisola is again well enough to resume command. The printing press of the rebels was bought from federation money, and it was then used by private persons. Luciano Muñoz was invited to help edit the newspaper, but he made excuses for lack of knowledge. There is also considerable rambling discussion of rather inconsequential matters. He feels that the desire for total removal of troops comes from a desire for total independence.

From Colonel José Stáboli, August 18, 1833:

He has visited customs daily, but the cash box is empty since Lujero and Praga have collected all that was owed by business men. There were conflicting orders concerning payment of funds by the governor.

On the way from Santander to San Fernando 206 men died of cholera. Stáboli asks to be relieved of his command because of family difficulties and many things that he needs to take care of. In closing he again asks for orders to be relieved.

The contents of these letters, which corroborate other information that General Filisola was continually receiving from persons of complete veracity and good faith, were bound to make him aware of the patriotism that General Fernández exaggerated so much in his communication previously inserted and the cruelty that he himself and all those of his party showed against the army, the commanding generals and every class of general government employees. He recognized no other motivation than his own personal interests and his very clear intention to set himself and others up as feudal lords in those areas and remain there without the presence and difficulties of the military who would have stood in the way of their appropriating all the income from the maritime and overland customs and would have protected the introduction of clandestine shipments for the interior of the Republic. With these disorders they fomented the insolent rebellion of the Texans and agreed to pave the way for the separation of these states.

[38]

His followers and favorites proceeded in the same manner as Señor Vital Fernández; these he had placed in the most important posts in the state, or that it was in his power to name. Among these we shall make mention only of the interim administrator of accountant for that customs office, Don N. Leal, who was his relative. The truth is that Leal had no knowledge in the field of his improvised employment. He had not been able to acquire this in his profession as violinist in the church of the poverty stricken village of Reinoso in which he played from time to time, earning about fifty centavos for each time that he did so.

On the other hand, he was not very backward when it came to knowing about his gain from the interests of the public treasury which he manipulated with greater dexterity than his instrument. In less than a year that he was administrator of that customs office it was public knowledge and notorious that he had acquired more than eighty thousand pesos, and so he was able to afford handsome carriages, excellent teams of mules and house furnishings comparable to those of a prince. However, this was as much in obvious contrast with the wretched hovel in which he lived as it was the butt of jokes to which his absurdities gave rise. Because of this he wound up working for another man who cheated his family out of all that he had managed to accumulate before he was attacked by the cholera which was ravaging that coast at the time.

The fact was that since Leal had to rationalize the immense fortune that he had built up, he intrusted its management to another person of the same port and with even less conscience than he had. This person had given no guarantee or statement of what he had received, and taking advantage of the sudden death of Leal betrayed the trust and even threw the family into the street. He told the widow that he was reclaiming from her the property belonging to her husband, and that she should not try to discredit his memory unjustly because the deceased had been very honorable in the management of the customs office. Since he had no other means of subsisting beyond his small salary, whence came that furniture, those carriages, mules, money, etc., etc., if he had not loaned it all to him? Consequently, neither she nor the children had anything left except debts to pay. The widow and children then were left out in the street until he provided them with another small hut like the one that they had had before.

Finally General Don Francisco V. Fernández had found out that all the proceeds from the customs were pledged for many months and that *the enemies of the liberty of their country* (Tamaulipas), as he called the commanding generals, the whole army and the employees of the federation, would no longer have anything to live on there, and consequently they would be unable to undertake anything to contain the advances of the *free and enlightened Texans*. He went to see what could be gotten from Soto la Marina, Victoria and Tampico, which were reputed to belong to him as his feudal possessions. We shall leave him on this excursion for the time being in order to turn ourselves again to his other stunts later on and to direct our attention to the immediate results that must inevitably come from such a state of affairs to the irreparable damage to the national service.

Hence the fact that the general command of the Eastern Interior States could no longer count on the proceeds that should be forthcoming from the ports of Matamoros and Tampico, but rather that on the contrary day by day the returns from those customs offices were less and less, and every day they fell even shorter of covering the debts that were being incurred. There remained absolutely no hope that any other places could make available the most necessary items for the subsistence of the few troops that had remained in the country. For that very reason they could not be reduced because of the lack of security which would result for the coasts and frontiers of that vast military area.

In order to make a better case it seems to be very fitting to see what Filisola had to say on these particulars to the Supreme government a short time after the occurrence of the events that we have just related, so that the reflections that we shall express may be in place.

Summaries of three communications from Vicente Filisola to

the Minister of War and Navy, Monterrey; First Communication, September 12, 1833:

The great difficulty for the suffering of the people because of the Indians is the lack of supplies. Until the central government provides funds properly organized there will be no improvement. Executive orders for payment from Tampico and Matamoros customs disrupt the presidio companies and other demands. Receipts for both places should be budgeted exclusively for the commissary and presidio companies with only the excess, if any, used for other things.

Second Communication, September 25, 1833:

The Tampico commissary has furnished only 20,000 pesos for the needs of the vast command of the Eastern Interior States, and these have already been used for the budgets of April and May. Salaries for various troops of Tamaulipas, Nuevo León and Lampazos are nine and ten months in arrears. Without funds the men are almost naked and barefooted, and only a few have arms. They are vulnerable to unreliable promises. Needs reach the sum of 50,000 pesos per month. There are many other obligations, and the honor of the government is at stake. Filisola again asks for 20,000 pesos from Tampico and Matamoros exclusively for payment of troops for three states. Otherwise, it will be necessary to retire troops to their homes. The government of Tamaulipas on its own has been giving orders to the military commands of Tampico and Matamoros, even arming militias maintained by the federation. This is done perhaps without the knowledge of the supreme government. Filisola asks that the Vice-President order that these abuses be stopped. Without unity and cooperation this command cannot answer for results.

In all the commanders there is one commander to assist inspectors, two principal commanders, two permanent cavalry companies in Tamaulipas, a presidio company of Nuevo León and seven in Coahuila and Texas, three active armed cavalry companies in Tamaulipas, two of the same in Nuevo León, one armed, the other not. These are located at immense distances from each other. On the coast there is only the company of La Bahía del Espíritu Santo against Indian raids.

Communications are difficult and much delayed. Proposals for vacancies are made years after they occur. Inspection reviews are held seldom or never. Time is wasted in questions and answers: the service deteriorates, discipline declines, the people despair. Filisola recommends two commands: one Tamaulipas and Nuevo León, the other Coahuila and Texas — the budgets of the first from Tampico, and the other from the customs offices of Matamoros, Matagorda and Brazoria.

Third Communication, October 9, 1833:

The ills lamented by the legislature have since increased as the mob in Matamoros has given rise to expenses to the customs offices, the only points where Tampico and Coahuila and Texas companies could have received help. These have been reduced to a third of the strength promised. No attempt has been made to replace casualties because of almost total lack of supplies. The commander has been forced to give license for the troops to forage for themselves in Río Grande, Agua Verde, Béxar and Alamo de Parras. There are left only 34 men at Béxar and 30 at La Bahía. If nothing is done soon, three other companies will have to be released. If something is not done soon, the three militia companies of Tamaulipas will have to be released, and perhaps three other companies, so that they may find something to eat and to wear.

There is a state of complete decay and insecurity among the peoples and businessmen of Coahuila and Texas because of Indians. This is also true along the Texas coast and ports. It is impossible to stop smuggling. There are sufficient men willing to enlist, but there are no supplies. To do something about present ills is not sufficient, but there should be a new military command in the whole command. Filisola again expounds on the vast expanse of territory and the great distances. He describes the endless forest, rivers and great uninhabited places. Everything must be taken along, often even water.

Tamaulipas and Nuevo León have adequate men available but no supplies. Likewise they have no Indians, and the settlements along the Río Grande form a barrier. Coahuila and Texas are almost without population. Filisola again urges division of the command into two units. Finally he lists again his main points: Division of the general command into two parts, with reassignment of officers of the two companies of Tamaulipas and one of Lampazos to Coahuila and Texas.

[39]

Meanwhile, the Texans were completely at ease without having the slightest obstacle put in the way of their advances, either in the matter of smuggling or in the plans for rebellion and independence that they were constantly occupied with. General Filisola, downcast because of his illness, his work and his sufferings, was constantly petitioning the general government for release from a task that was consuming his strength and his life uselessly. This was because not only did he bear the burden, but he was prevented from carrying it out because of the lack of resources that he had to deal with, and that he could not do anything about even if he had enjoyed the best of health.

On November 22, 1833, Brigadier General Don Pedro Lemus was named to succeed Filisola, and the latter turned the command over to him on January 4, 1834, in the city of Saltillo with an *instructive memorial of the situation of the Internal Eastern States, their borders, customs offices, military points and all the provisions that had been made or could be made for their better defense arrangement and good service to the nation.* And since his details seem to us worthy of major interest, this material will form a new chapter in which to give this portion that will complete the sketch that we have proposed to set forth in this first part of the present MEMOIRS.

The interesting, truthful and opportune exposition from General Filisola which we have just mentioned was not so much directed to his successor as to the supreme government. The profound respect which that chief wished to show suggested no other way to call with greater urgency and advantage than he had previously attempted for the energetic and effective attention demanded by the

195

numerous objectives that he proposed to touch upon in those instructions. This is set forth in the present terms which follow:

Summary of a letter on the situation of the Internal Eastern States from General Filisola to his successor Brigadier General Pedro Lemus, Monterrey, December 30, 1834:

In his transfer of command Filisola reviews the unrest and difficulties which he has set forth so frequently. He again discusses the lack of supplies and funds and the consequent poor morale of those troops still in the army. A number have been disbanded in order to go in search of food. Ammunition and guns have been found useless because of humidity. Buildings and quarters are in ruins, and hospitals are closed. There is no protection against highway robbers. Although gravely ill, Filisola's reason for seeking discharge is his lack of authority and frustration at the lack of support.

He cites the case of a band of 25 robbers when he found it necessary to ask the governor for horses for his men to ride. The Texas colonists follow their own ways and laws and pay no duties.

There are ample men who would enlist if funds were available. In the past company commanders have issued promissory notes which have been sold, often for only five percent of their face value. The holders then collect the full amount from customs receipts of Tampico, Soto la Marina or Matamoros. Filisola has attempted to stop this but with little success. Government and economic regulations of 1772 are long out moded, but Filisola's bad health has hindered his desire for reform.

The administration of justice has suffered a setback; this is due to inadequate judges and legal advisers, poor communications and almost complete lack of organization. There is also a grave problem of immorality and fraud in fiscal affairs. Up to 1830, there was sufficient income and to spare from customs duties, but government employees have become rich, built fine houses and bought beautiful coaches while the treasury has suffered. Various kickbacks on port duties have drained funds and much merchandise goes duty free. If the government happens to name an honest worker, he is soon corrupted, or some scandal is brought against him to get rid of him.

Summary and Observations

What we have sketched out in broad strokes up to this point has been no more than the contours of a rough outline, but one that is exact and proven, of the history of the Texas colonies upon which antecedents the history of the war with the same must begin. Although in no manner could we propose to fill out with less effort the idea that a great man has left as contained in these wonderful phrases:

> The truly useful history would be that one which taught us our duties and our rights, without appearing to attempt to do so,

nevertheless, neither shall we deny having had a plan as we undertake the present one, whatever may have been the difficulties that have been placed in our way up to this first part.*

But such a plan has been none other than to offer to our country in this small book a tribute of our loyalty, of our experience and of our thoughts. And although we are also far from having the presumption to believe that our task could have been at any time avoided, to amend or diminish the failures, the errors or the misfortunes which have ultimately followed the absolute loss of Texas, we have no doubt but that it will serve well so that in the future they may not suffer similar losses, nor an ignominy as painful as the one through which we have passed as we saw ourselves forced to purchase peace with the United States at the cost of such costly sacrifices as those which since the founding of the first colony it has been necessary to make for the defense of our ancient and disputed frontiers.

Attentive to the truth of all of the events that have been outlined in the preceding chapters, we will not be considered as too confident of our opinions if we insist upon affirming, as we do, that the loss of the territory of Texas has been rather a necessary consequence of the lack of foresight, the carelessness or the error of our governments of other times, and which had contributed in large measure the spirit of novelty, the indiscretions and even the lack of loyalty of some of our

---

[* In the introduction of Chapter 29. (Author's note.) — TRANS.]

own brothers, than the other causes to which it is generally attributed, however powerful and evident they might be.

It is as evident that only to the former should there be attributed in these latter times the surprising realization of the profound projects of our neighbors of the North, as it is also that it is likewise apparent that with more careful attention, a more foresighted policy and a more loyal circumspect conduct on the part of Mexico, these would have been sufficient to destroy such projects, or at least to keep them for many years among the mysteries of the cabinet in Washington. That government would have been as far from being able to carry them out as it was from being able to forge other greater projects to which we have given space and which with general surprise it has just consummated in like manner.

Let us then take advantage of the costly experiences that we have just bought. Let us generalize as much as possible among ourselves, and we shall begin to know and to pay attention to our own true concerns. Indeed we are reminded of something as easy to understand as it is apt, which is what Señor General Don José María Tornel wrote back in 1837, concerning *Texas and the United States*; we also cited his book at the beginning. Easy to understand because his testimony is all the more to be respected since he was writing after having visited the Republic of the North, in his character as one of first rank among nations, and one who has served in our own on various occasions in the war ministry. It is also fitting because since we assume that the material which he makes use of was taken from the official documents which he found in the ministry, many of which we have reproduced ourselves, nothing could be more natural than the agreement that has come about between the observations of this worthy general of ours, however severe they may seem with regards to the projects and character of the North Americans, to the governments that have held control in our nation and to the irregularities of our men of all classes and parties in this particular. Consequently, we have adopted even his minor ideas in order to give greater proofs of our own impartiality and good faith with regard to all that we have to say concerning our purpose at this point.

The following then are his [Tornel's] words:

Here beings material attributed by Filisola to General José María Tornel.

As one born in America I cannot regret the triumph of the revolution in 1776, nor condemn the attempt at social perfectability which it has made on our continent. But that same revolution which

198

had happy results for the American people, although not so extensive, perfect and complete as its sycophants proclaim, was the offspring of American beginnings, adopted with fervor and lack of discretion by the young fighters who had marched at the command of their sovereign to seek on the American continent a battlefield upon which the pride of England might be battered down.

While the Anglo–American provinces were elevating themselves to the rank of nations and were enjoying the advantages of English civilization, augmented and consolidated by an independent existence, France was paying with the blood of her sons and with the head of her king for the services that both of these had rendered to the cause of democratic principles. Not only France, but Europe and the entire world are victims still of an upheaval that has produced the most perilous instability in the fate of nations.

It is undeniable that up to a certain point the condition of mankind has improved, but it is also problematical whether this is sufficient recompense for so many and such cruel sacrifices as it has cost. If the good fortune were sure and unfailing, France and the universe might console themselves for so many losses over the tombs of so many victims.* But the struggle between absolutism and liberal ideas is still with us, and the latter have established a complete alternative of domination and power. It is surely evident that England obtained a full and bloody revenge for the aid which her rival extended on this continent to the rebellious colonists.

If gratitude were to be measured by the size of the benefit, Spain would be entitled to have the Americans treat her with constant justice and unbounded kindness. Has this been the conduct observed by the government and the people of the United States toward the Spanish nation? Certainly not. Against her they have tried out the tortuousness of their Punic faith, and on her territory they have exercised their first usurpations. Thus it is that parisitic plants are born and grow at the expense and to the detriment of the leafy tree that offered them its protection.

The treaty of alliance celebrated between France and Spain on

---

[* This problem becomes all the more difficult to resolve at the present time with respect to the Mexicans, and little less so on the part of the natives of Northern America who have left those who destroyed them as masters of the vast lands where rest the bones of their ancestors. These masters are the sectarians of the philosophy and socialism of William Payne, who proclaim themselves as friends *par excellence* of the freedom of man, of thought and of conscience, but nevertheless think that they have the right to destroy and to enslave men of other races besides their own. —*Note by the [1848 Mexican] Editor of these MEMOIRS.* — TRANS.]

August 18, 1796, subordinated completely the destinies of the second power to the will of the directory of the French Republic. This peace and this alliance were a shameful consequence of the precarious situation to which the Peninsula found itself reduced by the rout of its armies in the Northern provinces. From then on it was reduced to a merely passive attitude and obliged in everything and throughout everything to move along the path marked out for it by the policies of France. The latter's government took advantage of the desire that Charles IV had shown for the enhancement of the Duke of Parma, whom because of family whims and concerns he wished to see elevated to the dignity of a king. France offered for His Highness an increase in territory that could consist of Tuscany, the three Roman Legations or any other continental provinces in Italy in exchange for Louisiana, *with the same extension which it had then under Spain and which it had when it was possessed by France.*

Thus it was stipulated in the preliminary and secret treaty of October 1, 1800, which was signed on behalf of France by Alexander Berthier, and of Spain by the minister Don Mariano Luis Urquijo. On her part France compromised herself in no way because nothing of what she was offering belonged to her, and she was gaining furthermore possession of a territory that she had discovered and settled, and whose control she had not relinquished until the year 1764. This territory could serve France in reestablishing her influence in America, and although bounded by territory of Spain and the United States, it assured her an important position on the Gulf of Mexico, which had been closed to her by the English cruisers.

Bonaparte, who was already considering reconciliation with the kings and himself assuming the purple was pleased at the setting up of another monarchy near France, whose republicanism was now no more than an empty and pompous name. Later, embarrassed by negotiations in Europe and contemplating perhaps the fact that it was no longer possible for him to hold on to Louisiana and defend it against attacks and expeditions from England, he sold it to the United States for seven million pesos.

Some who pretend to know the secrets of Napoleon's cabinet declare these negotiations were violently opposed by Talleyrand, but as always the energetic will of the emperor prevailed. Spain had objected since the celebration of the treaty of San Ildefonso that the occasion could arise that France might try to divest herself of Louisiana, and since in spite of the warnings given to her plenipotentiary Urquijo, it was observed that there was included this essential and saving condition; she claimed and obtained the statement by a formal agreement that France promised not to divest herself of the territory without the previous consent of Spain. Since this was not asked in 1803, nor was any attention given to the interests and rights of His Catholic Majesty, the cabinet in Madrid directed a futile protest, to which no answer was given.

The United States, which knew the immense value of an acquisition that had been for so long the object of their efforts, took care by means of skillful negotiations that the treaty of purchase should be conceived in obscure terms with sufficient elasticity in order to be able to take over territory that had never belonged to France. Since the latter power was venturing nothing of her own, and what mattered most urgently to her was the receipt of the stipulated sum in order to take care of the needs of the war in which she was engaged, she ceded gladly without manifesting any scruples concerning the ambiguity with which the territory sold was mentioned.

The United States flattered herself for having won for the modest sum of thirty-five million francs an expanse or territory of more than six hundred thousand leagues, because this is the ideal and imaginary perimeter that she tried to give to Louisiana. The boundaries that were designated were the Perdido River to the East and the Río Bravo del Norte (Río Grande) to the West, promising to give reality to this ambitious dream at the first favorable moment.

The American ministers Pinckney and Monroe presented these claims to the cabinet in Madrid, which indignantly rejected them because neither West Florida nor the interior provinces of Mexico had belonged to the district of Louisiana, nor did France by virtue of the so called treaty of *retrocession* receive those far flung territories. Alarmed by such reckless interpretations that might in time be backed by force, the cabinet in Madrid asked the government of the emperor of the French to declare in clear and peremptory terms that would remove all doubt and destroy the selfish wrangling of the United States, whether the boundaries which they were trying to ascribe to Louisiana were those agreed upon by the treaty of *divestiture* and the same as those of the *retrocession* proclaimed in 1800.

Prince Talleyrand on the twelfth day of Fructidor in the twelfth year answered the Spanish ambassador in Paris in the following terms: *The eastern boundaries of Louisiana are marked by the current of the Mississippi, by the Iberville River, Lake Ponchatrain, and Lake Maurépas. At this line of demarkation ends the territory ceded by Spain to France by virtue of the treaty of the thirtieth of Ventoso, year nine. France would not have asked anything of Spain beyond these limits, and since she has done nothing more than substitute to the United States her acquired rights, they cannot demand of Spain*

a concession of territory of greater extent unless this concession is negotiated be-
tween Spain and that country by some later agreement. The minister himself
wrote to that ambassador that he had declared to the United States
that *Louisiana had been delivered to them in the same manner and with the*
same extent that France had acquired it, and that this declaration would be re-
newed and in the most positive manner as often as His Catholic Majesty might
desire.

It is clear to any one that since the contracting parties in the
treaty of San Ildefonso had been France and Spain, only these two
powers were the ones who could explain the treaty, the only ones
who knew the extent of the territory that had been the object of their
agreement. It did not matter that France had possessed in a more
distant time — even permitting the use of the name of Louisiana —
a territory that was not given over to Spain in 1764, and that could
not be restored by the latter in 1800, because one does not restore
what one has not occupied or received.

All right. France declared officially that by the treaty of San Ildefonso she did not presume to have acquired any other rights than
those which she herself transmitted to Spain by the voluntary gift
that was made to her of the island and city of New Orleans and other
lands that belonged to her to the west of the Mississippi. Since the
final treaty of peace of Paris in 1763, the limits of Louisiana had
been fixed by a line drawn down the middle of the Mississippi River
from its mouth to Iberville, and from Lakes Maurépas and Ponchatrain to the sea. Then the port of Mobile was ceded to the king of
England with all that the most Christian king possessed on the left
bank of the Mississippi, with the exception of what was later given to
the king of Spain.

In order for the latter to recover Havana and that part of the island of Cuba occupied by the English, he gave them as compensa-
tion all that he possessed to the East or to the Southeast of the Mississippi, thus joining the French and Spanish territory under the
name of West Florida. In the war of 1779, the English were thrown
out of this interesting country by the arms of the king of Spain, who
continued in possession and tranquil control peacefully after the cession of Louisiana without the French ever having the idea of laying
claim to it as though included in the treaty of San Ildefonso.

During the three years that followed, and after the provision
contained in the treaty had been put into effect, Spain had possession likewise of the province of Texas, exercised there undisputed
acts of control, and without the slightest appearance of displeasure
of disagreement on the part of the French government. It was left to

202

the cabinet in Washington to give to the treaty of 1800 an interpretation as unusual as it was arbitrary.

As long as Spain retained some power and was supported in her alliance with the emperor of the French, her rights were respected with the Americans being content to announce from time to time to the cabinet in Madrid with a tiresome insolence that they understood the letter and the spirit of the treaty of San Ildefonso better than the two signatory powers. It all reduced to the exchange of a few diplomatic notes without the government of Spain showing any awareness of this voice of alarm that was alerting an evident danger, to which she might have been given attention while her sad destiny was not upon her. She did nothing, and she lost everything.

The events in Madrid and in Bayonne in 1808, the consequent uprising in Spain against the hosts of the Emperor Napoleon, the disorder that of necessity entered into the negotiations in the Peninsula, the weakness of the revolutionary governments that could scarcely maintain a precarious existence — this combination of circumstances — came to favor the plans of the United States. They gave themselves over to poorly disguised transports of joy, operating now without the hypocritical mask that once covered their attempts. The thinking men of the United States had grasped the idea that their freedom was the prelude to that of the whole New World and that sooner or later the important revelation that resistance to a distant and tyrannical power could be crowned with complete triumph would not be lost upon the Spanish colonies.

They were not blind to the fact that the length of their existence, their advances in the race of civilization and the experience of their own strength assured them a predominance of power and influence in the settling of the fate of the new nations; to cooperate in this great result was to contribute by the most unfailing means to the consolidation of their existence. In spite of the advantageous position of the United States, her growing maritime power, the warlike nature of her inhabitants, the strength that she had shown in her own contest, the abundant resources of her soil and the hopes of her industry, she could not aspire to a superior rank in the catalogue of nations as long as the basis for comparison was sought among the old and dominant powers of Europe.

The scene was changing with the appearance of other independent peoples in the American world. It was then an essential concern of the United States to support with her example, her advice and effective aid the insurrection in Spanish America. That provided for the United States the realization of her covetous objectives, because of the sympathy that was created and for the weakness that it supposed in the fleeting governments of the modern associations. Selfishness is a vice that is inseparable from the spirit of the Anglo–American. If he proclaims, if he supports the august rights of liberty and independence of nations, he is not led by the noble stimulus of a just and holy cause; his self-interest is what he is seeking, his own advancement what he is looking for tirelessly.

The time which has transpired since our fortunate emancipation, that time so fertile in disillusionment, has torn away the blindfold that lack of experience had placed over our eyes. Who is unaware today of the cause, the only factor in that decision so soon manifested in the United States in favor of the independence of the Spanish colonies? The general nature of the assertion does not exclude the existence of a few philosophers, in whose number I am pleased to include the names of the honorable John Quincy Adams; that Demosthenes of the West, Mr. Clay; the Cicero of New England, Webster; the unfortunate legislator from Louisiana, Livingston; and a few other sincere friends of the emancipation of the human race, who have cooperated with that of America through pure, philanthropic and disinterested motives.

But it cannot be denied that the vast majority of the American people took part in our melancholy catastrophes for the purpose of weakening the forces of Spain and of influencing with the energy of a people filled with life and energy the destiny of poorly educated peoples who were to be destroyed by the excesses of a continual civil war. Nothing could stop the triumph of the Anglo–American system; the limits of the power of Spain were marked by the Pillars of Hercules; the canopied throne of the new nations, raised upon the shoulders of a decrepit monarchy was one that was vacillating and easily overthrown.

The Americans chose the days of major conflict of her ally and benefactor to uphold the spirit of rebellion in the colonies, taking advantage of the demands of a necessity of which they were aware, and whose profitable results they calculated. In the city of Baltimore companies were organized that directly aided the dissidents, in New York expeditions were made ready; in New Orleans they poured forth money, munitions and arms to do Spain every harm possible, to harass and destroy her commerce. Thus was advanced the plan for undermining more and more the power of a friendly nation, to snatch from her immediately her richest territories.

They began by abetting in Baton Rouge a rebellion against the Spanish authorities; after this was successful, they influenced it in the direction of forming a party that sought to be added to the republic. The authors of the unrest seemed to fear for the consequences. Under the pretext of hindering the revolutionary contagion, they marched in some troops for the occupation of the territory, which they later were so brazen as to add to the United States by a solemn act of congress. The same intrigues were used to take possession of the island of Amalia, Mobile and West Florida as far as the Perdido River. However, since the result was not reciprocated, the government of the United States took off her easy mask, and took possession by pure force of what they were not able to gain by their cunning — this after a prior scandalous authorization by the congress. With the boundaries extended as far as the Perdido River, rounding out their territory to the south, it came into possession of the longed for supremacy of the Gulf of Mexico.

To protests which were warranted by such monstrous and Machiavellian conduct the Americans replied that the occupied land would be held in trust while friendly negotiations were taking place. However, without waiting for that, it was incorporated forthwith into the dominions of the republic by another act of congress.

Entering into the long range plans was the helplessness of Spain in the reconquering of what she had lost. In order to gain time and to reach the goal of their desires, they employed their old and never abandoned tactic of bringing up injustices, protecting insults and demanding indemnification for them. No one is unaware of the fact that overwhelmed by a mountain of misfortunes which weighed down upon her, Spain at last ceded the two Floridas to the United States, although at the latest possible moment. She contented herself then that the United States should not demand payment for damages done to American shipping, not by the Spanish but by French corsairs in the Peninsula ports, which were a consequence of the famous decrees of Berlin and Milan.

It is quite to the point to call attention to the fact that the cabinet in Washington, in order to take over the territory of the two Floridas, no longer sought support in the rights which were formerly founded in the negotiations for the purchase of Louisiana, but by urging Spain with the insistence of her demands for indemnification, the United States obtained by this means what had been handed over to her by the other. The matter is ended as far as the Floridas are concerned; let us observe how they have tried and will try to assure the same outcome for the question of Texas.

Nothing can be better established than the exclusive possession always by the Spaniards of the province of Texas, recognized and respected by the French as long as they were in control of Louisiana. Thus it is pointed out in the paragraph that we have copied from Señor Don Luis de Onys, envoy extraordinary and minister plenipotentiary of His Catholic Majesty to the government of the United States, in the Memoir which he wrote to clarify the rights of his nation, *which were being attacked with such shamelessness*. But the boundary treaty of February 22, 1819, yielded to the United States the *contested territory*, although they proposed to dispute another, based on inexact maps, and even on some that they were so shameless as to forge and gravely deposit in their archives.

It still has not been ascertained what reason they could have had for reopening negotiations concerning boundaries with the Mexican nation, when the latter upon gaining her independence had inherited without question the obligations as well as the rights of Spain with regards to the other powers. Perhaps an attempt was made to revoke these negotiations in order to secure a better deal from opening the matter again; this was to be supposed considering our lack of experience, and the embarrassments of our internal situation. However, sufficient patriotism was found among the directors of our affairs, and the necessary foresight to establish as the basis of all negotiations, even those relating to commerce and navigation, the boundary treaty of 1819. Thanks to this conduct of perpetual honor for the Mexicans on the part of all that observed it, we were safe from the net that had been spread with the flattering hope of finding a lesser dignity and firmness in the agents of our Republic than in those of the Spanish government.

Let us agree that it is very sad, that it is very burdensome, to live next door to a people who intervene in all the transactions of America, who proclaim their political school as a system that is complete and unique, that demand in short as their own everything that can make their republic great and strong, without paying any attention to ancient and accepted rights, nor to the peaceful occupation of some centuries.

Mr. de Tocqueville, who has studied and knows so well the characteristic features of the people of the United States, explains it this way:

"It cannot be denied that the English race has acquired a frightening preponderance over all the other European races transferred to the New World. So long as she remains surrounded solely by wilderness or sparsely populated countries, so long as she does not come face to face with dense populations that stand in her way, no doubt she will continue to expand. *Boundaries estblished by treaties will not hold her back,* but wherever she wishes, she will leap over these imaginary barriers."

This is not a prophecy; the French philosopher writes because of what the facts tell him, through observation of a line of conduct that is never changed or concealed. The boundary treaty of 1819 has contained the plans of that same race that now is not stopped by the wilderness? The renunciation that the United States made forever of her rights, demands and claims whatsoever to the territories located to the West and to the South of the line described has had any other value than that of an empty promise that was never intended to be carried out? These negotiations, far from checking the drive, excited it even more, and the government of the United States did not consider that she was nurturing embarrassment when she contracted an obligation. The passion of the Anglo–American [North American] people, that very pronounced passion for the acquisition of new territories, is an energetic power that she proposed to serve and aid with her industry.

A line ill defined, the source of a river as yet unknown, future scientific explorations to establish *the markers that will indicate precisely the boundaries of both nations,* all this left the field open to the combined forces of the people and the government for taking possession of what did not belong to them. Do not think that the march of aggression is to be open and above board; what the United States may lack in cunning our inexplicable naiveté will supply. The plan of operations will be conceived in Washington; that plan will be aided and abetted directly in Mexico City. The colonization of Texas, abandoned to the adventurers from the United States, will be the surest means of losing that territory, *without discredit, without harm to existing treaties.* Who does not feel the tortuous spirit of the policy that suggested this unfailing recourse to make a mockery of the most solemn and sacred obligations that are contracted among nations? Let us see, we shall admit its effect.

Since among the conditions of the treaty of cession of Louisiana to France there had been included that of permitting the inhabitants to move to any point in the dominions of His Catholic Majesty that they considered convenient, the Anglo–Americans [North Americans] skillfully took advantage of it to make their way to Texas, pretending in the name of some Louisiana families the appearance of a ridiculous loyalty to the Spanish government. This occurred at the end of the year 1820, and the beginning of 1821. The Americans had already obtained permission to bring in three hundred families; they were to be Catholics, with the obligation of swearing obedience and loyalty to the Spanish sovereign.

The concession was made as a gracious gift, and without a single one of those precautions the necessity of which was indicated by the circumstances of the new settlers. *Moses Austin* placed himself at the head of the undertaking, perhaps considering his name somewhat fateful in the invasion which he had in mind, passing through the wilderness until his arrival in the promised land. One is amazed at such skillfulness on the part of the leader of *the new people of God,* and at such ignorance and lack of foresight on the part of the Spanish authorities. The latter should have considered that the United States undertakes and carries out her conquests along silent paths, without risking peaceful relations with the nation that is going to be despoiled of her territory. That instead of open hostile preparations, they make use of hidden means and expedients, slow and ineffective on the surface, but which give an unfailing result. Thus they despoiled two very powerful European nations of their domains which they possessed nearby. How did it happen that this lesson so near at hand and so recent was not profitable? It was a great mistake to open the door to the Americans, and this mistake continued until the consequences were made evident.

But long ago the colonists, in order to justify their rebellion, alleged that they were incorporated into Mexican society under the condition that they were to continue to be governed by the system of federated republics, and that since this had been only an illusion, a deceit, the pact was broken with them, and they could be a liberty to be governed as they saw fit. Can there be anything more brazen? When Austin asked the Spanish authorities in the most humble terms that he be permitted to settle some families in the vicinity of Nacogdoches, promising to defend with arms the Spanish government, this was a monarchy, and no stipulation was agreed to; nor could it be, because it was completely absurd, considering the form of government of the nation, which so unwisely but generously was taking in its neighbors.

Moses Austin died in June of 1821. His son Stephen, whom all of us have known in Mexico City, placed himself at the head of the colonization effort, addressing the authorities of the interior provinces demanding new favors and a greater expanse of territory. Those authorities turned to the supreme one in Mexico City, indicating that the number of families brought in was now past the number of five hundred, and that adventurers were presenting themselves daily without any of the qualifications mentioned in the grant. Since in this year independence had been proclaimed, and the struggle to win it had continued to the end of the year, it was natural that with the nation occupied in negotiations of major importance the impresarios should have had every opportunity that they might wish to gain ground as always, *without being noticed or felt.*

Almost two years passed without a definite decision being reached on this serious matter, and it is clear that those most concerned in the abandonment lost no time. In February 1823, the imperial government confirmed the grants with the precaution of adjusting it to the imperfect colonization law of January of the same year. With new difficulties that produced also new changes another year passed, and it was August 1824. Another colonization law was set forth, which although incomplete contained at least some restrictions, which because of a stroke of fate, of which the nation may complain of many, was never observed. How much we ourselves have contributed to our own ruin and despoiling!

Policy as well as propriety made it advisable that the issuing of laws on colonization as well as the care for their most exacting fulfillment, should belong to the general government and not to one state of Coahuila and Texas. The former was more in touch with the designs of our apparent friend, and could dictate with better knowledge of the matter more precautionary means that might lessen if not eliminate completely a very imminent evil. It was easy to lead astray and surprise men who were newly entered on the career of government, who lacked personal experience, who had no reason to be aware of such subtle maneuverings, in short of being won over by the prospect of quick and unexpected fortune.

Not even this means of security occurred to our legislators because we were sleeping in absolute confidence. To the authorities of Coahuila and Texas was delegated the power to make colonization contracts, and these contracts were agreed upon with a truly frightening prodigality. Texas was handed over to the North Americans, sometimes granting them lands in their name, and other times giving them to Mexicans without the will or the resources to colonize, whose purpose, with few and honorable exceptions, was to sell what they acquired at a cheaper price to citizens of the United States. The soul of Pope Alexander VI seemed to have transmigrated into the persons who were functioning as authorities in Coahuila and Texas, and they scattered about with the free hand of that pontiff the rich, valuable and coveted lands.

It is noted by the tenor of these unwise grants that by virtue of them one tenth of the population of the United States could have been brought into Texas if the impresarios had had at their disposal adequate means for transporting

them. Because of this difficulty the speculators left the door open to all adventur-
ers who could come in on their own And they have even simulated the scum of
the United States, those who because of debts or crimes found it necessary to flee
the punishment imposed by the laws, to provide themselves with a safe refuge in
an undisciplined country that nominally belonged to a regular and organized so-
ciety, and in which selfishness supported a complete concealment of the actions
and morality of all those who were making their way to this new Botanical
Garden.

The contracts gave rise to the scandalous abuse of selling them in the market of the United States, and sometimes in those of Europe, because since the speculators were, generally speaking, deprived of sufficient means for carrying out the establishment of their colonies, there was nothing left for them but the very lucrative thing of disposing of the rights which had been so graciously given to them. Every time the property changed hands, the easy conditions imposed were more and more forgotten. The final speculators, who had no relation with the Mexican authorities, cared little or nothing for our civil laws and the obligations that they contracted in a society that had voluntarily incorporated them into itself. No rules were obeyed other than those given by the colonists themselves, who only turned to the authorities of the state to ask for more lands without ever tiring. The sovereign authority was that of the councils, composed exclusively of the most influential individuals among the colonists themselves; the councils raised taxes, parceled out lands, exercised a police power that was absolute and subordinate to no one.

The extremely moderate costs laid down by the laws were scarcely sufficient. The State of Coahuila from April 1832 to August 1834, received no more than the miserable amount of six hundred seventy pesos one real and six grains, and it should be noted that this is precisely the period when half of the territory of Texas was disposed of. The income from the lands of the United States is one of the richest resources of her treasury, and the one that has been most useful to her for amortizing her debt. We could have used this example to support our poor economy and have *sold* what we did not wish to conserve.

However, our blindness has been such that we have *given away* the lands of a paradise, we have granted them without stipend or any sort of advantage to our enemies. We believe what I am relating because we are seeing it with our own eyes, and because right now we are receiving the punishment that our lack of foresight has deserved.

As the colonists organized their departments they pretended to conform to the constitution of the Republic and of the State, because following the analogy with the institutions of their country, they started from a known point which allowed them to create legislation entirely in keeping with and adequate to their habits and customs. Trial by jury was established for all civil and criminal cases by the law of the State of Coahuila and Texas of April 17, 1834, completing thereby what was lacking so that nothing in Texas could be distinguished from the legislation of any one of the United States. I have cited this law because when Texas proclaimed their independence from the Mexican Republic, they dared to assert that we had exercised over them the unheard of tyranny of not permitting them the introduction of juries in their trials, which they considered as the safeguard of the basic rights.

The people of Texas are in the great majority natives of the United States, particularly of the distant states of the West. The land speculators belong to them in considerable part. Among the latter there are some who exercise great influence in the United States policy because of their offices and their representation, all of which was bound to contribute to the formation in Texas of a people more Anglo–American than Mexican. Neither inclinations, nor manners nor language nor policy removed them from their origins or inspired sympathy in them for the country which they had adopted. The settlers conspired to set up an entirely new association modeled on their customs, their habits and their beliefs.

What were bound to be the results? That the colony would organize and consolidate itself to turn its forces against the mother country in whose midst it had been formed. Who cannot see in this simultaneous and combined march the progress of the ancient attempt at the invasion of our territory? It is no longer necessary to invoke the treaty of the Louisiana Purchase. They are not doing that when Aaron Burr disguises with his personal ambition that of his government, nor when he submits to the farce of a trial in which he had every assurance that he would be found not guilty.

It is of no use to take advantage of the enthusiasm of Don Bernardo Gutiérrez and of Alvarez Toledo to introduce into Texas seven hundred Anglo–Americans [*sic* — North Americans] under the pretense of aiding in our independence. The country is definitely possessed by the Anglo–Americans [*sic*] — the physical and moral strength is theirs. What matters the empty name of domain for the Mexican nation? Thus, in the shadow of our carelessness, taking support in their confidence in our frequent revolutions, they were fortifying their resistance that one day was to oppose openly the nation's independence.

211

In the first colonization laws Texas was granted exemption from all duties, and this was extended for two years more. That is, along an extension of one hundred fifty leagues of coastline and the extended land frontier was brought in not only what was more than enough for the development of the colony but much more that found its way by contraband into the other departments of the Republic. The colonists enjoyed with this a privilege that was making them accustomed to not conforming with any kind of tribute for helping in the burdens of the nation, destroying our income by the facilities that were left to them for maintaining an illicit commerce.

As long as things went on like that there was no need for a proclamation of their independence by the Americans settled in Texas because they were in truth already enjoying it, and it was even to their advantage to say that they belonged to the Mexican nation in order to enjoy the favors that the laws grant to her sons. But it was quite certain that scarcely would the Mexicans turn from their lethargy and try to consolidate their control by the means that all nations avail themselves of in similar circumstances, when they would meet a determined opposition appealing even to recourse to arms, with which the colonists had carefully provided themselves.

The first years of our independence passed without crossing the dissimulated spirit of conquest which led the Anglo–Americans [*sic*] to the fertile and abandoned fields of Texas. It may even be said that this movement of the population of the North was whole heartedly seconded by us; the laws which authorized the colonization could not have been more lax, the carelessness could not have been greater. Unfortunately the idea was getting about that the powerful neighbor was our friend, and that since there should be created a system exclusively American, in contradiction to the European system, the United States was called by the length of time since her origin and the energy of her power, to place herself at the forefront of an alliance of republics.

The scouts, the undercover spies and later the accredited agents were advancing rapidly in the attainment of these goals. A very crafty minister was sent to Mexico, one quite versed in the customs of those places which had been Spanish colonies, skillful in political intrigue, aware of our weaknesses, and who knew how to take advantage of them. This able diplomat did as much good for his country as he did ill for ours. Today he cannot speak of things here and of our men without directing towards us a glance of scorn. The penalty has been long in coming because it has come when the work of iniquity has already been consummated.

212

With the population of the United States growing at an astonishing rate because of the extraordinary emigration from Europe, they began to feel as an embarrassment the continuance in their territory of the Indian tribes who inhabited it, and whose existence there was consecrated by treaties and solemn agreements. In no part of the globe are so noticeable as in the United States the prejudices of the white race against people of other colors, and this was sufficient to exclude the bronzed or *red men* from their lands and despoil them of it. It was convenient, because in the soil inhabited by some of these tribes there had been discovered masses of the fateful and coveted metal. These tribes had cleared the forests, and the lands were now productive.

What could stop the greedy Anglo–Americans? [*sic* — North Americans] Nothing; power was on their side and weakness on that of the natives. Treaties maintain their validity as long as it matters to the stronger. In those United States they declaim against the governments of Europe because they favor the powerful and oppress the weak; they themselves have not the least consideration for the weak when it fits in with the advance of their own interests. In 1830, the expulsion of the tribes from Georgia and Alabama was definitely agreed upon.

"The circumstances that make more regrettable," says Mrs. Trollope, "the expulsion of these unfortunate people from their native land is the fact that they were giving in rapidly to the force of the example. Their life was no longer that of wandering hunters; they had become farmers, and the tyrannical arm of brutal power has not cast them out now as before from the lands where they hunted, from their favorite streams, and from the tombs of their forefathers, but is despoiling them of their homes which their progressive knowledge has taught them to improve in appearance, from the fields recently opened by their lands and which are now their pride, from the crops watered by the sweat of their brows. And for what? To add a few miles of unpopulated territory to the wilderness which surrounds them."

As I relate this recent catastrophe of the primitive inhabitants of our continent it is not my intention to bring down upon the United States the curse of having exterminated innocent people and taking their remnants into an unknown wilderness. The universe has already pronounced its judgment upon this classic injustice, and it is excusable that I should arouse the sensitivity of those who lament the misfortunes of the human race. What is my purpose, is to lay out clearly the fact that as they were despoiling the natives of their ter-

213

ritory they were contemplating despoiling the Republic of Mexico of hers. All of these tribes have been ordered to locate along our borders because it is considered to be without defenses, and it will be easy for them to invade them and by this means they will be free of the colored population which they consider as a burden.

Greater still is the scandal that the United States presents to the world with the preservation of slavery, with its strong efforts to maintain and promote the institution when other nations have come to an agreement in the philanthropic purpose of bringing about an end to this scourge and ignominy of the species.

Don Lorenzo de Zavala in his VIAJE A LOS ESTADOS UNIDOS (*Journey to the United States*), a work which he wrote apparently to praise that country to the skies and to plunge his own into the abyss, when he was already considering an infamous act of treason against it, could not resist the feeling that is naturally inspired by the contrast between the human and truly liberal policy of Mexico and the atrocious and bloody one of the United States relative to the slaves.

"As one passes," he says, "from the Mexican Republic to the states that permit slavery in our sister and neighbor, the philosopher cannot fail to feel the contrast that is to be noted between the two countries, nor fail to experience a pleasant recollection of those who have abolished this degrading traffic and caused to disappear from among us the last vestiges of so humiliating a condition of the human race." *

In fact, without having trumpeted so pompously as the United States the rights of man, we have respected them better by abolishing the distinctions of origin and considering as brothers all the sons of our common father. The land speculators in Texas have tried to convert it into a market for human flesh, for selling their slaves from the South and for bringing others from Africa, now that it is no longer possible for them to do so directly in the United States. In the opinion of the celebrated Mrs. Trollope, there is a general and deep feeling in all America that the Negro race deserves no confidence. Since fear, according to all the ideas of the country, is the only thing that can have any influence upon a slave, it is no wonder that the conduct of the latter often justifies such accusation. This lack of trust, this reciprocal fear between the slave and his stubborn tyrant, must some day put an end to the condition of more than three mil-

[* Lorenzo de Zavala, *Journey to the United States of North America* (translated by Wallace Woolsey), Shoal Creek Publishers, Inc., Austin, Texas, 1980, p. 26. – Translator's note. — TRANS.]

lion men, and this is not concealed from the thinking men of the neighboring Republic.

In anticipation of this event the recent and magnanimous example of England, who has emancipated her slaves and taken upon herself the responsibility for the value to the owners, must have great influence. What is to be done with the slaves in the United States? Maintain and preserve as long as is feasible the institution of slavery; when the fatal hour of destiny sounds that is to destroy a systematic and hateful tyranny, set them to following the footsteps of the Indians — *cast them also into Mexican territory*. It was my good fortune to see this thought confirmed in a speech of Mr. North, president of a school in New York:

"It is impossible," he says, "to maintain any longer the abuse of our slavery in some of our states. It is not necessary," he says, "to have a domestic rebellion, nor foreign intervention in order to bring down an institution so repugnant to our sensibilities and so opposed to our institutions. Public opinion has declared itself against this, and the moral energy of the nation will sooner or later bring about its abolition. But the question which presents itself then is, what will be the condition of this class that is restored to liberty?

"In other nations the races have blended with each other, mixing and forming a general mass. Here we are not in the same situation. Our freed slaves would remain to the third, fourth, and the thousandth generation, the same as they are today; that is, a distinct class degraded and unfortunate. Consequently, when their chains have been broken, and this will evidently happen either all at once or by degrees, it is clear that this country will find itself covered with a population as useless as it is wretched, a population that with its increase will diminish our strength, and its numbers will only bring crime and poverty. Slave or free, it will always be for us a calamity. Why then must we hesitate for a moment in urging their departure from the country? "

Mr. North's arguments are so urgent that they are not satisfied by the establishment of a colony of freed Negroes on the coast of Africa, which has served only to entertain the philosophical spirit of some friends of humanity. The eyes of those who concern themselves henceforth with the fate of the colored population will turn their eyes on Texas and perhaps on New Mexico and the Californias. Since in the United States nothing is done by chance, and all work with common consent and through a marvelous instinct in the pursuit of an end that suits them, it is impossible that there has not entered into their calculations the slow preparation of the ways by which in time

215

they are to get out of certain difficulties, the extent of which they have been able to measure. Thus we see accumulating an indefinite number of interests of the United States to stimulate them to all sorts of aggression.

End of General Tornel's Comments.

The opinions that precede, although written with much authority, are seen to be confirmed in what we have related in these MEMOIRS. Many of these truths are also to be found pointed out in the pomp of our glorious struggle for national independence, and some of these are even alleged by North Americans themselves who are in favor of them. We shall for our part conclude with the very simple observations that remain for us to set forth to fulfill our obligation.

One of these is that we do not share in the view of some who think that the maxims and political religious doctrines that after the revolution of the United States, which took place in 1776, with their absolute independence from Great Britain, were carried to France by the youth who had fought with Lafayette helping them. Nor do we believe that they were the immediate cause of the revolution that cost the unfortunate Louis XVI his throne and his head and had been the same which after crossing the Pyrenees and the Atlantic came to germinate among the Mexicans and to stimulate their desires and their plans for independence from Spain.

Every one knows that the throne which was taken from the line of the Capets was very soon raised again and to the astonishment of Europe was occupied by the fortunate Napoleon Bonaparte, son of that same revolution. That with the invasion of the forces of this emporor of the Peninsula and of having tried to substitute his brother Joseph on the throne of the Bourbons, the idea was to give to this dynasty an asylum as Brazil did to the House of Braganza which was reigning in Portugal. That these purposes and religious intolerance, alarmed at the Jacobin doctrines, etc., were the cause and the origin of the first movement of the Spanish living in Mexico, and which began with the imprisonment of the Viceroy Iturrigaray in 1808. Otherwise, we would not have found ourselves perhaps still divided into parties and factions by the monarchy, the republic, etc., and our system of government would have been consolidated in spite of our charming and devoted neighbors of North America.

Also it seems to us fitting to observe that although, as Señor Tornel states, at the court in Madrid they were either so careless or so remiss in not preventing in an opportune manner the loss of the Floridas, the same thing cannot be said of this event with respect to

216

those who were preparing for the loss of Texas. This immense responsibility will always be borne less by the cabinet in Madrid than by the viceroyalty of New Spain. It has already been told in these MEMOIRS how the break with Great Britain in 1804 prevented the government in Madrid from carrying out the political as well as opportune colonization of Texas with Spanish families, the realization of which was so close to achievement in those days. At the same time it is well known that the troubles in the court in Madrid in the year 1807, and the war of the French invasion in 1808, from which Spain had not emerged when the revolution headed by Señor Hidalgo of this nation broke out, continued to prevent the return to the matter of carrying forward that enterprise.

On the other hand, there is not the least doubt but that the expeditions of Colonel Burr and other North American adventurers into the frontier lands of this Republic undertaken in subsequent years should have alerted the attention of the viceroyalty of Mexico so that it would have been less easy, less prodigal and more cautious in the granting of the lands which were given to Moses Austin, and with whose example the door was opened for those later obtained by other impresarios in the colonization of Texas.

Thus it is also that from the first days of their political existence the Mexicans should have understood that the protection given them by the United States to prosecute the war had, as Señor Tornel observes very well, less as its purpose the triumph of liberty and the promotion of republican principles than it did the promoting of the interests of the speculators and the trade of that country. These speculators saw in this a very opportune occasion for advancing towards the realization of the plan and of acquiring lands that they had coveted of the king of Spain long before.

Otherwise, and even less with the existence of the treaties of peace and friendship which linked that republic with our former mother country, it would have been very difficult, in our opinion, to have permitted the organization and departure from its ports of the expeditions of Miranda, Bolívar, Gutiérrez de Lara, Tres Palacios, Mina, Lallemand, Long and others. These expeditions were made up not only of merchant transport ships but also of corsairs which provided great advantages and resources of all sorts for the promotion of the war in Spanish America. They had forgotten so quickly that Spain had protected them in their struggle against England, and what that power did with so much greater generosity; and loyalty when one remembered the straitened circumstances in which Spain found herself for her part on the continent of Europe.

217

Therefore, all the more sad and unpardonable has been the carelessness of the viceroyalty in the grants to Moses Austin that have been cited, lavishing them without precautions and before having fixed the claims on the boundaries of Louisiana maintained by the United States, who one time extended them as far as the Pánuco, and again to the Río del Norte. Although these were reduced later by the treaty of 1819, this had not been ratified. Even if it had been at that time, they had made it very clear in the answer that there was left pending the matter of the land that lies between the Sabine and the Hondo Rivers.

Even less should the viceroyalty have forgotten the necessity in which it found itself often on our part of making frequent expeditions from Béxar and Saltillo in order to eject from that territory a host of North American families and adventurers who had settled there as in other parts of our borders without any authorization of any sort and with the well known purpose of alleging afterwards as title of ownership that same possession, according to the system and favorite means of acquiring new extensions of land for the republic from which they came. These means, even if they have been slower were less costly to them wherever they had been put into practice. As a consequence of their immediate results particularly the native nations for many years had been rolling down upon our frontiers. This had the advantage for the North Americans of serving as a sort of vanguard and an instrument at hand for despoiling our land and enriching themselves with the spoils. Tell me if this is not so with the states of Sonora, Chihuahua, Durango, Nuevo León, Coahuila, Tamaulipas and even with New Mexico itself.

But the fleeting government of the Mexican empire which replaced that of the king of Spain showed no less lack of caution. In 1823, the patents of Moses Austin were confirmed to his son Stephen Philip [sic: Fuller] without any substantial restriction or any condition in favor of Mexico; it was as shortsighted and as lacking in discretion in its grants as was the Viceroy Apodaca.

The constitutional congress which came afterwards did nothing either to remedy the flaws in the colonization law which it issued in August of 1824. Neither did that government foresee that the new grants that were to be made as a result of it were open to the same difficulties as the previous ones.

To ward off ill effects it should at least have ordered that if they were not families from other countries, they could only and of necessity settle on the right bank of the Nueces River, and that no settlements be made on the left banks of those that run within our frontiers until the first should be sufficiently populated and capable of defending our borders. In this manner those that would be established on the San Antonio, Guadalupe, Colorado, Brazos, San Jacinto and Trinity Rivers, etc., would advance gradually from the populated to the unpopulated areas, leaving no wilderness in between the two that would hinder and make difficult communications and mutual help that they might need. Nor would it be difficult for the government to guard and protect the line of the frontier to keep it covered against the inroads of the savages and the advances of our neighbors the Anglo–Americans or the North Americans.

In the second place, with settlements only on the right banks of the rivers and not on the left, in case of war with the United States or with the colonists themselves, communications, means of subsistence, transport and defense of those rivers would always have been on our side and not that of the others. This circumstance would have contributed to greater security at all times for the inhabitants of our country and made available for our governments greater advantages for protecting them and protecting their authorities and the treasury offices. All this was in addition to the greater difficulty that the enemy would always have had in attacking them if before anything else they had to cross a wilderness of many leagues, without roads and devoid of all the necessities for subsistence and then to cross the rivers which were not always fordable, and even less so if the crossing were defended by opposing forces and fortifications.

The third advantage was that with the colonists, even though they were the North Americans themselves, so far from their own frontiers such as a matter of two hundred leagues, it is probable that the influence and the aid of their compatriots would have been much less for the realization of their plans in every sense.

But if the colonization laws which were setting up were so shortsighted, for those of the State of Coahuila and Texas we can find no words to describe them unless they be that of advocates and backers for the colonists and absolutely harmful and unfavorable for the Mexicans. The triple grants of lands were made to Stephen Austin, the treasonous venality of the state commissioners who handed out an endless number of grants of land to adventurers and vagabonds given to the ones who paid the best, the scorn with which they allowed the laws and customs of the country to be treated, even overlooking the introduction of slaves, and the scandalous smuggling that was carried on in the shadow of exemptions and privileges of the colonies could not possibly have been only the result of an innocent mistake. However, in our opinion the results were no less due

219

to the carelessness, the lack of organization and even the ignorance and ineptitude of the governments, and consequently, they alone and the promoters of the continual uprisings in which they were always forced to fight are the ones who will bear throughout all time the immense responsibility for all these claims for which history has a right to demand an accounting, nor could the present generation have carried it out more effectively.

What else could be expected from so disordered and inadequate an establishment of customs, collection offices, etc., the employees of which were generally inexperienced young people without the knowledge or qualifications that could in any wise recommend them, and whose salaries were so small that they were not sufficient to cover their expenses, even for the prime essentials?

They could not therefore fulfill their delicate and important obligations, either with the intelligence or with the decorum that were necessary. Indeed, they compromised at will with the wealthy merchants and were rigorous and severe with the small traders and other people of limited or average means. A course of conduct as reprehensible as it was scandalous that went unpunished caused dissatisfaction, scorn and even the hostility that they so richly deserved, but which unfortunately was extended even to the laws themselves, the government and the country itself upon which the offices and the employees themselves depended.

On the other hand, the detachments of troops to support the decisions of those people and to uphold the due respect and prompt observance of the laws, the administration of justice and the peace and tranquility of the towns, in addition to being insufficient in strength and numbers, found themselves at great distances from each other. They could not even fulfill their principal obligations nor help each other mutually and opportunely on the frequent and awkward occasions which required it. And thus it was that for lack of supplies, clothing and help to subsist the soldiers were at the mercy of the colonists themselves, whose excesses and treasonous objectives they were supposed to restrain and head off at the beginning.

It is also true that the law of April 1830, tried to remedy these evils. However, since the authorities had awakened too late from their lethargy into which they were plunged, and from which they might have been brought with the proposals of the North American government concerning the sale of Texas in the years 1828 and 1829, the colonists were already too far along, and this type of decision could not remedy the situation. Other more energetic and more positive actions were needed; that is, it was necessary to use force; and this, which was done later, also was not done at the proper time.

Much progress would have been made, however, in the period to which we have referred if as soon as they had made the good choice in the selection of General Don Manuel de Mier y Terán to see that this law was carried out, they had been able to come to his aid with all the resources that he needed to carry his commission to a happy ending. To this lack, and unfortunately to the end of the existence of the general, could the colonists owe the advances that they achieved, in addition to the way they were favored by the revolution which broke out much to their benefit in the city of Veracruz and spread to the whole Republic in the year 1832.

Because of the learning, tact, foresight and knowledge of the matters of that patriotic general, although they fought under difficulties, at last these were overcome or neutralized. But after his death they again became insuperable because the strong interests that had been created in their shadow came at last to make of them a hierarchy over and above the power of the general command and of the government of the State of Coahuila and Texas, as became evident. In addition to having to face the rebellious and turbulent colonists, they also were faced with the spirit of rebellion, the weakness, the ineptitude and the ignorance of the civil authorities, and the defection of the military forces, upon whom they could lean for having the laws carried out and respected, as well as the decisions of the government in all branches of public administration.

Such was the state of affairs in the territory of Texas during the period to which we have arrived in these MEMOIRS, and which naturally was bound to produce the results that were a consequence of such irregularity and confusion. The action of the supreme power was too far away and weakened by the factions that disputed about this among themselves and fought it in the very capital of the Republic. Because of this, and with the attention of those who had succeeded in defending it against its adversaries so occupied that they were not able to do anything else.

I have proved here most clearly how carelessness, ignorance and mistakes on our part brought it about that all this was converted into a great burden for us, and that we were overwhelmed under the weight of the bold thinking of a handful of colonists who did not know how to control themselves or to submit, much less to make themselves profitable in any sense to our frontiers. Rather to the contrary, they were bad for the whole country by their bad example and their influence.

Therefore, we also are of the opinion that *after* the sad error of taking foreign loans, then without them and without any other sort of outside aid the independence of Mexico had been won, the mistake that most clearly points up the childish inexperience, the most regrettable lack of foresight of our statesmen, and the one responsibility for which rests so heavily upon the present and future generations was the mistake that was made by trying and planning to carry out the colonization of Texas in the manner in which it was done. In what is left to tell in these MEMOIRS we believe greater proofs of this line of thinking will be found.

> *Praves non est securus habere Dominus,*
> *qui ipsi magis indigest*
> *Custodia aliorum, quam possint alios custodire.*
> [It is not certain that God
> is on the side of these crooked people
> Who are more in need of having an eye kept on them
> Than of keeping an eye on others.]

[An additional section entitled APPENDIX TO VOLUME I has been omitted. This material is an attempt through limited notes to amplify some items already covered, and they seem to add little if anything to the text as translated and published. The INDEX TO VOLUME I is also omitted as it is a repetition of the Contents at the front of the book.]

INDEX

A

Abasolo, Señor, 17
Abumada, Mateo, 47, 48
Adams, John Quincy, 204
Aguayo, Captain, 8
    Marquis de, 6
Ahumada, Colonel, 56
    Commander, 49
Alcorta, 165
    General, 163, 166, 167, 173, 174
    Lina José, 162
Allende, Señor, 17
Alvarez, José María de Toledo, 24
Alvis, Captain, 176
Andrade, Colonel, 128
    General, 161
    Manuel de, 125, 160, 166, 167
Añorga, [Seaman], 74, 75, 92
    Juan, 73, 111
Araiza, Miguel, 87
Arango, Manuel, 34
Arcedo, de Antonio, 3
Arista, General, 156
    Mariano, 155
Arminan, Benito, 33
    Colonel, 34, 38
Arocha, Ignacio, 121
Arrendondo, 26, 27, 28, 29, 30, 31, 32, 33, 44
    Joaquin de, 25, 42
Arreola, Second Lieutenant, 30
Aspeitia, Alviz, 185
Astorga, 126
Aury, 35
Austin, 44, 85, 97, 98, 100
    Colonel, 145
    John, 78, 83, 84, 85, 86, 88, 95, 110, 112
    Moses, 42, 43, 148, 207, 217, 218
    Mr., 45
    Señor, 152
    Stephen, 43, 48, 49, 52, 81, 95, 100, 101, 102, 103, 107, 110, 142, 143, 144, 148, 149, 151, 153, 207
    Stephen F., 79, 96, 108
    Stephen Philip [*sic* Fuller], 218
Averzana, José, 109
Ayllon, de Lucas Vasquez, 1

B

Basadre, Agustín Mora, 94
Bastrop, Baron de, 42
Batres, José, 60, 61
Beanjin, Captain, 4
Beau, Elias [Ellis **Bean**?], 112
Belaunzarán, Señor Bishop, 170
Benito, Francisco de Luby, 7
Berlandier, Luis, 60

Berthier, Alexander, 200
Bolivar, 217
Bonaparte, 200
    Joseph, 216
    Napoleon, 216
Bonna, (Geographer), 3
Bony, (citizen), 113
Bowles, (Cherokee Agent), 48, 49
Bradburn, Colonel Davis, [See also: Davis], 104, 120
    John Davis, 91, 92
    Juan Davis, 69, 90, 100
Bravo, Nicolás, 56
Brazoria, (Schooner), 88
Burr, Aaron, 13
    Colonel, 217
Bustamante, Anastasio, 47, 76
    General, 48, 49, 50, 51, 54, 56, 57, 59, 63, 115
Butler, Mr., 63
    Señor, 131

C

Caddos [Indians], 138
Calderon, (General), 106, 107
Capets, The, 216
Carbajal, J. M. J., 70, 78
Casiano, José, 121
Castaneda, Jose Domingo, 47
Chargé d'affaires Butler, 130
Charles IV, 12, 200
Cherokees, [Indians], 49, 50, 68, 138
Choiseul, Duke de, 8
Chowel, Rafael, 60
Cioreapuz, [Indians], 138
Claiborne, Governor, 14
Clay, Mr., 204
Cocos, [Indians], 49
Comanche Indians, 127
Comanches, 16, 34, 49, 50
Constante, [War Schooner], 72
Constanza, Vicente, 166
    Vincente, 167
Cortina, 92, 165, 166, 168, 171, 172, 177, 178
    Colonel, 161, 163, 168, 169, 173, 175, 176, 181, 186
    Juan, 85, 87, 111, 125
    Lieutenant, 91
    R. Juan, 60
    Ramon, 180
    Second Adjutant, 126
Coushatta, [Indians], 17, 28, 31, 50, 68, 138
Crozat, Mr., 2
Cuellar, Jesus, 180
Cuevas, Juan, 161, 164, 166

223

D

Dalille, (Geographer), 3
Danville, (Geographer), 3
Davis, Colonel, [See also: Bradburn], 70, 73, 78,
    81, 82, 83, 84, 85, 86, 88, 90, 91, 93, 97
De Angulo, Fernández, xxxi
del Rivero, Don Luis Manuel, xxv
Delawares, [Indians], 138
De Soto, Hernando, 1, 3
DeWitt, Green, 69
Díaz, Onofre, 175, 185
Díez, Captain, 176
Domínguez, 92
    Ignacio, 126
    N., 83
    Second Lieutenant, 84
Duke of Linares, 5
Duke of Orleans, 6
Duke of Parma, 200
Duprast, (*History of Louisiana*), 6
    Mr., 3
Durán, Gabriel, 155
    General, 156

E

Edwards, 54
    Hayden, 48
Elizondo, 23, 26, 27, 28, 29, 31, 32
    Ignacio, 22
Elozúa, Antonio, 56, 116, 125, 126
Escalada, Ignacio, 155, 156
Esparza, Andrés Ruiz de, 60
Extremadura Battalion, 33

F

Fernández, Francisco V., 108, 178, 192
    Francisco Vital, 172, 173, 175, 189
    General, 172, 174
    Vital, 190, 191
Fields, Richard (Cherokee Agent), 48, 49, 54
Filisola, 130, 140, 162, 169, 172, 193
    General, 92, 125, 126, 127, 132, 133, 134,
        135, 136, 137, 138, 142, 144, 145, 146,
        151, 152, 153, 156, 163, 164, 166, 167,
        168, 171, 173, 174, 175, 177, 178, 179,
        180, 181, 182, 185, 186, 187, 189, 190,
        195
    Vicente, 176, 192
Fisher, [Customs], 70, 96
    George, 104

G

Gaona, Antonio, 57
Garay, Francisco, 3
Garcia, Luciano, 32, 44, 47
Garduño, José, 114
Garza, Felipe de la, 44, 47, 58
    General, 59, 60, 61
    José Antonio de la, 121
Girón, José María, 167
Gordon, Major, 36
Grimaret, Pedro, 15
Guerra, 105, 114
    Colonel, 95, 96, 103, 104, 108, 165, 166, 167,
        181
    General, 107

José Mariano, 105, 107
    Senor, 106
Guerrero, 93
    Vincente, 57, 76
Guimbarda, Licenciado, 169
Gutiérrez de Lara, xxxiii, 17, 22, 24, 25, 33, 38,
    47, 211, 217
Gutiérrez, 18, 20
    Bernardo y Lara, 21

H

Hale, [an American], 21
Hasinais, [Indians], 5
Herrera, 14, 24
    Governor, 21, 38
    Joé Manuel, 35
    José Joaquín de, 186
    Simón de, 13, 18, 26
Hidalgo, Señor, 16, 17
House of Braganza, 216
Hunter, Dr. John Dums, 48, 49, 54
Hurtado, Andrés, 85

I

Iturbide, Señor, 44
Iturrigaray, Viceroy, 216

J

Janvier, (Geographer), 3
Jark, 82, 91
Jiménez, José María, 107, 108
    Manuel, 121
Jujero, Francisco, 107

K

Karankawas, 45, 49
Kemper, 17, 20, 21, 28, 30, 38
    Colonel, 24, 25
Kerlerk, Mr., 8
Kickapoo, [Indians], 50, 68
King Charles II, 5
King Ferdinand VII, 24
King Philip V, 6
Kohanis, [Indians], 49

L

La Fuente, Captain, 171
La Salle, 3, 4, 5, 8
Lafitte, [the Pirate], 34, 35
Lallemand, 39, 217
    General, 38
Leal, N., 191
Lemus, Pedro, 195, 196
León, Alonso de, 5
    Captain, 8
    Juan Ponce de, 3
    Martín de, 50, 69
Lipan Apaches [Indians], 28, 31, 66
Lipan Indians, 66
Livingston, 204
Llano, Governor, 168, 169
    Julián Del, 134
    Manuel María Del, 168
Lockett, [Officer], 17, 20
Lojero, Francisco, 180
    Lieutenant Colonel, 181
Long [Expedition], 217

General, 41, 42
López, Gaspar, 44
Tomás, 3
Louis XIV, 2
XVI, 216
Lujero, 190
Luna, Vicente, 162, 166, 169

M

Madero, 77, 78
Francisco, 70, 120
Magie [Magee], 17
Colonel [Magie, *sic* Magee], 19
Maillard, Doran, xxv
Manzanares, Guerra, 77, 95, 185
José Mariano Guerra, 60, 180
Marín, Primo Feliciano, 7
Marta, (Schooner), 85
Martínez, 44
Antonio María, 38, 42
Brigadier, 39
Masicot, 21
Mason, General, 95
Medina, Captain, 113
Mejía, 94, 103, 105
Colonel, 95, 107, 108, 110
General, 107
Meléndez, Pedro, 1, 2
Menchaca, 25, 28, 30
Micheltorena, Major, 77
Manuel, 114
Mina [Expedition], 217
Francisco Javier, 35
General, 36, 38
Miracle, 174
Julian, 161
Lieutenant, 166
Pedro, 173
Miramón, Angel, 161
Miranda [Expedition], 217
Moctezuma, 177, 179, 186
Colonel, 77
Estevan, 165, 180
General, 93, 106, 108, 109, 115, 172, 176,
178, 180, 181, 182, 187, 188, 189
Monroe, [Minister, i.e., Ambassador], 201
Montaño, 56
Montero, 92
Manuel, 87, 111
Mora, Ignacio, 105, 109, 114
Morales, Assistant Inspector, 185
Colonel, 174
Juan, 185
Moreno, 126
Moscoso, Luis, 1
Muldoon, Father, 104
Munoz, Luciano, 166, 190
Musquiz, Ramon, 130

N

Napoleon, 13
Emperor, 203
Napolitano, Pascual Constanza, 134
Narvaez, Panfilo, 1
Navarro, Angel, 121
Nelson, (American Schooner), 78

Nieto, 92
Miguel, 83
Nolan, Philip, 10
Noriega, Lieutenant, 104
North, Mr., 215

O

Ocampo, 92
Carlos, 111
Lieutenant, 82
Olivan, Judge, 6
Onis, de Luis, 1
Onys, Luis de, 206
Senor, 9
Ortega, Captain, 113
Ortiz, Diego de Parrilla, 6

P

Pacho, Juan, 80
Juan Maria, 85
Padilla, 185
Captain, 176
Palacios, Lieutenant, 77
Second Lieutenant, 111
Paredes y Arrellaga, Colonel, 105, 108
Y Arrillaga, Colonel, 108
Colonel, 76, 77, 114
Parres, Ramon, 179
Payne, William, 199
Pedraza, Manuel Gómez, 57
President, 117
Pedrazas, Manuel Gómes, 111
Perry, [Officer], 17, 37
Colonel, 22, 35, 36
Piedras, 165
Colonel, 55, 85, 95, 112, 113, 158, 159, 163,
171, 173, 174, 178, 186
Colonel José de, 91
José de las, 54, 83, 90, 130, 157, 172
Pierro, Luis, 166, 171, 172
Pinckney, [Minister, i.e., Ambassador], 201
Pintado, N., 74
Poinsett, 63
J. R., 62
Praga, 175, 176, 177, 178, 185, 190
Colonel, 173, 174
Lieutenant Colonel, 182, 189
Prince Talleyrand, 201

R

Ramón, Captain, 8
Domingo, 5, 6, 7
Republic of Fredonia, 48
Ribaut, 1
Rivero, xxvii
Adeodato, 104
Robertson, 73, 74
Robinson, 73
Rodríguez, Ignacio, 94, 160
Lieutenant, 161
N., 76
Romero, Captain, 176, 186, 187
María, 185
Rondero, Juan, 161
Ross, [Officer], 17, 20, 22
Rubí, Marquis de, 7

S

Sabariego, Captain Manuel, 161
   Manuel, 159, 160, 170
Sabina[s], (American Schooner), 78, 80, 81, 88
Saens, Captain, 173
Salcedo, 20, 24
   Governor, 21, 38
   Manuel, 13, 18
   Nemesio, 10
Salinas, Captain, 8
   Gregorio, 5
Sambrano, [See Zambrano], José María, 121
Sánchez, José Joan, 162
   José Juan, 161, 166
   José María, 60
Sandoval, Manuel de, 7
Sans, Captain, 161, 166
Santa Anna, 107
   Anna, Antonio Lopez de, 61, 155
   Anna, General, 76, 101, 106, 111, 115, 131
   Antonio Lopez de, 164
Saucedo, José Antonio, 48
Seguín, Juan Angel, 121
Serón, Jorge, 3
Shawnees, [Indians], 138
St. Denis, 3, 5, 6
Stáboli, 167
   Colonel, 166
   José, 161, 163, 190
Surbarán, Colonel, 85
   Felix, 85, 87, 91
   Féliz, 111
   Major, 77, 114

T

Talleyrand, 200
Tarnaba, Constantino, 60
Tawehashes [Indians], 28, 31
Tehuacana Indians, 28, 49, 50, 127
Tejas Indians, 5
Terán, Captain, 8
   General, 56, 59, 60, 61, 62, 63, 64, 65, 67, 68,
      69, 70, 73, 76, 79, 80, 81, 90, 93, 95, 101,
      103, 104, 105, 106, 107, 108, 109, 133,
      137, 138
   Manuel de Mier y, 56, 96
Ternova, Constantino, 166
Terrán, Manuel de Mier, 79
Thompson, Mayor, 91
Ticson, (American Schooner), 78, 80

Tocqueville, Mr. de, 206
Toledo, 25, 27, 28, 29, 30, 31
   Alvarez, 211
Tonkawa Indians, 4, 28, 31
Topaz, (American Schooner), 72, 73, 91
Tornel, Don José María, xxxi
   General, 216
   José María, 198
   Senor, 217
Travis, [W. B.], 82, 90, 91
Tres Palacios, 217
Tres-Palacios, José Félix, 44
Trollope, Mrs., 213

U

Ugartechea, 84, 89, 110, 190
   Anastasio de, 169
   Colonel, 105, 114, 165, 182
   Commander, 169
   Domingo, 73, 83, 88, 176, 181, 185
   Domingo de, 168
   José Domingo, 180
   Lieutenant Colonel, 81
Urquijo, Mariano Luis, 200

V

Valero, Marquis de, 6
Varela, Mariano, 38
Victoria, Guadalupe, 47
Villafañe, Angel de, 3
Villareal, Enrique, 66
Villasana, Ignacio, 111
   Major, 77, 114

W

Wacos, [Indians], 49
Webster, 204
Wilkinson, General, 14
Williams, (American Schooner), 78
Williams, Mayor, 86
Woodbury, [an American], 75

Y

Yamparicas, [Indians], 49
Yeganis, 138
Yhari, Colonel, 143
Yhary, Captain, 93

Z

Zambrano, [See Sambrano], 29
   Manuel, 28
Zavala, Lorenzo de, 214
Zenteno, Andrés, 166, 167

226